Emotional Echoes

Emotional Echoes

Tanuja Maben

Copyright © 2024 by Tanuja Maben
All rights reserved. No part of this book may be reproduced in any manner whatsoever without written permission except in the case of brief quotations embodied in critical articles and reviews.
First Printing, 2024

CONTENTS

DEDICATIONS	vii
ACKNOWLEDGEMENT	ix
FOREWORD	xiii
FOREWORD	xv

1	SYNOPSYS	1
2	AUTHOR'S THOUGHTS	5
3	RAINBOW OF EMOTIONS	7
4	EMOTIONAL INTELLIGENCE	9
5	THE FIRST STEP	13
6	PROCRASTINATION – Seize The Today	23
7	ANGER – Harness the Power	51
8	FEAR – Unlock Courage	77
9	SELF-ESTEEM – Embrace Your Worth	93
10	CHILDHOOD TRAUMA – Reclaim The Innocence	109
11	REJECTION – Fuel For Resilience	151
12	SELF TALK – Shaping Self	177
13	BARRIERS TO EMOTIONS	225
14	SRISHTI'S TRANSFORMATION	235
15	EPILOGUE	257

DEDICATIONS

This book is dedicated to my husband, Jackie, and our daughter, Rayo, whose unwavering love, encouragement, and support have been the driving force behind every word penned within these pages. Your belief in me and your constant presence by my side have fueled my passion and inspired me to pursue my dreams with determination and resilience. Thank you for being my pillars of strength, my greatest cheerleaders, and my eternal sources of inspiration. This book is a testament to our journey together, and I dedicate it to you both with all my heart.

ACKNOWLEDGEMENT

I am grateful for the privilege and honor of being mentored and guided by Dr. Meghana Dikshit, (Founder, De Mantraa, Brain and Performance Expert) and Nayan Agarwal, (Co-founder, De Mantraa). Their wisdom and guidance have ultimately transformed my life in countless ways, from personal growth to finding a clear direction. They are more than just mentors; they embody compassion and profound insights, serving as role models with their unwavering support. Their teachings have given me a renewed sense of purpose and direction, allowing me to break through personal barriers and embrace challenges with courage. Through their guidance, I have learned to see life in a new light - one filled with positivity, hope, and endless possibilities. They have instilled in me the power of self-belief and the importance of maintaining a growth mindset. Their dedication to helping others reach their full potential is truly inspiring. Their genuine concern for my well-being and success has been a driving force in my life. I am forever grateful for the positive impact they have had on me. The values and principles they uphold have resonated deeply with me, guiding me towards a life of integrity, compassion, and authenticity. They have also taught me the importance of giving back to the community and making a difference in the lives of others.

Dr. Meghana Dikshit and Nayan Agarwal have played an instrumental role in shaping my journey towards personal and professional fulfillment. I am honored to have learned from such incredible individuals and am committed to carrying forward their invaluable lessons. Thank you both for everything you do. I would like to express my sincere gratitude to Blair Singer, (Founder of Blair Singer Training Academy), a highly respected Leadership Mastery Coach from the United States, whose teachings and insights have had a profound impact on my journey. His expertise in sales, leadership, and personal development has equipped me with invaluable tools and perspectives that have greatly influenced my personal and professional growth. It has been an honor to learn from such an exceptional mentor.

I am also immensely thankful to Thaddeus Lawrence, an accomplished Integral Coach from Singapore, whose guidance and mentorship have been instrumental in my development. Thaddeus is not just a coach; he is a transformative force who has helped shape my growth in both personal and professional aspects. His mentorship has empowered me to break through my limits and achieve what I once thought was impossible.

The mission of Mac Attram, Business and Wealth Coach (Founder & CEO of MindSpace Business Growth) to empower others has been truly inspiring, and his mentorship has been invaluable in helping me realize my full potential. Mac's infectious enthusiasm and positive energy have fueled my motivation, and his wisdom has been a guiding light.

Commander Bimal Raj's (Retd., Mindset Mentor and Mind Kinetics Coach) unwavering dedication to excellence and ability to inspire those around him have continuously

motivated me. His mentorship has given me the confidence and clarity needed to pursue my goals with determination.

I am deeply grateful to Pallavii Walia Raj, (Charizmatic Communication Coach| TEDx Speaker| TV Host) whose expertise and encouragement have played a crucial role in my transformation. Her patient guidance, personalized coaching strategies, supportive nature, and keen insights have empowered me to overcome barriers and build meaningful connections with others. Her unwavering support and positive influence will always be appreciated.

I also want to thank Prameela Sreemangalam, (Founder Mindscan and Life Transformer) for instilling in me a sense of confidence and resilience that has allowed me to pursue my goals with renewed determination. Her wisdom and patience have provided me with the clarity needed to overcome countless challenges and seize new opportunities.

I am deeply grateful to Hemsingh Patle, (Habit Coach & Author) for his unwavering support and encouragement throughout this writing journey. His constant motivation was instrumental in bringing this book to life.

I would also like to extend my sincere appreciation to Manoj Sonawane, Author and founder of BLISS Books, for his invaluable assistance in helping me organize my thoughts and write this book. Without his dedication and collaboration, this project would not have been possible.

A special thanks goes to Sudhir Bhandarkar Bantwal, Management Consultant, whose guidance and inspiration have been a guiding light for me. His decision to assist me in this writing journey was a turning point, and his unwavering motivation and tireless efforts were crucial in driving the project forward. I am truly grateful for Sudhir's wisdom and his willingness to push me beyond my limits. His hands-on support was invaluable in completing this book, and I am thankful for his assistance towards achieving this feat.

FOREWORD

Tanuja, an exceptional student of my class has encapsulated her journey of growth and triumph into a compelling book.

Drawing from her own experiences, she sheds light on the internal barriers that impede our progress in life. Through her insights, readers are encouraged to recognize their role as architects of their destiny.

Within these pages lies a roadmap for uncovering the obstacles that hinder personal success, our own patterns of belief and behaviour.

Tanuja's guidance serves as a catalyst for readers to seize control of their life, a transformative opportunity to break free from self-imposed limitations as you embark on a journey of self-discovery and empowerment.

It's time to take charge and propel yourself forward.

- Dr. Meghana Dikshit
Founder De Mantraa, Brain and Performance Expert

FOREWORD

I have known Tanuja for a few years now; she is one of my star students. She has been an excellent student in learning & implementing the concepts. From her experience of growth & success, she has shared her learning in this book.

It is a great book to understand what is happening in your life & inner space, that stops us from our success in all areas of our life. The wisdom that I take from this book is that I am the creator of my own destiny.

Take the reins of your life in your own hands dear Reader, let go of what is stopping you, the obstacle in your path.

You will be amazed to realise that it is our own patterns of belief & behaviours that become our limitations.

Go all out, take this helping hand from Tanuja & shake yourself free.

- **Nayan Aggarwal**
Co-founder, De Mantraa

1

SYNOPSYS

"Emotional Echoes" is a self-help book written by Tanuja Maben, a seasoned mind therapist with decades of experience in helping individuals navigate the complexities of their emotions. In this book, Tanuja shares her expertise in emotional intelligence through the story of Srishti, a young woman facing multiple setbacks in her personal and professional life.

Srishti is a bright and hardworking individual who has always strived to achieve excellence in everything she does. However, in recent times, she has been struggling with depression and mood swings, which have affected her ability to perform at work and maintain healthy relationships. Despite having a supportive family and friends, Srishti finds herself trapped in a cycle of negative emotions, unable to break free.

It is at this point that Srishti's friend Susan suggests that she seek guidance from Tanuja, an accomplished mind therapist who has helped many individuals overcome emotional challenges. Initially hesitant, Srishti eventually decides to approach Tanuja and seek her counsel.

Over the course of the ensuing weeks, Tanuja and Srishti embark on a journey of self-discovery, exploring the complex nature of human emotions and the ways in which they shape our thoughts and actions. The sessions are structured around seven key emotions - procrastination, anger, fear, self-esteem, childhood trauma, rejection, and self-talk - each of which is explored in depth through the interactions between Tanuja and Srishti.

Through Tanuja's patient guidance and profound wisdom, Srishti learns to understand and master these emotions, gaining invaluable tools for navigating life's challenges. She discovers that procrastination is not simply a lack of motivation but a symptom of deeper emotional issues that need to be addressed. She learns to recognize the warning signs of anger and fear and to channel them into positive actions. She confronts the traumas of her childhood and learns to heal from the wounds of rejection.

Throughout the therapy sessions, Tanuja provides Srishti with practical exercises and techniques that help her to regulate her emotions and develop emotional resilience. She encourages Srishti to cultivate a positive self-image and to use affirmations and positive self-talk to counter negative thoughts and beliefs. Through it all, Srishti emerges as a stronger, more confident individual, empowered by her newfound emotional intelligence.

In the final session, Tanuja imparts the transformative power of understanding emotional triggers and breaking through the barriers that hold us back. She teaches Srishti how to recognize the patterns of behaviour and thought that have been limiting her potential and how to overcome them. Armed with this knowledge, Srishti emerges as a woman emboldened by emotional intelligence, fortified by renewed confidence and resilience.

As Srishti applies the lessons she has learned to her personal and professional life, she begins to see positive changes. She secures the promotion she deserves at work and rekindles her relationship with Amith, her boyfriend, their bond strengthened by her newfound maturity. Srishti's journey is a testament to the power of self-discovery and the indomitable human spirit. Tanuja's guidance illuminates the path to emotional mastery and ignites a flame of hope within Srishti, empowering her to embrace life's challenges with grace and resilience.

In summary, "Emotional Echoes" is a book that offers practical guidance and wisdom to individuals who are struggling with their emotions. Through the story of Srishti and her interactions with Tanuja, readers will gain insight into their own emotional patterns and learn how to develop emotional resilience and intelligence. This book is a must-read for anyone who wants to lead a fulfilling and meaningful life.

2

AUTHOR'S THOUGHTS

Emotions are the vivid colours that paint our inner world, shaping our experiences and defining who we are. But what happens when these hues become chaotic, blurring our rationality and causing us to react impulsively? How do we navigate through the storms within us and find peace amidst the chaos?

Welcome to 'Emotional Echoes - A Transformational Journey

This book will take you on a transformative journey, guiding you towards understanding and mastering your emotions. Imagine a life where stress doesn't overwhelm you, setbacks don't paralyze you, and conflicts don't ignite uncontrollable anger. Through research, personal experiences, and philosophical wisdom, this guide offers a comprehensive roadmap to managing your emotions.

Whether you are a student striving for success, a parent seeking harmony in your family, a teacher facing challenges in the classroom, or an educator shaping young minds, this book is tailored to empower you on your unique journey. We will explore the multifaceted nature of emotions, breaking down their different types and unravelling the complex web they weave within our minds and bodies. This is a practical guide for transformation, with step-by-step strategies and exercises to help you navigate through life's challenges with resilience and grace.

Through self-awareness, emotional intelligence, and mindfulness techniques, you will learn how to harness the power of your emotions and create balance in your life. Join Tanuja as she embarks on an adventure with Srishti, that will change the way you perceive and manage your emotions forever. As the journey unfolds, you will unlock the potential within yourself to nurture healthier relationships, embrace authenticity, and discover profound self-discovery. In the pages ahead, you will find the keys to unlocking your emotional potential and living a life guided by wisdom, compassion, and inner harmony. Get ready for an extraordinary journey where the most remarkable destination lies within yourself.

Let's begin!

3

RAINBOW OF EMOTIONS

A kaleidoscope of emotions swirls within us, ever-changing and unpredictable. They have a mind of their own, capable of lifting us up to the highest mountaintop or dragging us down to the depths of despair. But don't be fooled by their mischievous nature – emotions serve a purpose. They are intricate psychological and physiological responses that occur in our bodies and minds. Sometimes triggered by external events, and other times by internal thoughts and memories.

Our emotional palette spans a vast range, from elation and euphoria to heart-wrenching sorrow and seething anger. And yet, each emotion has its own unique message to deliver. When we feel fear, it's our built-in alarm system, preparing us for potential danger. Joy sparks feelings of warmth and connection with others, while anger can ignite a fierce desire for justice. Emotions are not just fleeting sensations – they hold power and purpose.

Every day, our emotions shape our experiences, coloring how we perceive and react to the world around us. Imagine watching a movie without emotions – it would be like staring at an empty canvas. Just as toppings add flavor to a pizza, emotions add depth and richness to our lives. They motivate us to reach new heights and protect us from harm.

But emotions aren't just individual experiences – they also influence our relationships with others. They give us the ability to empathize and understand their perspectives, deepening our connections with them.

Emotions may sometimes feel like wild beasts, but they are not enemies to be tamed or suppressed. Instead, they are an integral part of what makes us human. We wouldn't want to live without them because they allow us to love, show compassion, and experience the full spectrum of what it means to be alive.

4

EMOTIONAL INTELLIGENCE

Emotional intelligence, the elusive yet essential skill of understanding and managing our emotions and those of others, has taken the world by storm in recent years. Its allure lies in its ability to improve relationships, overall well-being, and professional success.

This mastery surpasses traditional measures of intelligence, delving into the intricacies of our emotional interactions with the world. Through this exploration, we unlock a deeper understanding of ourselves and those around us, empowering us to navigate life's complexities with greater ease.

But perhaps most thrilling is how emotional intelligence enhances our connections with others. By honing this skill set, we can truly empathize and comprehend the perspectives and feelings of those in our lives. This leads to more effective communication, stronger bonds, and healthier relationships. And so it is imperative that we develop strategies and skills to cultivate emotional intelligence for better connections with our loved ones.

Furthermore, this invaluable trait greatly contributes to our overall well-being and mental health. With high emotional intelligence, we can regulate our emotions and manage stress in a healthy manner. This results in reduced anxiety, improved self- esteem, and a profound sense of happiness and fulfilment. In this book, we will dive deep into practical techniques for enhancing our emotional well-being.

And let us not forget its impact in the workplace. Employers now recognize the value of hiring individuals with high levels of emotional intelligence as they make exceptional leaders, skilled at conflict resolution and collaboration. In this book, we will delve even deeper into this topic and explore how it contributes to professional success while providing practical strategies for honing these crucial skills.

The potential of emotional intelligence to positively transform every aspect of our lives is nothing short of enthralling. So let's continue our journey through this book and discover ways to master our emotions for a fulfilling life filled with meaningful connections.

Why do emotions need to be mastered? Emotions are like volatile chemicals that can either ignite our passions or burn us to ashes. They add depth and dimension to our experiences, but they must be handled with caution and precision. Imagine a world without emotions - it would be like living in a constant state of numbness, devoid of any highs or lows. But when we master our emotions, we can harness their power and use them as tools for growth and fulfilment.

So why does mastering emotions matter so much? Because they are the driving force behind everything we do. From the moment we open our eyes in the morning, to the last thoughts before we drift off to sleep at night, our emotions guide our every action. They can propel us towards success or cripple us with fear and doubt. By mastering our emotions, we gain control over our destiny and can navigate through life's challenges with courage and resilience.

Let's consider relationships - one of the most emotionally charged aspects of our lives. When we fail to master our emotions, they can cause irreparable damage to the connections we hold dear. Have you ever been consumed by rage during an argument with a loved one, hurling insults like daggers? Or have you felt overwhelmed by sadness, pushing away those who care about you? These destructive patterns only lead to fractured relationships and heartache. However, when we learn to manage our emotions, we can communicate effectively, show empathy towards others, and build strong foundations for lasting connections.

But perhaps most importantly, mastering our emotions is crucial for our overall well-being. Uncontrolled emotions can manifest in physical symptoms like chronic stress, weakened immune systems, and even life-threatening illnesses. On the other hand, when we learn to regulate our emotions, we can reduce stress levels, boost our immunity, and live longer, healthier lives.

In short, mastering our emotions is not just a luxury - it is a necessity for a fulfilling and thriving existence. So let us not shy away from the intensity of our emotions, but instead embrace them, understand them, and master them for our own growth and well-being.

Emotions are the invisible puppeteer, pulling the strings of our every move and thought. They have the power to consume us, to dictate our state of mind based on mere triggers - a place, a person, even a faint scent can send us tumbling into a torrent of emotions. But we must learn to control this force within us, for it holds the key to our well-being.

It is our emotions that drive us, that dictate how we feel - happiness or sadness, joy or despair. And if we are not conscious of them, they can easily take over our lives, leaving us as mere slaves to their ever-changing whims. But when we awaken to this truth, we can begin to weaken their hold on us and choose which emotions serve our purpose and growth.

As humans, we will inevitably experience both happy and sad emotions, but it is up to us to decide which ones we will allow to prevail. We must not let sadness drain us of our energy and rob us of our passion for life. Instead, we must learn to control our emotions so that we may live with purpose and intention. No longer shall we be at the mercy of our emotions - for now, we hold the reins in our own hands.

Our minds are moulded and shaped by those around us, conditioned to fear and doubt our own power. In the epic Ramayana, even the mighty Hanuman was made to forget his incredible abilities as a child, only to be reminded and pushed by others when it was time to cross the ocean. We all have limitless potential from birth, but it is often suppressed and overshadowed by the fears instilled in us by our parents and society. We must break free from these limitations and reclaim our strengths. Instead of seeking external motivation and inspiration, we must tap into our own inner fire and water, conquer the heights that once intimidated us. This book delves deeper into the emotions that hold us back from reaching our full potential. Thru the therapeutical journey of Srishti under Tanuja's guidance, we will learn to control and harness these emotions like a well-trained muscle, unlocking our true power and achieving greatness.

5
THE FIRST STEP

Srishti's childhood in the beautiful coastal Mangalore had been mostly idyllic, surrounded by a close-knit family who stressed the importance of education and a good career. Nourished by their love and support, she had flourished academically, her intelligence shining like a beacon from an early age.

"Remember when you won the state rank in the tenth standard?" her mother would fondly recall, pride evident in her voice. "And your essay on environmental conservation earned you that prestigious award in college!"

"Ah, and how could we forget your role as the captain of the debate team?" her father would chime in with a beaming smile. "You were unstoppable."

These memories, while precious, served to highlight the lofty standards Srishti had set for herself over the years. With every accolade, her desire to excel grew stronger, pushing her to scale greater heights.

The phone buzzed on the table, pulling Srishti back to the present. It was a text message from Susan, her best friend since college: "Hey, just checking in. How are you feeling about your appointment with Tanuja today?"

"Apprehensive but hopeful," Srishti typed out, her fingers hovering briefly over the screen before hitting send. Her heart fluttered with a mix of anxiety and anticipation as she considered the upcoming therapy session with Tanuja.

"Taking the first step is always the hardest," Susan replied, her words offering reassurance and comfort through the screen. "You're not alone, Srishti. Remember that."

"Thank you, Susan." Srishti felt warmth spread through her chest, gratitude for her friend's unwavering support mingling with the resolve to change her life for the better.

As she sat on the edge of her bed, Srishti allowed herself a moment of introspection. She thought of her achievements, the victories that had propelled her forward, and of the darker moments, the emotional struggles that had threatened to consume her. It was a delicate balance, one she longed to understand and manage more effectively.

"Today is the first day of the rest of my life," Srishti whispered to herself, willing the words to infuse her with courage. With a deep breath, she gathered her belongings and stepped out the door, ready to face the unknown with an open heart and a determined spirit.

*****

A few days ago... Srishti sat at her desk, the soft glow of the computer screen casting shadows on her face. She stared blankly at the report she had been trying to complete for hours, her mind wandering back to memories tucked away in the recesses of her heart.

"Perfect scores again, Srishti? You do make us proud," her father's voice echoed in her head, a bittersweet memory from her early teenage years. She remembered standing there with her report card, the words "Straight A's" emblazoned across the top, feeling both triumphant and terrified. The expectations that came with each achievement weighed heavily on her shoulders, a burden she carried well into adulthood.

"Good job, dear, but why didn't you get the first place in the science fair?" her mother's voice chimed in, another instance of praise laced with an insidious reminder of her perceived shortcomings. Srishti could feel the sting of disappointment even now, as though the memory had been etched into her very being.

"Is everything okay, Srishti?" her coworker, Ravi, asked, breaking her out of her reverie. His concern was evident, but she knew he couldn't fully understand the turmoil within her.

"I'm fine, just a bit tired," she replied, her voice wavering. She forced a smile, hoping it would mask the pain she felt behind her eyes.

"Alright, just let me know if you need anything," Ravi said before returning to his own work, unaware of the depth of Srishti's struggles.

As she attempted to refocus on her task, Srishti's thoughts drifted to the frequent mood swings that plagued her days, ranging from periods of restless energy to crippling despair. Her work performance suffered, deadlines often slipping through her fingers like sand. It wasn't just her professional life that bore the brunt of her emotional turmoil; her relationships were strained as well.

As she stared at the unfinished report on her screen, Srishti's heart ached with the weight of unspoken emotions and unaddressed pain. She knew that something needed to change, that continuing down this path would only lead to further suffering.

"Maybe Susan is right," Srishti thought, remembering her friend's suggestion to seek help from Tanuja. "I need to face my fears and seek guidance."

In that moment, Srishti made a silent promise to herself: she would confront her past, untangle the web of emotions that had ensnared her for so long, and learn to navigate the murky waters of her own psyche. It wouldn't be easy, but she knew that taking the first step was the only way forward.

*****

Srishti's hands trembled as she clutched the ceramic mug, the steaming tea within doing little to calm her racing thoughts. The room around her seemed to close in, its walls a suffocating embrace that mirrored the weight on her chest.

"Hey, Srishti. What's going on?" her brother Sathwik asked, his concern evident as he sat down beside her at the kitchen table. "You look really upset."

"I... I don't know," she stammered, struggling to find the words to express the whirlwind of emotions churning inside her. "It's just... everything feels too much right now."

"Is it work?" Sathwik prompted gently, knowing all too well how the pressure of deadlines and performance had been affecting his sister lately.

"Partly," Srishti admitted, tears welling up in her eyes. "But it's not just that, Sathwik. It's everything - my relationships, my expectations, these mood swings. I feel like I'm drowning, and I don't know how to swim."

Sathwik reached out, placing a comforting hand on her shoulder. "We'll figure this out together, okay? You're not alone, Srishti. We care about you, and we want to help."

"Thank you, Sathwik," she whispered, allowing herself to lean into his embrace for a moment. She knew that her family and friends were there for her, even when it felt like she was fighting her own internal battles. Their support was a lifeline that kept her afloat amidst the stormy seas of her emotions.

In that instant, surrounded by love and understanding, Srishti felt the first glimmer of hope. She recognized that her emotional challenges were not insurmountable, and with the support of those who cared for her, she could begin to mend her fractured spirit.

"Maybe I should talk to someone," she said softly, the idea taking shape in her mind like a fragile seedling pushing through the soil. "A professional who can help me understand what's happening and how to cope."

Sathwik nodded, his eyes lighting up with encouragement. "I think that's a great idea, Srishti. Mom and Dad will support you too, you know that. And we'll all be here every step of the way."

As they sat together in the comforting warmth of their childhood home, Srishti allowed herself to believe that maybe, just maybe, things could get better. The road ahead would be long and filled with challenges, but she knew that she didn't have to walk it alone. With the unwavering support of those closest to her, Srishti was ready to take the first tentative steps towards healing and self-discovery.

*****

The sun dipped below the horizon, painting the sky in hues of orange and pink, as Srishti sat on her balcony, cradling a steaming cup of masala tea. Her eyes traced the intricate patterns etched onto the ceramic surface of the cup, seeking solace in its delicate beauty. She took a deep breath, inhaling the soothing aroma of the tea. It was in moments like these that she found a small measure of peace amidst the turbulence of her emotions.

"Hey, have you thought about seeing a mind therapist?" Susan's voice echoed in her head, a gentle suggestion offered during one of their many heart-to-heart conversations. Srishti had initially brushed it off, uncertain if embarking on such a personal journey with a stranger would truly bring her the healing she sought. But now, as she contemplated the supportive network of friends and family that surrounded her, she couldn't help but wonder if Susan's advice might be worth considering.

Srishti set down her teacup and reached for her phone, her fingers tapping out a message to Susan. "What was the name of the therapist you mentioned? The one who helped your cousin?"

"Tanuja Maben," came the swift reply, accompanied by a smiling emoji. "She's amazing, Srishti. I think she could really help you."

As much as Srishti longed for self-improvement, the idea of laying bare her vulnerabilities in front of a stranger filled her with trepidation. Her heart raced at the thought of discussing her deepest insecurities and fears with Tanuja, a woman she had never met.

"Can I really do this?" she wondered, her thoughts swirling like leaves caught in an autumn breeze. "Can I trust someone I barely know to guide me through my darkest moments?"

"Take your time, Srishti," Susan had said when she first suggested therapy. "It's not an easy decision, but remember that you're never alone in this journey. We're all here for you."

With Susan's words echoing in her mind, Srishti took a deep breath and made a decision. She would at least give therapy a try, for herself and for those who cared about her. Steeling her resolve, she typed out a message to Tanuja, inquiring about the possibility of booking an appointment.

"Hello, my name is Srishti, and I was referred to you by a friend," she wrote, hesitating for a moment before pressing send. As the message disappeared into the digital ether, she felt a mixture of trepidation and determination settle within her.

"Maybe this will be the first step towards finding my way back to happiness," she thought, sipping her tea and watching as the last light of day faded from view.

*****

The sun poured a warm, golden light through the office window as Srishti nervously fiddled with the hem of her pastel blue dress. Her heart hammered in her chest as she stood outside Tanuja Maben's door, her hand poised to knock.

"Is this really going to help?" Srishti questioned herself, her thoughts racing. But then, she remembered the encouraging words of her friend Susan and the support of her loved ones. She took a deep breath, steadying herself. "For them, and for me," she whispered before finally knocking on the door.

"Come in!" Tanuja called out, her voice gentle yet firm.

Srishti hesitantly pushed open the door, stepping into the serene office that seemed bathed in a comforting glow. The room was filled with bookshelves and adorned with plants, creating an ambiance of calm and warmth. As her eyes met Tanuja's kind gaze, a flicker of hope ignited within her.

"Hello, Srishti," Tanuja said warmly, gesturing towards the cozy armchair across from hers. "Please, have a seat."

"Thank you," Srishti replied, her voice barely audible as she settled into the chair, her hands clasped tightly in her lap.

"Before we begin," Tanuja started, her eyes soft and inviting, "I'd like to assure you that this is a safe space. You can share anything you wish, and I will do my best to help you navigate your emotions."

Srishti nodded, her throat tight but grateful for the reassurance. Tanuja's presence felt like a soothing balm, easing some of the tension that had knotted itself within her.

"Would you like some tea or water?" Tanuja offered, noticing Srishti's unease."Water would be nice, thank you," Srishti responded, her voice slightly stronger. As Tanuja poured her a glass, Srishti took the opportunity to collect her thoughts. She knew that opening up about her emotional turmoil would be difficult, but she also recognized that it was time to break free from the relentless grip of negativity.

"Where would you like to begin, Srishti?" Tanuja asked gently, handing her the glass of water.

Srishti hesitated for a moment, her fingers tracing the condensation on the glass. "I think... I want to start with why I came here," she said quietly, drawing in a shaky breath. "I've been struggling for a while now, and I'm tired of feeling this way. I need help," she admitted, her voice cracking.

"Thank you for sharing that, Srishti," Tanuja said softly, her empathetic gaze never leaving Srishti's face. "It takes courage to seek help, and I want you to know that you've taken an important first step by coming here today."

As Srishti listened to Tanuja's reassuring words, she felt a small weight lift from her chest. Perhaps, with Tanuja's guidance, she could begin untangling the complex web of emotions that had held her captive for so long. For the first time in what felt like ages, hope began to blossom within her heart.

*****

Determined to voice her struggles, Srishti leaned forward in the comfortable armchair, her fingers gripping the edge of the seat. "I've been dealing with... depression and mood swings," she began hesitantly, searching for the words to describe her inner turmoil. "One day, I'm on top of the world, feeling like everything is possible, and the next, I'm drowning in a sea of despair. It's exhausting."

Tanuja nodded gently as she listened, her compassionate gaze encouraging Srishti to continue. "Tell me more about these mood swings. When do they usually occur? Are there any specific triggers?"

Srishti considered Tanuja's question, delving into her memories. "It's not always clear what sets them off. Sometimes, it's when I'm under immense pressure at work or when I feel like I'm not living up to my own expectations." She paused, swallowing hard as she admitted, "And other times, they seem to come out of nowhere, leaving me feeling helpless and lost."

As Srishti spoke, Tanuja maintained eye contact, creating an atmosphere of trust and understanding. "It's important that you recognize these feelings, Srishti," she said, her voice strong but soothing. "Our emotions can be powerful teachers if we learn to listen to them. They can show us where we need to heal and grow."

Silently reflecting on Tanuja's insight, Srishti felt a spark of curiosity flicker within her. Could she truly learn from her emotions instead of being controlled by them?

"Over the coming weeks," Tanuja continued, "we will work together to uncover the root causes of your emotional challenges and develop strategies to help you navigate these difficult moments more effectively."

The prospect of facing her emotional wounds was daunting, but Srishti knew that she couldn't continue on her current path. "I'm ready to do the work, Tanuja," she said with a newfound determination. "I want to better understand myself and find ways to manage my emotions."

"Your willingness to engage in this process is admirable, Srishti," Tanuja praised as she offered a warm smile. "As we progress, remember that it's normal to feel overwhelmed or uncertain at times. The key is to remain patient and compassionate with yourself."

Hearing Tanuja's words of encouragement, Srishti felt her confidence grow – a seed of hope taking root within her soul. Embracing the challenge before her, she knew that she had taken the first step towards reclaiming control over her emotional well-being.

*****

As Srishti took a deep breath, she felt a sense of relief wash over her like a gentle wave. The tension in her shoulders began to dissipate, and for the first time in what felt like ages, she allowed herself to believe that there could be a way out of her emotional labyrinth.

"Thank you so much, Tanuja," Srishti said with heartfelt sincerity, her eyes glistening with gratitude. "I didn't realize how desperately I needed someone to listen and understand."

"Of course, Srishti," Tanuja replied warmly, placing a reassuring hand on her arm. "It's incredibly brave of you to seek help and open up about your struggles. Remember that healing is a journey, and I'm here to guide you every step of the way."

As she listened to Tanuja's words, Srishti felt a surge of hope rise within her chest. She clung to the possibility that these therapy sessions would not only provide her with the tools to manage her emotions but also transform her life in ways she couldn't yet imagine.

"Alright, let's take this journey" Srishti resolved, her voice steady and determined. "I'm ready to learn and grow."

"Excellent," Tanuja beamed, pleased by Srishti's resolve. "We'll begin our next session by exploring your past experiences in more depth. This will help us gain a clearer understanding of how certain events may have shaped your emotions and thought patterns."

Srishti nodded, accepting the challenge ahead. As Tanuja rose from her chair and opened the door, the sunlight streamed into the room, casting a warm glow over the space. Srishti felt as though it was a symbolic representation of the light that had begun to shine within her own heart.

"Take care, Srishti," Tanuja said with a genuine smile. "I look forward to seeing you soon."

"Me too," Srishti replied, her eyes shining with newfound hope.

As she stepped out of Tanuja's office and into the sunlit afternoon, Srishti knew that the path to healing wouldn't be easy. There would be challenges, setbacks, and moments of self- doubt. But with each step forward, she was inching closer to a brighter, more fulfilling future – one where she held the power to shape her emotional destiny.

And as the door closed behind her, the end of this chapter marked the beginning of a new one: a journey of self-discovery, growth, and transformation that would redefine the course of Srishti's life forever.

6

PROCRASTINATION – Seize The Today

Tanuja observed Srishti, fidgeting in the chair across from her, her gaze drifting towards the window where a pigeon had perched on the sill, seemingly postponing its next flight. The sun spilled into the room, casting a warm glow on Srishti's face, which seemed to be caught between the desire to soak in the light and the weight of an invisible burden.

"Procrastination," Tanuja began in her calm, reassuring voice, "might sound like a complex term, but it's quite a common experience. It's when we delay or avoid tasks that need our attention." She noticed the slight nod from Srishti, an acknowledgement wrapped in hesitation.

"Whether it's about preparing for exams, clearing up your space, completing a project, or even sending out an email," Tanuja continued with a gentle smile, "instead of addressing the urgent and essential, we often choose something more amusing or less demanding. Watching a show, scrolling through the phone, engaging in games, or daydreaming."

Srishti's eyes met Tanuja's, carrying an unspoken question. "Why do we do it, though?" she asked, her voice barely above a whisper, but laden with curiosity. Her hands stopped their nervous dance and rested in her lap, signalling her readiness to dive deeper into understanding her own patterns of avoidance.

Tanuja leaned forward slightly, her expressive eyes holding Srishti's in a soft but firm embrace. "It's a question worth exploring," she affirmed. "What's really happening in our minds when we choose to procrastinate? What are we seeking or, perhaps more importantly, what are we avoiding?"

The room was filled with a silence that seemed to invite introspection. Srishti took a deep breath, her thoughts gathering like clouds before a downpour - charged, expectant.

"Sometimes," Tanuja offered, breaking the silence with her therapeutic cadence, "it might feel as if we're standing at a crossroads. One path leads to the known comforts, the immediate gratifications. The other to the necessary, yet less appealing tasks ahead."

"Exactly," Srishti found herself saying, her own understanding beginning to crystallize. "It's like there's this voice inside me, arguing for just one more episode, one more level in the game, or a few more minutes lost in fantasies."

"Ah," Tanuja nodded, "the inner dialogue that negotiates with time and priorities." She paused, allowing the words to settle, before adding, "But remember, Srishti, every moment of realization is a step towards change. Recognizing this pattern is where your power lies."

Srishti's posture straightened, a subtle shift that did not go unnoticed by Tanuja, who saw it as a sign of Srishti's rekindled resolve. "So, what can I do about it?" Srishti asked, a spark of determination igniting in her almond-shaped eyes."Let's start by embracing this awareness," Tanuja suggested, her tone imbued with hope. "And together, we'll explore strategies to navigate through the temptation to procrastinate, towards a path where you're in control."

"Sounds like a plan," Srishti replied, a small yet genuine smile tugging at the corners of her mouth. They both knew it wouldn't be an easy journey, but the commitment to understand and overcome was already taking root, promising a fertile ground for growth.

Srishti perched on the edge of the cushioned chair, her fingers absentmindedly tracing the soft fabric as she contemplated the pattern of her own behaviour. Tanuja observed her, the patient silence between them thick with unspoken thoughts. "Consider this," Tanuja began gently, her voice a soothing balm to Srishti's restless mind. "Our brain is designed with a simple preference: pleasure over pain. It's instinctual."

"Like choosing chocolate over chores?" Srishti quipped, a wry smile flickering for a moment. "Exactly," Tanuja affirmed with a nod, her warm eyes reflecting empathy. "The piece of chocolate is immediate joy, tangible and sweet. But when it comes to tasks that require effort and focus..."

"Studying... cleaning..." Srishti sighed, her gaze dropping to her lap. The weight of undone tasks seemed to press down on her shoulders. "Those can feel like mountains at times," Tanuja continued, leaning forward, her presence a pillar of support. "Your brain protests against the climb, luring you towards easier paths."

"Video games. TV shows," Srishti added, lifting her eyes to meet Tanuja's steady gaze. "They promise fun, an escape from the uphill battle." Tanuja said softly. "Procrastination whispers in your ear, offering comfort. It says, 'Why endure discomfort when bliss is just a click away?'"

"Yet afterward, the mountain looms larger, doesn't it?" Srishti murmured, understanding dawning in her eyes. "Indeed," Tanuja agreed, her tone laced with encouragement. "But there's depth to this pattern, layers waiting to be uncovered."

Srishti leaned back, her mind churning. Tanuja's words painted a clear picture, one that resonated within her. She was beginning to see the landscape of her mind - the valleys of avoidance and the peaks of necessity. "Procrastination isn't just about seeking joy or shunning duty," Tanuja explained, her hands gesturing subtly as if drawing the concept into existence. "It's entwined with our inner narratives, the stories we tell ourselves."

"Stories that I can rewrite?" Srishti asked, hope threading through her voice. "Absolutely," Tanuja confirmed, her smile a beacon of assurance. "And together, we will explore those stories, understand their origins, and learn how to pen a narrative of resilience and action."

"Sounds empowering," Srishti said, her earlier hesitance giving way to a budding conviction. "Empowerment starts within," Tanuja stated, her words like seeds planted in fertile soil. "We'll cultivate it, bit by bit, with patience and persistence."

"Patience and persistence," Srishti repeated, the phrase becoming a mantra of possibility. The journey ahead didn't seem so daunting now, not with a guide like Tanuja by her side, ready to traverse the intricate pathways of the mind.

*****

Tanuja observed Srishti as she fidgeted with the hem of her blouse, a subtle dance of anxiety at the edges of her fingers. A silence had settled between them, rich with unspoken truths. "Procrastination," Tanuja began, breaking the stillness with her serene voice, "isn't merely a game of hide and seek between pleasure and responsibility." She paused, watching Srishti's guarded expression soften. "At its heart lies fear."

Srishti met Tanuja's gaze, her own eyes a mirror of vulnerability. "Fear?" she echoed, the word a breath, a whisper of admission. "Specifically, the fear of failure," Tanuja clarified, her tone gentle yet unwavering. "It's a shadow that looms over many, cloaking potential in doubt." A nod from Srishti, slight but significant, acknowledged the truth in Tanuja's words. Her shoulders, once tense, eased fractionally under the weight of recognition.

"Failure, it's paralyzing." Srishti murmured, tasting the bitterness of the concept. "Yet it is through understanding this fear that we find our courage," Tanuja said, her voice a balm to Srishti's apprehension. "It's not about never failing, but about embracing each stumble as a step forward."

"Embracing failure," Srishti pondered aloud, her mind wrestling with the paradox. "How?"

"By reframing it," Tanuja suggested, her hands coming together in a steeple, reflecting thoughtfulness. "See it not as an endpoint, but as a teacher. A guide, even."

"Guide me to success?" Srishti asked, a tentative smile curving her lips."Exactly," Tanuja affirmed, her smile reflecting Srishti's. "And remember, every great story has its trials. It's how the hero grows."

"Am I the hero, then?" Srishti's question was half-teasing, half- hopeful."In your story? Always," Tanuja said, her conviction clear and strong. "You hold the pen, Srishti. Write your next chapter with courage inked in every line."

"Courage..." Srishti whispered, the idea unfurling within her like the first rays of dawn dispersing shadows of doubt."Let's explore this more," Tanuja offered, inviting deeper reflection. "What does courage look like to you in the face of procrastination?"

"Action, I suppose,to act despite the fear." Srishti replied, her thoughts crystallizing."Indeed," Tanuja nodded, proud. "And with each action, you chip away at the barriers holding you back."

"Small actions, they could lead to big changes.", Srishti mused, finding strength in the simplicity. "Often, they're the only thing that ever does," Tanuja confirmed, her voice a testament to countless journeys witnessed and guided."Then let's start small," Srishti decided, a newfound resolve lifting her stance. "One task at a time."

"One task at a time," Tanuja echoed, "and soon, you'll be on the other side of procrastination, looking back at how far you've come."

"Thank you, Tanuja," Srishti said, gratitude shining through her like sunlight piercing clouds. "For helping me see that."

"Always," Tanuja responded, the warmth in her eyes promising continued support. "Together, we'll walk this path."

"Step by step," Srishti added, her voice a note higher, filled with the music of potential. "I'm ready to take the first one."

"Then let's begin," Tanuja said, a soft determination in her tone. "Your journey awaits."

*****

Tanuja leaned forward, her gaze soft yet penetrating as she probed into the layers of Srishti's mind. "It seems we've unearthed the fear of failure," she said gently, "but tell me, what about the fear of acceptance? How often do you find yourself worrying about judgment from others?" Srishti's fingers toyed with the hem of her shirt, a nervous habit that spoke volumes. "All the time," she admitted in a quiet voice. "It's like I'm on a stage, and everyone's a critic waiting for me to slip."

"Ah," Tanuja murmured, her nod slow and understanding. "The imaginary audience can be quite unforgiving, can't it?" The room was still, the air itself seemed to hold its breath, acknowledging the weight of shared truths.

"Especially when they're not just in my head," Srishti added, her cheeks colouring slightly. "I replay conversations, imagining disdain in every pause, criticism in every word."

"Yet here you are," Tanuja pointed out, her tone infused with hope, "braving the spotlight to face these fears." She gestured toward the space around them, an invisible arena where battles were fought and won within the confines of the mind.

"Because I want to break free," Srishti declared, her voice stronger now, echoing her inner resolve. "To live without the constant dread of disapproval looming over me."

"Bravo," Tanuja applauded softly. "And what of the fear of the unknown? How does that shape your procrastination?" Srishti's eyes flickered, reflecting an internal struggle. "It paralyzes me," she confessed. "Not knowing what might happen if I act... it's easier to do nothing."

"Uncertainty is life's constant companion," Tanuja said, her voice a soothing balm. "But consider this: each step into the unknown is also a step towards possibility."

"Towards growth," Srishti finished, her earlier anxiety giving way to contemplation. "It's just hard to take that first step."

"Indeed," Tanuja agreed, "but each journey begins with exactly that—a single step, taken with courage." Her words floated between them, seeds of encouragement waiting to take root. "Courage doesn't always roar," Srishti reflected aloud, surprising herself with the insight. "Sometimes, it's the quiet voice at the end of the day saying, 'I will try again tomorrow.'"

"Beautifully put," Tanuja said, her expression proud. "And remember, Srishti, it's not the absence of fear but the triumph over it that defines courage."

"Triumph," Srishti repeated, rolling the word around in her mouth like a new taste. "I like that."

"Then let's build on that," Tanuja proposed. "Let's cultivate acceptance—beginning with accepting ourselves, our efforts, regardless of the outcome."

"Sounds liberating," Srishti mused, a tentative smile blossoming on her lips."Because it is," Tanuja confirmed, her voice resolute. "Liberation from our own harsh judgments, from the chains of uncertainty. You have the strength within you, Srishti."

"Strength," Srishti echoed, testing the power of the word. "To accept. To face the unknown."

"Exactly," Tanuja affirmed. "You're not alone in this. Each step you take, I'll be right beside you, cheering you on."

"Thank you, for believing in me, even when I struggle to believe in myself." Srishti said, gratitude lacing her words. "Always," Tanuja replied, her eyes shining with conviction. "Together, we'll conquer these fears—one small, brave step at a time."

"Step by step, I'm ready." Srishti vowed, standing a little taller, ready to march into battle against her inner demons. "Then onward we go," Tanuja said, a beacon of support in the quest for self-improvement. "Toward growth, toward healing, toward freedom."

"Freedom," Srishti whispered, embracing the word, the concept, the future. And in that moment, the fears that had once loomed large began to shrink back, diminished by the light of hope and the promise of change.

*****

Tanuja leaned slightly forward, her hands clasped together in a gesture that radiated both focus and comfort. The room was quiet except for the gentle hum of the air conditioner—a soothing white noise against the backdrop of their conversation.

"Procrastination often has deeper roots," Tanuja began, her voice as warm as sunlight breaking through clouds. "Beyond fear, there's another layer. Let's explore that."

Srishti nodded, her almond-shaped eyes reflecting a pool of curiosity tinged with apprehension. She tucked a strand of hair behind her ear, a small act of preparation, as if bracing herself to dive into the depths of her psyche. "Sometimes," Tanuja continued, "the seeds are sown early in our lives. Think back to your childhood—were there moments when you were labelled as lazy or not serious enough by parents or teachers?"

A frown creased Srishti's forehead, her pastel blouse almost mirroring the vulnerability etched across her face. Her voice, usually so measured, wavered slightly. "Yes," she admitted. "I was always trying to be perfect, but... sometimes it felt like my efforts were never enough. If I hesitated or took too long, they'd say I was procrastinating, being lazy."

"Those labels," Tanuja said gently, "they stick, don't they? They become a part of your narrative."

"Like a shadow," Srishti whispered, "following me, even now."

Tanuja nodded, her expressive eyes holding a well of empathy. "But shadows only exist because of light. You have the power to change the narrative, Srishti. You're not that child anymore. You can choose which labels define you."

"Choose..." Srishti mulled over the word, a tentative seedling of empowerment taking root within her. "Exactly," Tanuja confirmed, a soft smile playing on her lips. "You're meticulous, intelligent, resilient. These are your truths. Hold on to them."

"Resilient," Srishti repeated, the word resonating within her like a struck chord. "I like that."

"Let's replace those old labels," Tanuja suggested. "Every time you hear that echo of 'lazy' in your mind, counter it with 'resilient', 'diligent', 'capable'. Your self-talk shapes your reality, Srishti."

"Capable," Srishti tested the word, feeling its solidity. "I am capable."

"Indeed, you are," Tanuja affirmed. "And with each step, you'll peel away those layers of doubt that were once wrapped around you by others' words."

Srishti sat up a little straighter, her spine aligning with the newfound strength that seemed to fill her. "I've allowed those labels to dictate how I see myself for so long," she said, her voice steadier now, carrying a hint of revelation."Recognizing that is the first step to unlearning it," Tanuja encouraged. "You are not the procrastinator they claimed; you are someone who carefully considers her actions."

"Careful consideration," Srishti repeated, rolling the words in her mouth like a comforting balm. "That's not laziness, is it?"

"Far from it," Tanuja replied warmly. "It's a sign of your thoughtful nature. It's about being strategic with your energy and attention."

"Strategic," Srishti contemplated. "I need to embrace that. To be kind to myself when old patterns emerge."

"Kindness is key," Tanuja agreed, her voice a tender melody. "And remember, it's okay to pause, to breathe. You're not on anyone's timeline but your own."

"Thank you," Srishti managed, her almond-shaped eyes brightening with unshed tears of gratitude. "For helping me see that."

"Always," Tanuja assured her. "And together, we'll work on strategies to keep moving forward, even when it's hard. Procrastination doesn't define you. Your actions, your choices – that's where your true power lies."

"Choices," Srishti echoed, feeling the weight of her years of self-doubt beginning to lift. "I choose to move forward."

"Excellent choice," Tanuja said, her smile reflecting the pride she felt for Srishti's breakthrough. "And remember, every small step counts. Consistency conquers, Srishti. Consistency conquers."

*****

Srishti shifted uncomfortably in the plush armchair, her fingers tracing the soft fabric as if seeking solace from its texture. The room, bathed in the gentle glow of the afternoon sun, felt like a sanctuary, yet her heart raced with the familiar flutter of anxiety.

"Think of our mind as a home," Tanuja began, her voice steady and soothing. "One that prefers the coziness of known spaces."

"Safe spaces," Srishti murmured, her gaze fixed on a patch of light dancing across the floor."Exactly," Tanuja affirmed. "But sometimes, growth lies beyond those walls. Stepping out invites discomfort, it's true. That feeling is your body responding to perceived threats, trying to coax you back to safety."

"Back to procrastination," Srishti added quietly. Tanuja nodded.

"That's one way to see it. But let's try another perspective. Imagine these signals not as stop signs, but as markers on a path to better understand ourselves."

"Markers..." Srishti considered the word, rolling it around her thoughts. She exhaled slowly, a deliberate breath to calm her racing heart."Procrastination isn't an immovable obstacle," Tanuja continued. "It's a challenge, a chance for self-discovery and empowerment."

"Empowerment," Srishti echoed, the concept resonating within her. "That sounds more...hopeful."

"And it is," Tanuja said, her eyes locking onto Srishti's with unwavering belief. "You hold the power to redefine your relationship with discomfort. To move through it and come out stronger on the other side."

"Stronger," Srishti repeated, feeling the stirrings of conviction. "How do I start?"

"Small steps," Tanuja suggested. "Identify what you're avoiding, then take one small action toward it. Acknowledge the discomfort, but don't let it dictate your actions."

"Action, not avoidance," Srishti said, a mantra forming in her mind. She pictured herself standing at the edge of her comfort zone, ready to step over the threshold."Remember," Tanuja said, leaning forward slightly, "every step is progress. Guilt and overwhelm are unnecessary burdens. You have the capacity for growth and the strength to improve."

"Capacity for growth," Srishti whispered, a smile tugging at the corners of her lips. It was a new narrative, one she could write herself, with Tanuja's guidance lighting the way."Indeed," Tanuja smiled back, her expression a mirror of encouragement. "So, shall we plan your first step together?"

Together. The word wrapped around Srishti like a warm embrace, dispelling the last tendrils of trepidation. With Tanuja by her side, the journey ahead seemed filled with possibility. "Yes," Srishti answered, her voice steadier now. "Let's do that."

"Excellent," Tanuja replied. "Your journey begins with belief, and belief sparks action. You're already on your way, Srishti."

"Belief sparks action," Srishti repeated, letting the words anchor her newfound resolve. She was ready to face procrastination head-on, transforming it from foe to teacher. One step at a time.

*****

Srishti's fingers hovered over the keyboard, the cursor blinking mockingly at her. The deadline for her report loomed like a thundercloud, and yet here she was, paralyzed by the familiar clench of procrastination. She glanced at the clock, feeling the first tendrils of panic winding their way through her chest.

"Last-minute rushes can be quite addictive," Tanuja's voice was calm as it sliced through Srishti's mounting anxiety. "They flood us with adrenaline, convincing us we're more productive under pressure."

"Yes, but then why do I feel so overwhelmed?" Srishti asked, her voice tinged with frustration."Because, Srishti," Tanuja said gently, "the body's response to stress isn't sustainable long term. It's meant for survival, not for writing reports or meeting work deadlines."Tanuja leaned forward, her eyes locked onto Srishti's. "Tell me, how do you feel when you submit your work at the eleventh hour?"

"Relieved, yes. But mostly exhausted and jittery," Srishti admitted, her shoulders slumping. "Exactly. That exhaustion is a sign. It's your body telling you that this pattern might not be serving you well." Tanuja's tone was not one of reprimand but of understanding.

"Then, how do I change it?" Srishti's voice was small, almost lost in the room's quiet. "First, by recognizing it's just a pattern, Srishti." Tanuja's words were soothing, the rhythm of her speech like a balm. "And patterns can be reshaped."

"Reshaped," Srishti echoed, allowing the idea to plant itself in her thoughts. "Let's start with acknowledging the emotions that come with these last-minute rushes," Tanuja suggested, her hands folding neatly in her lap. "Do they make you feel empowered or drained?"

"Drained," Srishti answered without hesitation.

"Then, we find a new pattern. One that includes proactive steps, time management, and—most importantly—self-compassion.", chimed in Tanuja. "Proactive steps," Srishti repeated, her mind beginning to edge away from the precipice of panic. She could see the shape of a plan forming, something tangible she could grasp onto.

"Break down the task," Tanuja guided, "set smaller deadlines leading up to the final one, and reward yourself for each step completed. This way, you create a series of successes, rather than a single moment of rushed relief."

"Successes," Srishti murmured. The word felt good, solid, achievable. "Remember," Tanuja concluded, her expression warm and hopeful, "you have the power to rewrite this narrative. Each decision to act before the rush is a victory over old habits."

"Rewrite... my narrative," Srishti whispered, a newfound determination flickering in her eyes. She turned back to her computer, taking a deep breath. Her fingers began to dance across the keys, each word a deliberate step away from procrastination and towards control, towards calm.

"Victory," she said, a soft smile curving her lips. With each sentence crafted, Srishti felt the old pattern loosening its grip, replaced by the steady heartbeat of progress. And within that rhythm lay the promise of change, the echo of Tanuja's wisdom guiding her forward.

*****

Tanuja leaned forward, her hands clasping together in a gentle display of solidarity. The afternoon light filtered through the blinds, casting a soft glow on the quiet space between therapist and client. "Let's explore the roots of what's holding you back," she said, her voice a soothing balm to Srishti's frayed nerves. "Understanding why we procrastinate can be our most potent weapon against it."

Srishti nodded, her eyes tracing the patterns on the carpet as if they held the answers she sought. "I guess I'm just scared of... not being enough," she admitted, the words tumbling out like reluctant confessions. "Ah, the fear of inadequacy," Tanuja acknowledged, recognizing an old adversary. "It can paralyze us, make us believe that unless it's perfect, it's not worth doing at all."

"Exactly," Srishti whispered, feeling the weight of countless unfinished tasks pressing down on her. "But nothing I do ever seems perfect enough."

"Perfection is an illusion, a mirage that keeps moving the closer you get," Tanuja offered gently. "What if we shift our focus from being flawless to simply making progress?"

"Progress..." Srishti rolled the word around her mind, tasting its potential. She lifted her gaze, meeting Tanuja's steady one. "But how do I start? How do I stop this cycle?"

"By embracing your imperfections," Tanuja replied, her expressive eyes conveying deep empathy. "Every stumble, every falter, is part of your journey. Mistakes are not failures; they're stepping stones to growth."

"Stepping stones," Srishti echoed, the concept resonating within her. A small smile played on her lips as she imagined herself hopping from stone to stone, moving forward despite the occasional slip. "Remember, Srishti, you are more than your productivity," Tanuja continued, her tone warm yet imbued with conviction. "You are a work in progress, and that's beautiful."

"Work in progress," Srishti repeated, the phrase wrapping around her like a comforting embrace. She could feel the tendrils of hope weaving through the fog of her doubt, clearing a path for courage to take root."Let's set some small, attainable goals," Tanuja suggested, "and celebrate each achievement, no matter how modest. It's about consistency, not speed. You can conquer procrastination one step at a time."

"Consistency," Srishti affirmed, a newfound strength rising within her. With each syllable, she felt more equipped to face the tasks ahead, armed with the knowledge that perfection was not the goal—movement was."Will you try that for me?" Tanuja asked, her question more of an invitation than a challenge.

"I will," Srishti said, determination etching its way into her features. She could almost see the chain of procrastination breaking link by link, each victory over hesitation a testament to her growing resilience.

"Good," Tanuja smiled, the pride in her protégé palpable. "Now let's begin."

*****

Tanuja leaned forward slightly, her gaze locking onto Srishti's with an intensity that conveyed both assurance and challenge. "Srishti," she began, her voice a soft yet stirring force, "I want to introduce you to a very simple yet powerful tool. It's called the 5 Second Rule."

"Five seconds?" Srishti echoed, her eyebrows knitting together in curiosity."Exactly. Five seconds can be the difference between staying stuck and moving forward," Tanuja explained. "When you notice you're hesitating before a task, count down from five to one. And then—start immediately."

"Is it really that simple?" Srishti asked, scepticism giving way to intrigue."Deceptively so," Tanuja replied, a knowing smile touching her lips. "This rule engages your prefrontal cortex, empowering you to take action before your doubts can take over."

"Five... four... three... two... one..." Srishti murmured under her breath, as if tasting the words.

"Start!" Tanuja interjected with gentle firmness. "In those moments of doubt, this mantra propels you into action. The countdown is your launch pad."Srishti sat up straighter, her mind visualizing the countdown like bright neon numbers against the backdrop of her tasks. Her heart thrummed with the prospect of breaking free from the chains of procrastination.

"Alright," Srishti said, her voice now steadier than before. "The next time I find myself hesitating, I'll count down."

"Remember, the goal here isn't just to start but to break the cycle," Tanuja reminded her, her eyes radiating confidence. "It's not about the size of the step you're taking. It's about the decision to take it at all."

"Five seconds to beat the brain's hesitation," Srishti repeated, internalizing the strategy. She could already feel the gears shifting, the usual paralysis waning as the simplicity of the technique settled in."Exactly! And watch how much you'll accomplish," Tanuja affirmed, her tone brimming with optimism. "Let's practice. Think of a task you've been putting off."

"Emailing my mentor," Srishti admitted quickly."Good. Now close your eyes," Tanuja instructed. "Picture yourself opening your laptop, starting the email. Ready?"

With a deep inhale, Srishti nodded, her eyelids fluttering closed. "Five, four, three, two, one—start!"

Srishti's eyes snapped open, a spark igniting within them. "I'm doing it right after our session," she declared, a hint of excitement seeping through her resolve."Perfect," Tanuja said, her approval clear. "See how you transformed hesitation into action? That's the power you hold."

"Five seconds to change course," Srishti whispered, almost to herself, feeling the weight of potential in that tiny span of time."Those five seconds are yours, Srishti," Tanuja emphasized. "Use them to fuel your journey forward."

"Thank you, Tanuja. This... feels doable. Like I'm regaining control," Srishti expressed, gratitude lacing her words.

"Because you are," Tanuja confirmed. "One five-second countdown at a time."

*****

Tanuja leaned forward, her hands clasped gently on the table between them. "Srishti, let's explore the ABCDE method now," she said, her voice a soft melody of guidance. "It will help us understand your procrastination patterns more deeply."

"ABCDE?" Srishti echoed, curiosity threading through her skepticism.

"First, AWARE. Recognize the task you're avoiding," Tanuja explained. "Reflect on why it's remained untouched." Srishti's gaze dropped to her hands, fidgeting in her lap. "I've been dodging the research proposal I need to write. It feels so massive, daunting."

"Good awareness," Tanuja nodded. "Now, BELIEFS. What thoughts circle around this task?"

"I believe if it's not perfect, it'll be a failure. That I'll be a failure," Srishti confessed, a shadow crossing her features.

"CHALLENGE those negative perceptions," Tanuja prompted gently. "Is perfection truly attainable? Does it define your worth?"

A faint shake of Srishti's head. "No, but it feels like it does," she admitted.

"DISPUTE your excuses, the justifications for delay," Tanuja continued, her eyes holding Srishti's with an unwavering warmth. "Replace them with thoughts that empower you. Can you try?"

Srishti breathed in deeply, searching for the courage within Tanuja's words. "I... I am capable. The proposal is a work in progress, not a measure of my value."

"Exactly," Tanuja's smile was radiant, lighting up the room. "Every step, no matter how small, is progress."

"Progress, not perfection," Srishti repeated, the mantra settling into her bones. "Write that down," Tanuja suggested. "Your new belief." Srishti obliged, her pen scratching across paper, the sound a testament to her shifting mindset.

"See? You're already taking action." Tanuja's approval was palpable."Because of you," Srishti said, lifting her eyes, brimming with newfound determination."Because of you," Tanuja corrected softly. "You chose to challenge and dispute. And you can choose it every time."

"Every single time," Srishti agreed, her voice stronger now. "Remember," Tanuja concluded, "your thoughts have power. Use them to forge your path ahead."

Srishti stood, shoulders squared, a ripple of energy coursing through her veins. She paced the length of Tanuja's office, each step a drumbeat to her newfound rhythm of action. The room was awash with the golden light of late afternoon, lending a glow to the scene that felt like a tender nod from the universe itself.

"Let's break the cycle," Tanuja said, her voice the very essence of encouragement."Breaking it," Srishti echoed, a small but genuine smile playing on her lips.

"Good." Tanuja unfolded a fresh sheet of paper, placing it on the table between them—a procrastination worksheet, a map for the journey ahead. "Now, let's energize your plan."

"ENERGIZE," Srishti repeated, rolling the word around like a promise.

*****

Srishti bent over the worksheet, pen in hand. Her fingers gripped the instrument as if it were a key turning in the lock of her potential.

"Small steps," Tanuja reminded her. "Break it down."

"Divide and conquer," Srishti murmured to herself, scrawling headings on the paper—steps that once towered over her now downsized into manageable tasks.

"Set deadlines," Tanuja guided, calm and steady.

"Deadlines," Srishti nodded, scribbling dates next to each task, a timeline materializing from the mist of postponement.

"Eliminate distractions," Tanuja continued, her words a gentle nudge.

"Clearing my space," Srishti affirmed, envisioning her desk at home, free of clutter and ready for focus.

"Create a schedule," Tanuja's suggestion floated across the room.

"Allocating time," Srishti responded, assigning slots to each activity, her heartbeat syncing with the intention of every line she drew.

"Reward yourself," Tanuja's eyes twinkled.

"Sweet victories," Srishti smiled wider now, imagining the joy in little celebrations, picturing herself basking in the satisfaction of tasks completed.

"An accountability partner can be a pillar," Tanuja offered, a lighthouse guiding ships to shore.

"Sharing my goals," Srishti acknowledged the strength found in vulnerability, the power in partnership.

"Reflect often," Tanuja's final piece of advice landed softly.

"Adjust and grow," Srishti finished, her voice a murmur of empowerment.

"Consistency conquers," they said together, an anthem rising in the quiet office.

"Consistency," Srishti whispered to herself, her eyes tracing the neat rows of her worksheet. Each word she had written was a stepping stone away from the quagmire of delay. She could almost feel the shackles of procrastination melting away, replaced by a vibrant energy ready to propel her forward.

"Remember," Tanuja spoke, her tone imbued with hope, "this is a process. There will be days when it all feels too much. But look at what you've created here, Srishti. This is your blueprint for action."

"Thank you," Srishti breathed out, gratitude swelling in her chest. She clutched the worksheet like a talisman, knowing its true magic lay not in the paper and ink but in her own resolve.

"Thank yourself," Tanuja corrected gently, "You are the architect of your change."

"Architect," Srishti repeated, standing a little taller. They both knew; the real building was just beginning.

*****

Srishti hesitated for just a moment before her pen touched the paper, the silence of the room wrapping around her like a cocoon. She drew in a deep breath, steadying her jittery nerves, and began to write.

"Email to my supervisor," she murmured, the words etching into the worksheet, "proposal for the community project, doctor's appointment..." The list grew, each task a whispered confession of delay.

Tanuja watched, her eyes reflecting pride. She leaned forward slightly, her presence an anchor in the vast sea of Srishti's anxieties. "That's it," she encouraged. "Let them flow out of you and onto the page."

"Register for the workshop," Srishti continued, her voice a notch stronger. With each word, the fog in her mind seemed to lift, revealing a path that had been obscured by the mists of indecision. "Good," Tanuja said, nodding. "Now, let's look at these tasks. Which one needs your attention first?"

Srishti scanned her list, biting her lip as she considered each entry. "The email," she decided, feeling the weight of its importance. "It's been hanging over me for weeks."

"And after that?" Tanuja prompted, her gaze steady and reassuring.

"The proposal," Srishti replied, feeling a newfound clarity. "Then the doctor's appointment." She arranged them neatly, the priorities aligning like stars charting her course.

"See how they start to order themselves when you face them?" Tanuja's voice was soft but filled with conviction. "One step at a time."

"One step," Srishti echoed, her pen pausing as she felt the truth of those words settle within her. Each task, once a source of dread, now transformed into a stepping stone toward her goals.

"Exactly," Tanuja affirmed, a smile gracing her lips. "You're already on your way."

"Thank you," Srishti said again, this time with confidence blooming in her chest. The daunting mountain of procrastination now seemed a series of manageable hills, and she felt ready to climb.

*****

Tanuja leaned forward, her eyes reflecting the glow of determination in Srishti's. "Now that we have priorities," she said, capturing Srishti's gaze with a gentle intensity, "it's time to break them down."

"Break them down?" Srishti asked, tilting her head slightly. The concept felt foreign yet inherently logical.

"Into smaller steps," Tanuja clarified, her hands moving as if she were visually dividing an unseen challenge into segments. "It makes the task less daunting, more achievable."

Srishti considered this, her mind racing through the tangled threads of her pending email. "I suppose I could start by outlining what I want to say."

"Exactly," Tanuja encouraged, her voice a melody of support. "And then?"

"Draft the introduction," Srishti continued, feeling the weight lift with each imagined step. "Followed by the main points I need to cover."

"Good," Tanuja nodded, her approval like a warm blanket around Srishti's shoulders. "And for the proposal?"

"Research first," Srishti answered, gaining momentum. "Then, create a rough structure, and finally, flesh it out."

"Perfect," Tanuja's affirmation was a soft but powerful nudge. "Now, let's assign some deadlines."

"Deadlines..." Srishti echoed, the word often a harbinger of stress, now transformed into a signpost of progress. She pulled her calendar closer, the dates suddenly allies in her journey.

"Tomorrow, for the email outline." Srishti's voice was firmer, surer than before.

"Reasonable," Tanuja agreed, her nod a silent cheer.

"End of the week for the research?" Srishti proposed, testing the waters of her newfound resolve.

"Excellent pacing," Tanuja confirmed. "How does that feel?"

"Realistic," Srishti allowed herself a small smile, the taste of potential progress sweet on her tongue. "Doable."

"Remember," Tanuja's words were deliberate, wrapping around Srishti like a protective shawl, "you're not alone in this."

"Thank you," Srishti breathed out, the gratitude mingling with a budding sense of empowerment. "For making it seem possible."

"Because it is," Tanuja said simply, her smile speaking volumes. "One step, one deadline at a time."

Srishti left the session with her list, now a map to a treasure trove of self-accomplishment. Each step was a brick in the foundation of her recovery, each deadline a promise to herself. They were commitments etched not in stone, but in hope – a testament to the power of breaking things down, of shaping chaos into order, one manageable piece at a time.

*****

Srishti's fingers hovered over her laptop, the screen a blank canvas waiting for her thoughts. Tanuja watched from across the room, a serene presence in the quiet space. "Let's talk about your environment," she suggested gently.

"Environment?" Srishti glanced around, as if seeing her workspace for the first time. "It's comfortable, I guess."

"Comfortable is good," Tanuja acknowledged with a nod. "But what about distractions?"

"Distractions..." Srishti repeated, her gaze drifting to the window where the world bustled by, oblivious to her struggle. She thought of her phone, its siren call often too alluring to resist. "Identify them," Tanuja encouraged. "What pulls you away from your work?"

"Notifications," Srishti admitted, "social media, even just... daydreaming."

"Start there," Tanuja said. "Turn off notifications. Give yourself the gift of uninterrupted time."

"Uninterrupted time, I can do that." Srishti mused, feeling the weight of each syllable. "Good," Tanuja smiled. "Now, let's create a schedule. What does your typical day look like?"

"Chaotic," Srishti confessed. "I try to do everything at once."

"Ah," Tanuja leaned forward, her eyes locking with Srishti's. "Let's change that. Allocate specific time slots for each task. Start with the most important."

"Okay." Srishti took a deep breath, picking up her pen with newfound purpose. "Mornings for writing, afternoons for research..."

"Excellent," Tanuja approved. "How does that feel?"

"Structured," Srishti answered, the word a new friend. "Focused."

"Remember," Tanuja's voice was soft, yet potent, "your time is precious. Guard it well."

"Yes," Srishti agreed, her heart swelling with hope. "I will guard it."

"Promise yourself," Tanuja prompted. "I promise," Srishti said firmly, the two words a pact sealed between her present and future self. "No more yielding to distractions."

"Your time, your rules," Tanuja affirmed. "You're creating a space where progress can bloom."

"Progress," Srishti whispered, loving how the word felt on her lips. She envisioned her days, each moment a step toward her goals, every task completed a victory over procrastination.

"See?" Tanuja's voice was the gentle tide against the shore of Srishti's consciousness. "You have the power to shape your day, your life."

Srishti nodded, her schedule now a sacred text, her commitment etched deep within. This was more than a plan; it was a testament to her resolve, a declaration of her agency in the relentless flow of time.

"Thank you," Srishti said, her eyes bright. "For helping me see I can."

"Always," Tanuja replied, her smile the warm embrace of a proud mentor. "One task, one time slot at a time."

*****

Srishti settled into the familiar chair, hands clasped, a small smile tugging at her lips. The room, awash with soft light, seemed to hold its breath, awaiting her next step. "Tell me," Tanuja began, her voice a soothing melody, "what would make completing a task feel rewarding to you?"

"Something small but meaningful," Srishti mused, eyes alight with thought. "Like a cup of my favourite jasmine tea after finishing a report."

"Good," Tanuja nodded, her eyes encouraging. "Rewards should be savoured, moments of acknowledgment for your efforts."

"Jasmine tea," Srishti repeated, the imagery vivid and fragrant in her mind, a symbol of tranquillity earned, not given. "Let's talk about sharing your goals," Tanuja steered gently. "An accountability partner can be a touchstone, someone to share your triumphs and setbacks with."

"Someone I trust," Srishti added, warmth spreading through her at the thought. "My friend Susan, she's always been there."

"Perfect," Tanuja said, her smile a shared secret. "Opening up to her, letting her support you—it's another layer of commitment."

"Susan will be honest, push me when I need it," Srishti reflected, picturing her friend's determined gaze, a mirror of her own resolve. "Accountability isn't a leash," Tanuja clarified, her tone gentle. "It's a partnership, rooted in mutual respect and encouragement."

"Respect... Encouragement..." Srishti echoed, the words weaving a safety net around her intentions. "Imagine her joy, seeing you succeed," Tanuja painted the picture, broad strokes of camaraderie and celebration. "Her joy... my success," Srishti whispered, a future built on today's promises, vibrant and within reach.

"Small rewards, trusted friends," Tanuja summarized, the pillars of Srishti's blueprint for change standing firm.

"Step by step," Srishti affirmed, her path now dotted with tea leaves and the steady gaze of companionship. "Step by step," Tanuja echoed, her approval the gentle push of a fledgling towards flight.

"Thank you," Srishti breathed out, gratitude mingling with newfound strength.

"Always," Tanuja replied, as they both knew the journey ahead was Srishti's to walk, but never alone.

As Srishti left the room, her steps were lighter, her spirit buoyed by clarity and determination. The path ahead was hers to tread, each tick of the clock a reminder of her newfound command over the dance of her daily life.

*****

Srishti sat cross-legged on her terrace, the soft glow of dawn painting the sky in hues of promise. Her journal lay open before her, a silent witness to the thoughts spilling across its pages. She scribbled furiously, the pen dancing with her racing mind—a tango of reflection and resolve.

"Let's see," she murmured, her eyes scanning the words of the past week. "What worked? What didn't?" The questions were whispers, each one a stepping stone towards clarity.

"Consistency," Tanuja's voice echoed in her memory, a mantra for those moments of doubt. "It's your rhythm, Srishti. Find it, live it."

"Rhythm," Srishti repeated, tasting the word. Adjusting strategies meant listening to her own beat, crafting a tempo that sustained, not strained.

"Monday was good," she acknowledged, nodding at her recorded victory. "Tuesday... less so." Honesty colored her analysis, no room for excuses—this was about growth, not guilt.

"Patterns emerge," Tanuja had taught her, eyes alight with the wisdom of experience. "Spot them, understand them, and then you can change them."

"Patterns," Srishti said, tracing the cycles of her efforts like constellations in the night. There were bright spots, dim ones, and some yet to be discovered.

"Maybe smaller steps on Tuesdays," she pondered aloud, the solution budding like spring's first bloom. "And a morning walk to clear my head."

"Adjust, adapt." The words felt like keys unlocking doors she'd once thought sealed. "Reflection isn't rumination; it's renovation."

"Renovation," she whispered, embracing the concept of self as both architect and home. With every insight, she laid a new brick, strengthened a foundation.

"Consistency," she breathed into the growing light, her gaze steady. "It's not about perfection; it's persistence."

"Remember, Srishti," Tanuja's guidance was a gentle nudge, "a river cuts through rock not by force, but by persistence."

"Persistence," Srishti affirmed, a vow made to the rising sun. The rock of procrastination would erode under her relentless stream of effort.

"Success is an accumulation of consistent actions," Tanuja had said, her smile an encouraging lighthouse in the fog of uncertainty.

"Consistent actions," Srishti resolved, the phrase now a beacon guiding her forward. Today was another chance, a fresh page waiting to be written.

"Change is incremental," she recalled the therapist's soothing tone, "Celebrate each step, no matter how small."

"Small victories," she promised herself, envisioning a future crafted from today's tiny triumphs.

"Reflect, adjust, persist," Srishti declared, her voice a steady drumbeat against the silence. "This is how I conquer."

"Indeed," Tanuja would agree, her pride a silent ovation. "This is how you soar."

"Today, I soar," Srishti vowed, closing her journal with a sense of purpose. The day awaited, a canvas ready for the strokes of her newfound consistency.

*****

Srishti stared at the stack of envelopes on her desk, each one screaming deadlines and responsibilities. She had been here before, locked in a dance with delay, the music of procrastination leading her steps astray. But today, she halted mid-twirl, aware of the familiar tune and determined to change the rhythm.

"Procrastination," Tanuja's voice echoed in her mind, "is a shared struggle, not a personal failure." Srishti clung to those words, letting them be her anchor as she reached for an envelope.

"Understanding is the first step," Srishti murmured, echoing Tanuja's wisdom, peeling open the flap with deliberate care. She laid out the contents, facing what she had once avoided—a mosaic of tasks that now seemed less daunting.

"Break it down," she whispered, pen in hand, dividing the workload into fragments small enough to conquer. Tanuja had taught her this—divide and prevail. With each task segmented, Srishti felt a weight lift, her breath coming easier.

"Set a goal," she said, scribbling a deadline next to each micro-task, her heart steadying with every line drawn. The goals looked back at her, reasonable and attainable, allies rather than adversaries.

"Imperfection is human," she recited, a mantra against the critical voice that so often whispered insufficiency. Her therapist's understanding gaze seemed to penetrate the walls, filling the room with compassion.

"Small victories," Tanuja had said, her tone rich with encouragement. Srishti allowed herself a smile when the first checkmark adorned her list—a triumph in the tiniest but mightiest of forms.

"Persevere," she urged herself, feeling the power in persistence. Each task completed was a declaration of war against the inertia that had once claimed her days.

"Deadlines are promises," she realized, treating each as a commitment to herself, a pact sealed with intention. Tanuja's nod of affirmation was palpable, even in her absence.

"Celebrate," Srishti decided, allowing pride to bloom in her chest for every deadline met, every promise kept. In these moments of joy, the shadow of procrastination cowered and shrank.

"Productivity blossoms from within," she acknowledged, her actions a testament to the strategies woven into her daily tapestry. They were threads of resilience, patterns of growth.

"Conquer with ease," she affirmed. With each passing hour, the mountain of avoidance became a field traversed, her footsteps marking the path of a warrior who had learned to wield the sword of effective planning.

"Goals within reach," she breathed, her eyes alight with the vision of her accomplishments. Tanuja's teachings were her armour, her shield against the arrows of delay.

"Ease," Srishti savoured the word, its simplicity a balm to her once-frayed nerves. It was not the absence of challenge but the presence of strategy that crafted this newfound serenity.

"Embrace, break, set, celebrate," the cycle continued, a harmonious cadence of action and reflection. And in this dance of diligence, Srishti found her rhythm, composing a life score no longer marred by the dissonance of procrastination.

*****

Consistency was the gentle drumbeat guiding Srishti's days. Each morning, she sat at her small desk, bathed in the soft gold of sunrise that slipped through her curtains, a silent promise to begin anew. Today, like yesterday, and the day before, she opened her journal, its pages no longer blank but adorned with her steady progress.

"Small steps," she whispered to the quiet room, her mantra for the journey ahead. The tasks listed on the paper were her daily milestones, each one a testament to her commitment. She picked up her pen, the weight familiar and comforting in her hand, and checked off the first task completed.

"Consistent action, consistent results," Tanuja had said during their last session, her voice a soothing tide that washed over Srishti's doubts. The words echoed in Srishti's mind now, a lifeline thrown across the turbulent sea of past procrastination.

"Today is a victory," she affirmed, acknowledging the power of her routine. Her once daunting to-do list had transformed into a series of stepping stones, each crossed off leading her closer to her goals. The pleasure of ticking boxes became a cherished ritual, the ink marks symbols of her persistence.

"Consistency conquers," Srishti repeated, allowing the syllables to fill the space around her, reinforcing her resolve. It was not about grand gestures or monumental leaps; it was the steady hum of effort, the pulse of perseverance that mattered.

With each task she undertook, Srishti felt the chains of avoidance melt away, replaced by a growing confidence. The fear of failure, which once loomed like an insurmountable peak, now seemed like rolling hills she knew she could navigate.

"Keep going," she urged herself when weariness crept into her limbs. Her breaks were as intentional as her work, moments to recharge, not to retreat. She rose from her desk, stretching tall like the pines outside her window, reaching for the sky with open palms.

"Every step counts," she reminded herself, returning to her tasks with renewed vigour. The rhythm of her actions was a dance she had choreographed carefully, moving to the beat of progress and the melody of self-compassion.

"Tanuja was right," Srishti mused, a smile playing on her lips. Consistency was not just a strategy but a form of self-respect, a way to honour her dreams and the hard work they demanded.

"Tomorrow, I'll do it again," she promised as twilight painted her room in shades of lavender and rose. And when she closed her eyes that night, it was with the knowledge that she had taken yet another step towards her aspirations, each one steady and sure.

"Consistency conquers," she breathed out, the truth settling deep within her bones. Tomorrow awaited, and so did she, ready to meet it with the same unwavering dedication that had brought her this far.

7

ANGER – Harness the Power

The sun filtered through the sheer curtains, casting a serene glow across the room where Tanuja sat opposite Srishti. Their chairs were close enough, yet spaced for comfort, a silent acknowledgment of the delicate dance between therapist and client.

"Anger," Tanuja began, her voice as soft as the light, "is much l ike this sunlight. Natural, inevitable. I t touches everyone."Srishti nodded, her hands folded in her lap, a tiny earthquake of tension running through her fingers. "But it burns sometimes, doesn't it?" Her voice was carrying the weight of many sleepless nights.

"Indeed, it can," Tanuja agreed, her eyes never straying from Srishti's face, reading her like a cherished book. "If we let it rage unchecked, it scorches our wellbeing, our peace, our relationships."Srishti admitted, "Feels like I've been holding a torch to everything lately," a sad smile flirting with the corners of her mouth.

Tanuja leaned forward slightly, empathy etched into every line of her face. "And yet, just as we manage the heat of the sun by seeking shade or wearing sunscreen, we can manage anger. It requires the right mindset, the willingness to apply those strategies."

"Strategies..." Srishti echoed, rolling the word around like a new flavour on her tongue. "Think of them as tools," Tanuja offered, "tools that help us build rather than tear down." Her hand gestured as if laying bricks, one atop another. "With these, we construct a happier, more fulfilling life."

"Is it really possible? For someone like me?" Srishti's eyes searched Tanuja's, seeking an anchor in the storm of her doubts."Especially for someone like you," Tanuja affirmed, her tone unwavering. " Your intelligence, your self- awareness—they are your allies on this journey."

A pause settled between them, heavy with potential. Then, slowly, Srishti's posture shifted, a subtle straightening of the spine—an embodiment of the hope beginning to take root."Then I suppose," she said, with a cautious optimism, "it's time I learn how to use these tools.

"Tanuja's smile was like a warm embrace. "And I'm here to guide you through each step, Srishti. Together, we'll navigate this path."

As they delved into the heart of their session, Srishti felt the first stirring of empowerment. Anger, that familiar foe, might have left its mark, but the promise of healing whispered through the air, as soothing as the daylight that surrounded them.

*****

"Anger," Srishti whispered. "It's like it has a life of its own."

"Let's sit with that feeling," Tanuja said gently. Tanuja's presence was calming, an anchor in the choppy waters of Srishti's inner turmoil."Try to step outside yourself for a moment, and observe this anger. Can you see it without judgment?"

Srishti nodded slowly, closing her eyes. She pictured her anger as a separate entity, a shadow looming over her. It was powerful and dark, yet when she dared to look it in the eye, it seemed less intimidating—merely a part of her vast emotional landscape.

"Good," Tanuja continued, sensing the subtle shift in Srishti's demeanour. "Now, let's become aware of what happens to you physically when this emotion arises."

"Physically?" Srishti echoed, her voice a mix of curiosity and scepticism."Notice any tension, any changes in your breath or heartbeat," Tanuja said with a calm authority.

Srishti focused inward, attuning to her body's signals. Her jaw was tight, her breaths shallow. With each breath, she felt a thrumming in her veins, a slow burn in her chest.

ANGER – HARNESS THE POWER

Acknowledging these signs, she began to realize how her body mirrored her emotional state.

"See? You're beginning to understand the language of your body," Tanuja praised softly, offering Srishti a warm, affirming smile that reached her eyes. "By being aware of these cues," Tanuja explained, "you can catch your anger before it escalates. Recognition is your first tool in managing it."

Recognition. The word resonated with Srishti. She could feel the beginnings of control, a sense of mastery over the wildness of her emotions. "Recognition leads to understanding," Srishti mused aloud, "and understanding to control."

"Exactly," Tanuja affirmed. "And through control comes peace."

Srishti opened her eyes, meeting Tanuja's gaze with newfound resolve. There was work to be done, paths to be explored, but the journey no longer seemed insurmountable. In the safety of this room, with guidance, she could learn to dance with her anger rather than be consumed by it.

"Thank you," Srishti said, her voice stronger than before. "For helping me see that my anger doesn't define me—it's just another part of who I am."

Tanuja nodded, her expression one of quiet pride. "And a part you are learning to live with, in harmony."

*****

Srishti inhaled deeply, her chest rising and falling with a measured rhythm that filled the room with an aura of tranquility. She closed her eyes, envisioning her breath as waves lapping against the shore—steady, constant, soothing. The air swirled into her lungs, a cool stream that tempered the simmering heat of her anger.

"Focus on your breathing," Tanuja's voice guided her from across the room, gentle yet resonant. "Let each breath be deeper than the last. Feel your body relaxing."

With every exhalation, Srishti felt the tension uncoil from her muscles, the knots of frustration loosening their grip. Her mind, once a tumultuous storm, settled under the calming influence of the rhythmic breathing. She could feel herself stepping back from the edge, the precipice of impulsive reactions now a distant threat.

"Good," Tanuja encouraged, observing the subtle shift in Srishti's demeanour. "Deep breathing is like a bridge, leading you away from anger to a place of clarity." Srishti nodded slightly, eyes still closed, acknowledging the truth in Tanuja's words. The simple act of controlling her breath empowered her to control her response to the world around her.

"Remember," Tanuja continued, "anger can be a signal, not a verdict. It alerts you to something that needs attention, but it doesn't have to dictate your actions." Opening her eyes, Srishti met Tanuja's gaze with a spark of revelation. "I've always let it push me to react... Now, I see there's another way."

"Exactly," Tanuja said, her smile encouraging. "Now, think about healthy outlets for your emotions. Physical activity or speaking with someone can transform the energy of anger into something constructive."

"Like jogging," Srishti reflected. "When I , my mind clears. I could use that time to process what I'm feeling instead of letting it fester."

"Or writing," Tanuja suggested. "Sometimes articulating your emotions on paper can provide release and insight."

"Writing," Srishti echoed, picturing herself pouring her thoughts into words, her pen channeling the raw intensity of her feelings into structured sentences. It was a safe space, a blank canvas that would not judge but absorb.

"Or talking," Tanuja offered gently. "Sharing your feelings with friends, family, or even here, with me—it's a way to externalize what's inside. It helps to lessen the burden."

"I've always feared being a nuisance," Srishti admitted, a shadow of old anxiety flitting across her face. "But maybe it's okay to lean on others sometimes."

"More than okay," Tanuja reassured. "It's brave. It's human. And it connects us."

Srishti sat there, absorbing the compassion in Tanuja's words, feeling the warmth spread through her. There was hope in this new understanding, a promise of strength drawn from vulnerability. Her journey was far from over, but with these strategies, she felt equipped to walk the path ahead—one deep breath, one honest word at a time.

*****

Tanuja leaned forward, her hands clasped lightly on the table between them. The soft glow of her office lamp cast a serene light across her features as she addressed Srishti with a calm, steady voice.

"Communication is key, Srishti," she said, her eyes holding a gentle firmness. "It's how we bridge the gap between our inner world and the outside one. When anger arises, it's often signalling that something within that connection needs attention."

Srishti nodded, her posture relaxing slightly as the weight of Tanuja's words settled on her shoulders like a comforting shawl. She had always seen communication as a means to an end, but never as a tool for healing.

"Think of it as a dance," Tanuja continued, illustrating her point with a graceful hand gesture. "When both partners are in sync, the movement flows effortlessly. But if one missteps, the harmony is disrupted."

"Disrupted harmony," Srishti echoed softly, picturing her recent conversations that had ended in frustration—a misstep in her own relational dance.

"Exactly. And to maintain that harmony, active listening is vital. It allows you to truly hear what the other person is saying, beyond just their words." Tanuja's voice was like a melody, each note resonating with wisdom. "And with assertiveness, you can express your own feelings without aggression or passivity. It's about being honest, yet kind."

"Kindness..." Srishti tasted the word, finding its flavor sweet against the bitterness of past conflicts. "It sounds so simple, and yet..."

"And yet it requires practice," Tanuja finished for her, an encouraging smile on her lips. "Like any skill, it takes time to develop. But I believe in you, Srishti. You have the insight and the strength to master this dance."

Hope flickered in Srishti's heart, a small flame ignited by Tanuja's belief in her. She could learn this dance, step by careful step, until the rhythm of understanding flowed through her interactions. "And remember," Tanuja added, her tone shifting to one of profound sincerity, "anger held too long turns to poison. Forgiveness is the antidote."

"Forgiving doesn't mean forgetting," Tanuja clarified, sensing Srishti's hesitation. "It's about releasing the hold that past hurts have on you. When you forgive, you reclaim your power. You choose peace over pain."

"Peace," Srishti whispered, the idea expanding within her like dawn's first light. She could envision it now—a future where her grip on old resentments loosened, making room for new growth.

"Start with forgiving yourself," Tanuja suggested, her voice a tender nudge. "For the times you've stumbled in anger, for the harsh words spoken to your reflection. Self-compassion is the soil from which forgiveness blooms."

Srishti closed her eyes, allowing the truth of Tanuja's words to seep into her soul. She imagined offering kindness to herself, her own heart a garden awaiting her care. "Will it hurt?" she asked, a vulnerable question that hung in the air between them.

"Sometimes," Tanuja acknowledged, her expression softening further. "But the pain is part of the process. It's the breaking of the shell that encloses your understanding."

"Then I'm ready to break that shell," Srishti declared, her voice gaining strength. "To dance, to listen, to forgive. To heal."

Tanuja's approving nod was all the confirmation Srishti needed. Together, they would navigate the delicate steps of this new dance, each session a rehearsal for the grand performance of life—where Srishti would take the stage not as a perfect dancer, but as a brave one, ever-learning, ever-growing.

*****

"Think of two scenarios," Tanuja began, her voice imbued with the calm of a lullaby. "First, someone acts against your wishes. Second, they fail to act as you hoped. Both can be sources of anger."

"Like when my colleague disregarded my ideas," Srishti murmured, the memory igniting a flicker of irritation within her chest. "Exactly," Tanuja affirmed. "Your anger is a spectrum, Srishti. Sometimes it's a whisper of annoyance, other times a shout of fury."

"Srishti nodded, envisioning her emotions as colours, each hue representing a shade of vexation. She pictured her own silence in some moments, the unspoken words heavy like stones in her throat.

"Anger can also be silent," Tanuja said, as if reading her thoughts. "Unvoiced, it echoes loudest in the caverns of our heart."

"Silence has been my shield," Srishti confessed, her voice barely above a whisper, "and my cage."

"Let's reshape that shield," Tanuja proposed, her eyes reflecting a well of wisdom. "Turn it into a lens through which you see yourself with kindness, not critique." "Anger doesn't define you," Tanuja continued, her tone painting hope in the air. "It's merely a signpost, pointing to what matters deeply to you."

"Signposts," Srishti echoed, her grip on the mug easing. "I never thought of them that way."

"Every emotion has its purpose," Tanuja explained. "They guide us, teach us. Anger is no different."

"Then I'll learn from it," Srishti resolved, her gaze lifting to meet Tanuja's. "Not just react to it."

"Exactly! Recognize when it's just a ripple or the crest of a wave," Tanuja said, her hands gesturing the ebb and flow of emotions. "Each has a different call to action."

Srishti absorbed the metaphor, picturing her anger as water, fluid and variable. "But how do I stop the wave before it crashes?" she asked, earnestness lining her features.

"By observing the ripples! Identify the moments that start small

—those can grow into waves if left unchecked. And remember, Srishti, your emotions are like the weather —temporary and ever-changing," Tanuja reassured her, her voice a steady beacon. "You are the sky—vast, enduring, capable of weathering storms."

Srishti closed her eyes, allowing the words to imprint on her consciousness. She visualized her anger as clouds passing through her expansive sky, not permanent fixtures but transient visitors.

"Practice observing without attachment," Tanuja suggested, leaning forward slightly, bridging the space with her presence. "Acknowledge the cloud, then let it drift. You control the skies of your mind."

"Control," Srishti whispered, feeling the weight of the word, yet also its liberation. It was a dance of power and release, a balance she yearned to master. Tanuja smiled, her expression soft yet empowering. "And when you feel the tide rising, reach for your tools— the deep breaths, the timeouts, the clear communication."

"Tools, not weapons," Srishti corrected herself, a small smile tugging at the corners of her mouth. She imagined equipping herself with instruments of peace rather than arms for battle. "Peace begins within," Tanuja affirmed, her eyes mirroring the tranquillity she spoke of. "Cultivate it there, and watch it bloom around you."

The image of a budding flower took root in Srishti's mind—a symbol of growth amidst the struggle, a testament to resilience.

"Your journey is one of many steps," Tanuja concluded, her voice a gentle nudge. "With each step, you'll find more strength, more clarity, more peace."

"Steps toward peace," Srishti said, standing now, feeling steadier, taller. "I can walk that path."

"And I'll be here to guide you," Tanuja assured her, her presence a promise of unwavering support.

Together, they stood at the threshold of change, gazing ahead, where anger was no longer an adversary but a teacher—a guide leading Srishti toward a horizon of self-understanding and serenity.

*****

Srishti clasped her hands together, fingers interlacing as if to hold her own emotions in check. She sat across from Tanuja, the soft hum of the air conditioner the only sound between them for a moment. The room felt like a cocoon, safe and insulated from the chaos of the world outside.

"Sometimes," Srishti began, her voice barely above a whisper, "I get so angry over little things. It's like... it's like I can't stop myself. It feels normal, but..." Her voice trailed off as she searched for the right words. Tanuja nodded, encouraging her to continue, offering a silent strength that seemed to fill the space. "It's exhausting," Srishti admitted, meeting Tanuja's gaze. "Like I'm sick with it. It doesn't make me happy. It's just there, blocking... everything."

"Anger," Tanuja said softly, leaning forward slightly, "is often seen as a natural part of life. But think of it as a barrier, much like an illness, preventing you from experiencing true joy and connection."

"An illness?" Srishti asked, her brow furrowed as she considered the analogy. "Yes," Tanuja replied. "Something that neither you nor those around you find enjoyable or necessary. It's not essential to your happiness, Srishti. It's an obstacle that can be overcome."

Srishti pondered this, a sense of realization slowly dawning on her. She had never thought of her anger as something that could be separated from her, treated, and perhaps even healed.

"Anger is a habit," Tanuja continued, her tone still gentle but insistent. "And also a choice. Something we learn over time."

"A habit?" Srishti echoed. She recalled the countless instances where anger seemed like the only response, the only way to express her frustration. "Absolutely," Tanuja affirmed. "When we're angry, we're not thinking clearly. It's almost like... temporary insanity. Our rational mind takes a backseat."

"Temporary insanity," Srishti repeated, letting out a short, humourless laugh. "That sounds about right."

"Remember, though," Tanuja added quickly, reaching out to place a comforting hand atop Srishti's, "it's temporary. And since it's a habit, it means it can be unlearned. You have that power, Srishti."

"Unlearned," Srishti said, feeling the weight of the word. She looked down at Tanuja's hand on hers, the contact grounding her. "How do I start?"

"By recognizing that each moment of anger is a choice," Tanuja explained. "And by choosing differently. Every time you feel the anger rising, acknowledge it, then decide to take a different path."

Srishti leaned back in the chair, her fingers drumming softly against the armrest. The room was still, save for the subtle hum of the air conditioner and the gentle ticking of the wall clock. She could feel the remnants of anger like a fading echo in her chest, an emotion she had often held onto tightly.

"Expressing anger," Tanuja continued, her voice a calm ripple in the quiet atmosphere, "is important. It's healthier than bottling it up inside. But have you noticed how it feels afterward?"

"Drained," Srishti admitted, recalling the hollow sensation that often followed her outbursts. "Like I've run a marathon with my emotions."

Tanuja nodded, encouragingly. "That's because while expressing anger may release pressure, it doesn't address the root of the problem. Once you're calm, you'll find you can communicate what you truly need or want much more effectively."

The idea seemed to hover in the space between them, a new possibility. Srishti considered this, her almond-shaped eyes reflecting a dawning understanding.

"And," Tanuja continued, "when we trace the path of our anger, we often find it begins with our thoughts."

"Thoughts?" Srishti echoed, her voice tinged with curiosity.

"Thoughts lead to feelings, which lead to actions," Tanuja elaborated, her expressive eyes locked onto Srishti's. "If we change the thoughts, we can change the entire sequence."

"Change the thoughts..." Srishti mused, the notion unfurling like a new leaf in spring. "How do we do that?"

"By challenging the automatic ones that fuel your anger," Tanuja said, gesturing with an open palm as if presenting a key. "By asking yourself if they are true, helpful, or necessary."

"True, helpful, necessary," Srishti repeated slowly, tasting the words. Each one a filter, a sieve for her simmering frustrations.

"Let's take a scenario," Tanuja suggested, leaning forward slightly. "Imagine someone cuts you off in traffic. What's your first thought?"

"That they're reckless, and they did it on purpose," Srishti responded, feeling the familiar stir of irritation at the memory."Could there be another explanation?" Tanuja probed gently.

"Maybe they didn't see me... or were in a rush," Srishti conceded, the tension in her shoulders easing as alternative narratives spun in her mind."See? You've just practiced reframing your thoughts," Tanuja said, her smile conveying warmth and pride.

"Reframing," Srishti whispered, the word a soft promise of control regained, of power reclaimed over the tempest of her own emotions."Remember, Srishti," Tanuja said, her tone infused with hope, "anger doesn't define you. It's simply a signal, and you can choose how to respond to that signal."

"Choose," Srishti affirmed, feeling a spark of empowerment amidst the waves of past indignation. "I can choose."

"Your brain has two parts at play when anger flares up. First, there's the feeling brain—the amygdala," Tanuja continued, her hands unfolding in the air like blossoms. "It's quick to light up, like a match struck in the dark, at the slightest hint of threat or frustration."

Srishti nodded, her brow knitting together as she visualized her mind like an intricate dance of light and shadow."Instant reaction," she murmured, recalling the countless times her chest had tightened before reason could take hold."Precisely," Tanuja affirmed. "It floods you with emotion, a surge of heat without a moment's pause for thought." She paused, ensuring Srishti was following. "It's primal, protective, but not always precise."

"Like a guard dog that sometimes barks at friends," Srishti offered, a tentative smile touching her lips at the analogy.

"An apt comparison," Tanuja replied with an approving nod. "And while it serves a purpose, we must also learn to recognize when it's merely reacting out of habit rather than necessity."

They sat in a brief silence, the metaphor settling over Srishti like a whispered secret. She envisioned her amygdala, vigilant and fierce, quick to defend yet often too hasty, sparking flames where there need only be warmth.

"Understanding this," Tanuja said, drawing Srishti's gaze once more, "is your first step towards mastering the art of calm. Recognizing the spark before the flame catches."Srishti exhaled slowly, imagining the knowledge seeping into her, dampening the kindling of her past anger with a soothing balm."Mastering calm," she echoed, a note of hope threading through her voice. "I'll remember that."

"Good," Tanuja said, her eyes reflecting the resolve forming within Srishti. "Next time you feel that flash of heat, take a breath. Acknowledge your guard dog, but remind it that you're safe, and you can choose a different response."

"Choose," Srishti repeated, the word now a familiar mantra, each syllable a stepping stone away from the precipice of rage."Remember, Srishti," Tanuja said softly, her tone imbued with unwavering support, "you are not at the mercy of your emotions. You have the power to understand them, to guide them."

"Guide them," Srishti whispered, a sense of agency blooming within her. She no longer felt adrift in a sea of anger but rather like a sailor charting a course through previously uncharted waters."Take this knowledge with you," Tanuja said. "Let it be the lighthouse guiding you back to shore when the waves of emotion rise high. Think of your prefrontal cortex as an experienced captain," Tanuja's voice was a lifeline amidst the chaos, "navigating the ship through rough waters."

Srishti nodded, her breath slowly synchronizing with Tanuja's calm pace. She pictured herself at the helm, the vast ocean of her anger stretching before her, dark and daunting. "Your feeling brain is quick to react," Tanuja continued, "like a first mate who spots danger and sounds the alarm."

"Too quick sometimes," Srishti admitted, her voice a whisper of vulnerability. "Indeed," Tanuja affirmed with a nod. "And when the alarm blares too loudly, it can drown out the voice of reason. Your thinking brain struggles to be heard, to plot a safe course."

Srishti closed her eyes, her mind conjuring the image of a lighthouse in the distance, its beam cutting through the fog of her fury. It was her prefrontal cortex, offering guidance, but the waves of anger crashed relentlessly against her resolve. "Remember, the captain doesn't ignore the first mate's warnings," Tanuja said, her tone both empathetic and encouraging. "But he also doesn't let them steer the ship into the rock. Take a deep breath, let the feeling brain sound its alert, but then let the captain take over. Deliberate, considerate actions will bring you back to tranquillity."

Srishti felt a shift within her, the gears of her thinking brain grinding into motion, slow but steady. She inhaled deeply, letting the air fill her lungs, feeling the grip of her intertwined fingers loosen.

"Sometimes the waves will be high, Srishti," Tanuja added. "The anger may seem insurmountable. But trust in your ability to navigate. Trust in the wisdom of your captain."

"Trust," Srishti echoed, opening her eyes to meet Tanuja's gaze. There was a spark there now, a flicker of confidence where doubt once reigned. "Anger is powerful, but so are you," Tanuja's words were like a beacon. "With practice, the captain grows wiser, stronger, and more skilled. You'll learn to sail through the tempest and reach the serenity of clear skies. Let's now explore some strategies to keep the captain in command," Tanuja proposed, her voice both a challenge and a promise. She leaned forward, her hands folded neatly on the desk separating her from

Srishti. A beam of sunlight filtered through the sheer curtains, casting a soft glow that danced on the surface of the wooden table.

"Imagine walking through a garden, Srishti," Tanuja began, her voice a gentle breeze stirring the leaves of thought. "Your senses absorb everything—colors, scents, the rustle of leaves." Srishti nodded, picturing herself amidst a myriad of flowers, each petal and blade of grass vivid against the backdrop of her mind.

"Yet two people might walk the same path and notice different things," Tanuja continued. "One sees the blossoms, another spots the thorns. It's not the garden that differs but the lenses through which they view it."

"Like how I sometimes only see what's wrong in a situation?" Srishti interjected, her almond-shaped eyes reflecting a dawning understanding. "Exactly," affirmed Tanuja, a smile touching the corners of her mouth. "Our senses gather the world, yet it's our past experiences, beliefs, and values that paint the picture we see."

"Then my anger..." Srishti hesitated, searching for the words. "Your anger is a reaction to that picture," Tanuja clarified, her eyes warm with compassion. "By recognizing the filters you're using, you can begin to change them, shift your focus."

"Change my filters," Srishti mused, her tone tinged with curiosity. "Look for the blossoms instead of the thorns?"

"Indeed," Tanuja said, nodding encouragingly. "When you alter these internal filters, you can transform your responses. Anger doesn't have to be your default."

"Transform," Srishti echoed, the syllables a soft promise to herself. She envisioned her own garden of perception, ready to prune away the tangled vines of instinctive ire, to nurture the buds of calm and reason. "Communication blooms when we tend to it with intention," Tanuja added, her metaphor extending roots into Srishti's consciousness. "Healthy interactions grow from soil rich with understanding and patience."

"Intention... patience," Srishti repeated, her voice stronger now, a declaration of her commitment to cultivate a new inner landscape.

"Have you ever tried smiling when you're angry?" Tanuja asked, her voice a soothing hum in the calm space. Srishti's eyes flickered with confusion and curiosity. "Smiling? But isn't that... counterintuitive?"

"Perhaps," Tanuja conceded with a small, knowing smile. "Yet it's a simple technique that can change the intensity of your anger. It's about taking control. When you smile, even if it's not genuine at first, it can send a signal to your brain that things are not as dire as they seem."

Srishti considered this, her brow creased in thought. She took a deep breath and let it out slowly, a practice she was learning to use often. Then, tentatively, a smile tugged at the corners of her mouth. It felt odd, forced, but she held it.

"Notice any shift?" Tanuja encouraged. "It feels... lighter," Srishti admitted, surprise coloring her tone. The smile became more natural now, a glow from within that seemed to soften the sharp edges of her frustration.

"Good," Tanuja nodded. "It's about managing the emotion, not letting it manage you. And part of that management is setting boundaries for yourself and others."

"Boundaries?" Srishti's smile faded slightly as she grappled with the concept.

"Clear lines that define what you are comfortable with," Tanuja explained. "Communicate your needs and limits. This way, you protect your energy and emotional well-being. It's crucial for healthy relationships."

"Protect..." Srishti murmured, the word resonating with her. She pictured an invisible sphere around her, safe and intact, a barrier against the demands of the world. "Exactly," Tanuja affirmed. "When you assert those boundaries, you honour your worth. It's not about building walls, but rather nurturing respect—for yourself and from others."

Srishti nodded slowly, the idea settling in her mind like a seed ready to sprout. "I can do that," she whispered, more to herself than to Tanuja. "I can set my boundaries."

"Indeed, you can," Tanuja said. "And I'll be here to help you learn how."

Srishti inhaled deeply, folded her hands in her lap, a conscious gesture of containment, a physical manifestation of the boundaries she was learning to define. "Sometimes," she began, voice steady though her heart raced with the vulnerability of her admission, "I feel like I'm giving too much. To my job, my family... I don't know where I end and they begin."

"Ah, the delicate dance of give and take," Tanuja mused, nodding knowingly. "But remember, Srishti, boundaries prevent burnout. They're not just lines drawn on sand; they're your declaration that your needs matter too."

"Resentment," Srishti reflected out loud, "it builds when I stretch myself too thin." Her fingers intertwined, squeezing slightly. "How do I stop that cycle?"

"By stating what you can and cannot do, openly, without guilt. It allows others to understand and respect your limits." Tanuja's eyes were soft but insistent. "Mutual respect is the cornerstone of any healthy relationship."

"Even at work?" Srishti asked, skepticism threading through her curiosity. "Especially there," Tanuja confirmed. "Clarify your capacities. You'll find that it leads to healthier teamwork and more realistic expectations."

"Okay," Srishti breathed out, a tentative smile curving her lips. "It's not selfish, then? To say 'no' or 'enough'?"

"Far from it," Tanuja reassured her. "Caring for yourself empowers you to offer your best self to others. And that's a gift to them, not a deprivation."

Srishti let those words swirl around her, seeping into the crevices of doubt. With each repetition, they etched a little deeper, forming a mantra of self-preservation. "Setting these boundaries," she said, her voice gaining strength, "it's going to take time, isn't it?"

"Indeed," Tanuja agreed, her tone warm and encouraging. "Like nurturing a garden, it requires attention and care. But oh, how it thrives once those boundaries are in place."

"Thrive..." Srishti echoed, holding onto the word, letting it fill her with hope. "A balanced life, where my needs are met, and I still meet theirs."

"Exactly," Tanuja smiled. "And with each step, your self-esteem will flourish, stress will wane, and you'll find harmony in the space you've claimed as your own."

"Harmony," Srishti mused, a concept once foreign now dawning within reach. She pictured herself encircled by a gentle buffer, one that allowed her to move freely, to breathe without constraint. A boundary that didn't isolate, but rather, defined where her garden ended and another's began.

"Thank you, Tanuja," Srishti said, her gratitude genuine, her resolve firming. "I think I'm ready to start drawing my lines." Tanuja's eyes gleamed with pride. "And I'll be right here, cheering you on, every step of the way. Let's take a look at this together," Tanuja suggested, pointing to the item on the worksheet. "Identifying what triggers your anger is a crucial step towards managing it."

Srishti nodded, clutching a pen with determined fingers. The first trigger leaped out from her memory—a missed deadline, the sharp sting of self-reproach. She scribbled it down, each word a tiny release.

"Deadlines," she murmured, feeling the familiar pulse of anxiety. "They make me feel like I'm constantly racing against time."

"Understandable," Tanuja empathized, leaning forward. "And when you're racing, any obstacle seems larger, more frustrating."

"Exactly," Srishti confirmed, her voice steady as she listed another trigger—unmet expectations, those she set for herself and those imposed by others. "It's like I'm setting myself up to fail, and then the anger just comes roaring in."

"Look at that insight," Tanuja praised, her tone rich with encouragement. "Seeing these patterns is a powerful first step."

Srishti's pen paused over the paper, her thoughts turning inward. "Criticism," she added, almost whispering. "Even when it's constructive, it sometimes feels like an attack."

"Your awareness is key, Srishti," Tanuja said softly. "Recognizing these moments gives you the choice to respond differently."

"Choice," Srishti reflected, the concept resonating within her. The pen moved once more, its trail a testament to her growing understanding.

"Good," Tanuja affirmed. "Now, remember, recognizing triggers doesn't mean you'll never feel anger again. It means you're learning to anticipate and navigate it."

"Navigate," Srishti echoed, allowing herself a small smile. "Like charting a course through stormy seas."

"Exactly," Tanuja said with a nod. "And with each voyage, you become a more skilled sailor."

"Skilled sailor..." Srishti let the words linger, finding solace in the metaphor. Her list of triggers, once daunting, now felt like coordinates on a map—a guide to better understanding herself.

"Thank you, Tanuja," Srishti said, her heart lighter, her pen ceasing its dance across the page. "This... it's helping more than you know."

"Helping is what we're here for," Tanuja replied, her eyes warm with the shared victory of a hard-fought realization. "Together, we'll turn these triggers into stepping stones."

"Stepping stones," Srishti repeated, a mantra of transformation. With each tick on the worksheet, she felt less like a prisoner of her emotions and more like an architect of her peace.

Tanuja leaned forward slightly. "Now, let's delve deeper," she said, her voice a beacon in Srishti's tumultuous inner world. "Recognizing the physical signs is crucial. It's your body speaking to you." Srishti nodded, her fingers tracing the edges of her worksheet as if to anchor herself. "Physical signs," she murmured, thinking aloud.

"Exactly," Tanuja encouraged. "What happens to your body when anger begins to surface?" A pause lingered, filled with self-reflection. Then, slowly, Srishti began to describe, "My heart... it starts to race, like a drumbeat growing louder and faster."

"Good observation," Tanuja replied, her words painting a picture of validation.

"Muscles tense," Srishti continued, her own hands clenching unconsciously at the memory, "as if preparing for a battle."

"Notice these things," Tanuja advised gently. "They signal your emotions escalating."

"Escalating," Srishti echoed, her breath hitching slightly with newfound awareness. She unclenched her fists, laying her hands flat against the cool surface of the desk. "And my breathing, it becomes shallow, quick." Tanuja offered an understanding smile. "That's your body's way of saying it's time to take a step back, to breathe deeply."

"Deep breaths," Srishti repeated, closing her eyes and inhaling slowly, practicing right there, right then. Exhaling, she opened her eyes, finding strength in the simplicity of the act.

"Describe the feeling that accompanies these signs," Tanuja prodded gently, coaxing the words from Srishti's newfound calm. "Anger," Srishti admitted, "it feels like heat rising within me, threatening to spill over." Her voice was steady now, a testament to her growing understanding.

"Good," Tanuja affirmed. "By identifying the feeling, you're beginning to separate it from your actions. Anger is just that—a feeling."

"Feeling," Srishti whispered, the word less daunting than it once seemed. "I see it now, like a wave that comes and goes."

"Beautiful imagery," Tanuja praised. "Remember, you can ride out the wave without letting it pull you under."

"Ride it out," Srishti mused, a sense of empowerment budding within her chest. "Without letting it control me."

"Control," Tanuja echoed. "You have that power, Srishti. You always have."

"Power," Srishti said, tasting the word, savoring the notion. The worksheet before her no longer felt like a confessional but a roadmap to self-mastery.

"Let's keep going, shall we?" Tanuja suggested, her tone both hopeful and confident in the journey ahead. "Let's," Srishti agreed, her pen poised to chart the course, her heart buoyed by the promise of calmer seas.

*****

Srishti's fingers tapped a staccato rhythm on the paper, each tap punctuating a heartbeat of introspection. "When I expressed my anger," she started slowly, "it was like unleashing a storm. Words would crash out, actions would follow without thought."

Tanuja nodded, her gaze steady and encouraging. "And afterwards? How did you feel?"

"Drained," Srishti confessed, her voice a low murmur against the silence of the room. "As if the storm had passed but left everything in disarray."

"Disarray can be sorted," Tanuja offered softly, a guiding light through the fog. "Reflect on the thoughts that fuelled that storm of anger."

Srishti's pen hovered over the worksheet, her mind sifting through the tumult of memories. "The thoughts...they were always so accusatory. 'They don't understand me,' 'They never listen,' 'I'm not valued.'"

"Accusations can sting," Tanuja acknowledged, her presence a balm to the discomfort. "They often speak more about our own fears than reality."

"Right," Srishti mumbled, a frown creasing her brow. "It was fear speaking, not me." She scribbled down the words, the act of writing them down stripping them of their power. "Let's reframe those thoughts," Tanuja suggested. "Consider alternative perspectives for those moments."

"Okay," Srishti breathed out, pausing to gather her resolve. "'They may not understand, but I can explain,' 'They might listen if I speak calmly,' 'My value doesn't decrease because of their inability to see it.'"

"Beautifully reframed," Tanuja praised, her voice a melody of warmth. "Do you notice a shift in how you feel, voicing these new thoughts?"

"I do," Srishti said, surprise coloring her tone. "It feels...lighter, more hopeful."

"Hope is the seed from which change blossoms," Tanuja responded, her metaphor wrapping around them like a comforting shawl. "Change," Srishti repeated, allowing herself to dwell in the possibility. The worksheet before her now a testament to her evolving narrative—a story rewritten with self-compassion at its core.

*****

Srishti clasped her hands, a silent signal to the rush of emotions that often threatened to spill over. "Coping strategies," she began tentatively, the phrase hanging in the air between them like a question mark. Tanuja nodded, her eyes holding Srishti's gaze. "Yes, let's explore that. When anger rises like a wave, how might we ride it safely to shore?"

"By finding balance," Srishti answered, a newfound steadiness in her voice. She reached for the pen, poised above the worksheet as if ready to chart a new course on a map only she could see. "I could write... or maybe go for a walk."

"Writing and walking," Tanuja echoed, the gentle cadence of her words encouraging exploration. "Both powerful ways to process your feelings from a place of calm."

"Right. To diffuse the anger before it defines my actions." Srishti's hand moved across the paper, each word a step toward reclaiming her agency.

"Let's consider a timeout plan," Tanuja suggested, guiding without pushing. "A strategy for those moments when stepping back can mean stepping forward later."

"Timeout..." Srishti pondered, the concept taking shape like a lifeboat amidst stormy seas. "A quiet room, deep breaths, counting to ten—simple acts to interrupt the anger."

"Simple, yet profound," Tanuja affirmed. "For in that pause lies the power to choose a different path."

"Choosing," Srishti murmured, the idea resonating within her. She envisioned the quiet room, felt the expansion of her lungs, the slow count dissolving the sharp edges of her ire."Exactly. It's about choosing," Tanuja smiled, her presence a beacon of hope. "Remember, Srishti, you have the tools and the strength to navigate these waters."

"Tools...strength..." Srishti repeated, the words becoming mantras of empowerment. She looked down at the worksheet—the blueprint of her journey toward peace—and felt a surge of gratitude."Thank you," she said, her eyes reflecting the resolve of a woman who had glimpsed serenity amid the tempest of her own emotions. "For helping me see that I am the captain of this ship."

"And a capable one at that," Tanuja replied, her voice brimming with belief. "Steer well, Srishti. Steer towards peace."

"Towards peace," Srishti whispered, the worksheet now a compass in her hands.

*****

Srishti leaned forward, the worksheet resting on her knees like a familiar friend. The air between her and Tanuja vibrated with unspoken words, a canvas waiting to be painted with new, calmer hues of expression.

"Let's practice," Tanuja said, her voice a gentle nudge. "Imagine I'm someone you're angry with. Tell me what you're feeling, calmly and assertively."Srishti inhaled deeply, her chest rising with the tide of challenge. She pictured herself standing before an invisible adversary, her previous fury morphing into something more poised, more controlled."I feel... upset when my efforts are overlooked," she began, her words measured, her tone even. "I need my work to be acknowledged."

"Good," Tanuja encouraged, her eyes reflecting pride. "You're stating your feelings without blame. Now, think of the negative thought that usually accompanies this anger."

Srishti closed her eyes for a moment, delving into the familiar dark spiral of 'I am never enough.' She held it there, examined it, then slowly released it, allowing space for something new. "Instead of thinking I'm always overlooked," Srishti opened her eyes, a spark of realization flickering within, "I can remind myself that my worth isn't defined by one person's recognition."

"Excellent." Tanuja's nod was an affirmation, a seal upon Srishti's newfound resolve. "Replace those negative thoughts with truth and kindness towards yourself."

"Truth and kindness," Srishti echoed, feeling the weight of old patterns lift, making room for healing affirmations. "My value is intrinsic, not contingent."

"Exactly," Tanuja smiled, witnessing the transformation from turbulent emotions to serene self-assertion. "Keep practicing this communication with yourself, and it will reflect in how you communicate with others."

"Reflect..." Srishti repeated, the syllables a soft promise of the growth yet to come. Her heart felt lighter, as if she had shed an armor that no longer served her. "Your voice is your power, Srishti," Tanuja reminded her. "Use it to build bridges, not walls."

"Build bridges," Srishti murmured, the image clear and comforting. With every word spoken, every alternative thought embraced, she could feel the landscape of her mind reshaping, blossoming into a haven of self-compassion and understanding.

*****

Srishti inhaled slowly, her chest expanding as she drew in the tranquillity of the therapist's office. Tanuja had rearranged the cushions on the floor into a circle, a silent invitation to grounding and peace.

"Who in your life can you reach out to?" Tanuja asked, her voice threading through the calm like a soft melody. "My friend Susan, perhaps," Srishti responded, the corners of her lips curving upwards at the thought. "We share everything."

"Good," Tanuja affirmed, eyes warm with approval. "Support is essential. It's a bridge connecting us when we feel isolated by our emotions."

"Bridge..." Srishti pondered, feeling the word resonate within her. She envisioned the strong cables of trust linking her to those she loved.

"Now, let's explore some relaxation techniques," Tanuja suggested, shifting seamlessly from emotional to physical healing. "Have you ever tried meditation or progressive muscle relaxation?"

"Only in passing," Srishti admitted, a flicker of curiosity lighting her features.

"Let's start with deep breathing," Tanuja guided, demonstrating a slow inhale followed by an elongated exhale. "Feel the air fill your lungs, then release it along with any tension."

Srishti mirrored the action, the rhythm syncing with Tanuja's. Breath by breath, her shoulders unknotted, her jaw unclenched.

"Notice the stillness that follows," Tanuja whispered, almost reverently. "The quiet after the storm."

"Quiet," Srishti repeated, embracing the hush. Her thoughts ebbed, leaving a clear expanse where anger once raged.

"Progressive muscle relaxation involves tightening and then relaxing each muscle group," Tanuja instructed, her hands gesturing fluidly. "Begin with your feet and move upward."

With each contraction and release, Srishti felt layers of unrest peel away. The tightness in her calves softened; the stiffness in her back melted.

"Let go," Tanuja encouraged, her words a gentle push towards liberation. "Release the hold anger has on your body."

"Letting go," Srishti echoed, a mantra taking root. Each word was a step toward serenity, each breath a stitch mending frayed edges.

"Imagine a wave of warmth spreading over you," Tanuja continued, her tone painting images of comfort in the air. "It's washing away residual bitterness, leaving only calm."

"Only calm," Srishti agreed, a smile playing on her lips. She basked in the imaginary sunshine, its rays dissolving shadows of doubt.

"Whenever you feel anger rising," Tanuja said, drawing the session to a close, "remember these techniques. They are tools for tranquillity in the palm of your hand."

"Tools for tranquillity," Srishti nodded, standing now with a newfound lightness. "I'll carry them with me."

"Carry them, use them, share them," Tanuja offered, her words an empowering benediction as Srishti stepped out into the world, equipped and hopeful.

*****

Srishti sat at the edge of her bed, a journal open on her lap. The pages, once blank, now held the footprints of her journey—a map of progress through the landscape of her emotions. She penned down a few more lines, reflections of the week that had passed.

"Each day, a little less sharp," she noted, the ink capturing her evolving relationship with anger. "Each conversation, a touch softer."

The words were simple, yet they revealed the intricate work of self-awareness that Srishti had been nurturing under Tanuja's guidance. As she reviewed her entries, she could see patterns emerging—triggers and triumphs laid bare on the page.

"Patterns," she murmured, tracing her fingers over the dates. "Time to weave new ones."

She thought back to the instances where her anger had threatened to surge, and how the deep breathing had steadied her pulse, how reciting mantras had grounded her thoughts. Adjustments were needed, perhaps in her expectations or reactions, but the foundation was there.

"Adjust, not admonish," Srishti reminded herself, her tone forgiving. "Change is a dance, not a race."

Her phone beeped softly from the nightstand, a reminder of her next appointment with Tanuja. Srishti smiled at the thought of sharing her insights, eager for the empathetic exchange that awaited.

"Managing, not muzzling," she said aloud, standing up as if in affirmation of her own capability. She closed the journal, its contents a testament to her resilience and determination.

"Anger is a visitor," she spoke into the mirror, rehearsing the perspective she had adopted. "I choose when it leaves."

"Indeed," Tanuja's voice resonated through the room a few hours later, "anger comes, but you hold the key to the exit."

"Managing it," Srishti reflected, "means I'm no longer its host, but a mindful observer, guiding it gently out the door without slamming it and without locking myself inside."

8

FEAR – Unlock Courage

Tanuja's office was a sanctuary of tranquillity, with the faint scent of lavender. Srishti sat across from her, legs crossed, hands clasped tightly in her lap. The therapist's eyes were warm and steady, inviting trust.

"Let's start by naming your fears," Tanuja suggested, her voice smooth as silk yet carrying an undeniable strength. "Write them down, one by one."Srishti hesitated, then reached for the pen and pad offered to her. She had always been meticulous, and now her handwriting mirrored her inner turmoil—neat yet tremulous.

"Public speaking..." she murmured, etching the words onto the paper. "Failure... being judged... losing control..."

"Good," Tanuja nodded encouragingly. "Now, rate these fears on a scale from one to ten. Ten means the fear is overwhelming; one means it's barely there."

The room was serene, the only sound was the scratching of pen on paper as Srishti considered each anxiety. "Public speaking, it's a nine. Failure, a solid ten." Her voice wavered, betraying the weight of her confession. "Being judged, that's another nine... And losing control, definitely a ten."Tanuja absorbed this information, her expression thoughtful. "You've taken an important step today, Srishti. Recognizing and rating your fears helps us understand their impact on you."

Srishti looked up from her list, finding solace in Tanuja's gaze. "It's hard to see them laid out like this," she admitted."Yet, it's brave and necessary," Tanuja replied, her tone empathetic. "This is how we begin to untangle the threads of anxiety. We'll work through each one, together."

Srishti's hands were still, yet her heart raced as the quiet hum of the air conditioner filled the room. Tanuja leaned in slightly, her eyes soft with empathy. "Let's explore what situations trigger these fears," she said gently. "Can you think of specific events or circumstances that heighten your anxiety?" Srishti inhaled deeply, grounding herself in the safety of the therapy room. "For public speaking... it's when I'm in a meeting and asked to present unexpectedly," she began tentatively. "My mind goes blank, my palms sweat, and I feel everyone's eyes piercing through me."

"And failure?" Tanuja prompted, her voice a steady beacon. "Deadlines at work," Srishti confessed, her voice barely above a whisper. "When I'm responsible for a project's success... the fear of not living up to expectations—it's crippling."

Tanuja observed her, noticing the slight tremble in Srishti's voice. "What about being judged? What brings that fear to the surface?"

"Social gatherings," Srishti replied, a hint of distress colouring her tone. "Especially around people I perceive as more successful or confident than me. I imagine them scrutinizing my every word and action."

"Lastly, losing control?" Tanuja asked, her words like stepping stones guiding Srishti across turbulent waters. "Uncertainty does it," Srishti admitted, her gaze fixed on the kaleidoscope of emotions swirling within her. "Not knowing how things will turn out, especially in relationships. It feels like standing on the edge of an abyss."

"Understood," Tanuja nodded. "Now, let's picture the worst-case scenarios for these fears. Start with public speaking. What's the absolute worst thing that could happen?" Srishti closed her eyes, confronting her inner demons. "I could freeze completely, become unable to speak. Everyone would see me fail, and my reputation would be ruined."

"Failure in your work projects?" Tanuja's question was a lifeline in the stormy sea of Srishti's thoughts. "I'd be seen as incompetent, maybe lose my job," Srishti said, the weight of her words heavy in the air. "I'd disappoint everyone who believed in me."

"Being judged at social events?" The therapist's inquiry was calm, a counterpoint to Srishti's quickening pulse."Laughed at, talked about behind my back. I'd become an outcast," Srishti's imagination painted a bleak picture.

"And if you lost control in uncertain situations?" Tanuja's voice held an unspoken promise of hope."Everything would fall apart, and I'd be helpless to stop it." Srishti's breath hitched as she voiced her darkest fear."Thank you for sharing, Srishti," Tanuja said warmly, acknowledging the courage i t took. "Acknowledging these worst-case scenarios is hard, but it's a crucial part of our journey. Now, we'll find ways to navigate through them."

In the compassionate space between therapist and client, Srishti found strength she didn't know she possessed. With each truth unveiled, the path to healing grew clearer, lit by the gentle glow of understanding and self-compassion.

*****

Tanuja's gaze was soft yet penetrating. "Let's consider the likelihood of these worst-case scenarios actually happening," she urged gently.

Srishti paused, a frown creasing her forehead as she weighed her fears against reality. "Honestly? I don't know. It feels like they could happen any moment, but..." Her voice trailed off, uncertainty lacing her words."Think about the times you've been in similar situations before," Tanuja prompted, her tone encouraging. "What has been the outcome more often than not?"

"Mostly... everything turns out okay." Srishti's admission was hesitant, a reluctant acceptance that her catastrophic expectations were seldom met."Exactly," Tanuja affirmed with a nod, her voice rhythmic and soothing. "That's an important piece of evidence to hold onto. Your experience tells us that the worst rarely comes to pass."

Srishti considered this, her mind racing through past presentations and social events. Her pulse slowed, the rhythm steadying as she acknowledged the truth in Tanuja's words. She had indeed faced her fears before and had come through largely unscathed.

"Can you think of any concrete evidence that supports the idea that these fears are likely to become reality?" Tanuja asked, her question hanging in the air like a challenge. After a long pause, Srishti shook her head, her almond-shaped eyes meeting Tanuja's compassionate gaze. "No, I can't," she admitted. The realization seemed to lighten the burden she carried, a subtle shift in her posture reflecting the change.

"Then that's what we focus on," Tanuja said with a reassuring smile. "Your fears, while deeply felt, aren't always supported by what actually happens. Remembering this can help you when anxiety tries to take hold."

"Right," Srishti breathed out slowly, feeling a glimmer of hope amidst the fog of her fears. Her intelligent mind, usually so adept at identifying problems, began to see the pattern of unfounded fears for what it was – an emotional response not always rooted in the present reality.

"Your strength lies in recognizing these patterns and challenging them with the evidence you gather from your own life," Tanuja continued, her words imbued with a hopeful cadence. "You have the power to rewrite the narrative of fear into one of resilience."

Srishti nodded, it was a small step, perhaps, but even the longest journey began with such increments. In the quiet office, surrounded by the empathy and wisdom of her therapist, Srishti felt the first stirrings of a courage that had long lain dormant.

"Let's keep building on this," Tanuja said, her voice a beacon guiding Srishti toward calmer waters. "Remember, Srishti, you've weathered storms before. You can do it again."

And in that moment, Srishti believed her.

*****

Tanuja leaned forward, clasping her hands together on the mahogany desk. "Srishti," she began, her voice a soft lull in the quiet office, "how has fear manifested in your life? In what ways has it shaped your decisions or behaviours?"

Srishti's eyes dropped to her own fidgeting fingers. "It's like I'm always on the edge of a cliff," she confessed, the metaphor painting a vivid image of her inner turmoil. "Every choice feels like it could be the wrong one, so I... I freeze up. I end up doing nothing instead of risking a mistake."

"Ah, the paralysis of indecision," Tanuja nodded, her understanding gaze never leaving Srishti. "And when you do make a decision?"

"Regret follows me," Srishti replied, her tone tinged with defeat. "Like a shadow. Even if things turn out well, I wonder if they could have been better. It's exhausting."

"Let's talk about strategies," Tanuja suggested, steering the conversation towards empowerment. "Coping strategies can serve as bridges over those cliffs of doubt. Have you tried any methods to cope with these fears?"

"Sometimes, I write lists," Srishti admitted with a hesitant shrug. "Pros and cons for every decision. But the lists get longer, and the fear doesn't really go away."

"Lists can be helpful," Tanuja affirmed, "but they're just the beginning. Let's explore visualization. Picture yourself facing a decision, but this time, imagine that you trust yourself completely. How does that feel?"

"Freeing," Srishti murmured, a tentative smile curving her lips for the first time. "Like taking a deep breath after holding it for too long."

"Good," Tanuja said warmly. "Hold onto that feeling. Visualization is not just fanciful thinking; it's a rehearsal for reality. You're training your mind to anticipate success rather than fear failure."

"And if I still make a mistake?" Srishti asked, her voice a mix of curiosity and concern. "Then you'll handle it," Tanuja stated with unshakeable confidence. "The same way you've handled every challenge in your life thus far. With intelligence, resilience, and now, with a healthier perspective."

Srishti nodded, absorbing the truth in those words. She had faced fears before; she had triumphed over them without even realizing her strength. Now, with Tanuja's guidance, she was learning to acknowledge that strength and use it as a foundation for coping with her anxieties.

"Remember, Srishti," Tanuja concluded, the session drawing to a close, "fear does not define you. It's simply an emotion passing through. You are much more than your fears."

Tanuja watched Srishti jot down a list, her pen making firm, decisive marks on the page. It was a physical representation of the fears that had been silently shaping her life, and now they lay exposed, ready to be addressed.

"Good," Tanuja nodded in encouragement, a small smile gracing her lips. "Now, let's discuss some strategies to cope with these fears. Healthy coping mechanisms are vital tools in regaining control."

Srishti looked up, her eyes searching for guidance. She found it in the steady gaze of her therapist—a gaze that spoke of unwavering support and belief in her potential.

"Firstly," Tanuja began, her voice a soothing balm, "let's explore relaxation techniques. Deep breathing exercises can be incredibly effective when you feel anxiety rising. Picture each breath as a wave, washing away tension." She demonstrated, inhaling deeply and exhaling slowly, inviting Srishti to mirror her actions.

"Feels better," Srishti admitted after a few cycles, a hint of surprise in her tone.

"Indeed," Tanuja agreed. "Now, problem-solving strategies are just as important. When fear arises, break down the situation into manageable parts. What can you control? What steps can you take? This helps shift focus from feeling overwhelmed to taking action."

Srishti considered this, her brows furrowing slightly as she processed the advice. "It makes sense," she said thoughtfully. "Breaking it down doesn't seem as intimidating."

"Exactly," Tanuja affirmed. "And always remember, you're not alone. Seeking support from friends, family, or professionals like myself can provide additional strength. Sharing your worries can lessen their hold over you."

"Talking does help," Srishti agreed, a softness entering her voice. "Sometimes I forget that others might understand."

"Never underestimate the power of a shared experience," Tanuja gently reminded her. "Fear thrives in isolation but diminishes in the light of connection and understanding."

Srishti nodded, her list of fears now accompanied by a growing list of coping strategies. Each item was a step toward reclaiming her life from the clutches of anxiety. With Tanuja's words echoing in her mind—simple, rhythmic sentences like a calming mantra—she felt hope stirring within her.

"Remember, Srishti," Tanuja said as their session came to a close, "these fears... they're not invincible. You have the power within you to face them, and you have tools at your disposal to help you through."

"Thank you, Tanuja," Srishti replied, her voice steadier than before. "I'll practice these strategies. I... I think I can do this."

"You can, and you will," Tanuja assured her, her expression radiating empathy and confidence. "One step at a time."

"Let's talk about some of the negative thoughts you've identified," Tanuja suggested, her tone encouraging yet gentle, as if she were coaxing a bird to take flight for the first time.Srishti nodded, taking a deep breath. "I... I often think that if I fail at something, it means I'm not good enough." The words came out in a rush, like water finally breaching a dam.

"Ah, the classic fear of inadequacy," Tanuja said, nodding knowingly. "Tell me, what makes these thoughts irrational?"

"They're based on an old belief that perfection is the only path to worthiness," Srishti replied, her voice gaining strength as she spoke. "But logically, I know that's not true. Everyone makes mistakes."

"Exactly," Tanuja affirmed, her warm eyes locking onto Srishti's. "Mistakes are how we learn and grow. Can you recall a time where a mistake led to a positive outcome?"

"Sure, there was the project at work I thought I'd ruined because of one oversight. But fixing that mistake actually made the final result much better," Srishti recounted, the corners of her mouth lifting slightly. "It turned into a success, not a failure."

"See? That's evidence challenging the irrational fear of not being enough," Tanuja pointed out, her words painting a picture of hope. "Your job isn't to be flawless, Srishti. It's to be human, to evolve."

"Evolve," Srishti repeated, tasting the word. "I like that."

"Good," said Tanuja, her head tilting in a subtle nod. "Now, let's consider another negative thought you've written down."

"Being rejected means I'm unlovable," Srishti read from her list, each syllable heavy with past pain.

"Does this thought hold up when you look at your life, the people who care for you?" Tanuja probed softly.

"No, it doesn't," Srishti admitted. "My friends and family—they love me even when I'm not at my best."

"Then that thought," Tanuja said with a smile, "is just a ghost from the past, whispering lies. You are loved, Srishti. Always remember that."

As they continued, Srishti felt the weight of her irrational fears lighten. With Tanuja's guidance, she began to unravel the tangled threads of negativity that had woven themselves into her psyche. The process wasn't easy; it required honesty and vulnerability. But each challenge to a negative thought was like a ray of sunlight piercing through the clouds—dispelling shadows and warming the once-cold ground of her self-perception.

"Thank you, Tanuja," Srishti said as the session drew to a close. "I feel... clearer now, like I can see beyond the fog."

"Clarity comes when we question the darkness," Tanuja replied. "Keep challenging those negative thoughts, Srishti. With time, they'll lose their grip, and you'll find yourself free to soar."

Tanuja's gaze was gentle but penetrating, as if she could see the turmoil beneath Srishti's calm exterior.

"Let's challenge these thoughts," Tanuja suggested, her voice a soft melody that seemed to harmonize with the quiet hum of the air conditioner. "Okay," Srishti replied, her voice barely above a whisper. She picked up the pen, poised to rewrite the script that had long dictated her life.

"Take the fear of rejection," Tanuja began, leaning forward. "What's a more balanced thought you can have about it?" Srishti hesitated, then the words tumbled out. "Rejection doesn't mean I'm not good enough; it just means someone else made a different choice."

"Exactly," Tanuja affirmed with a nod. "Not everyone will resonate with your ideas or actions, and that's okay."

They moved through each fear, dismantling the towering spectres into manageable truths. With every balanced thought, Srishti's breath came easier, and the grip on her hands relaxed.

"Now, let's try visualization," Tanuja instructed, her eyes inviting Srishti into a world of possibility. "Close your eyes. Picture yourself in a situation where you're confronting one of these fears." Srishti closed her eyes, her eyelashes casting delicate shadows on her cheeks. She took a deep breath, filling her lungs with the scent of lavender from the diffuser in the corner of the room.

"Imagine you're at a meeting," Tanuja continued. "You have an idea. Feel the fear of speaking up, acknowledge it."

Srishti's brow furrowed, her body tensing once again. But she nodded, signalling she was in the moment.

"Good," Tanuja said softly. "Now, shift that image. You're still in the meeting, but this time you speak up. Your voice is clear, your idea insightful. See the others nodding in agreement, hear them acknowledging your contribution."

In her mind's eye, Srishti saw herself standing confidently, her colleagues' faces reflecting respect and interest. The words flowed from her effortlessly, her heart steady, her fear a distant echo rather than a deafening roar.

"Notice how you feel," Tanuja whispered.

"I feel...powerful," Srishti admitted, surprise lacing her tone. "And...proud."

"Carry this feeling with you," Tanuja encouraged. "Remember it when fear tries to silence you."

As Srishti opened her eyes, they shone with the reflection of newfound strength. The visualization had offered a glimpse of a reality where fear did not reign supreme—a reality she was determined to manifest.

"Thank you," she said, her voice firmer now. "I'll hold onto this feeling."

"Remember, Srishti," Tanuja concluded with a warm smile, "you create your reality. Choose courage over fear, every single day."

Closing her eyes, Srishti imagined standing at the precipice of her fear, the vast auditorium stretching out before her like an ocean of anticipation. She could feel the weight of every gaze upon her, could hear the whisper of her own accelerated heartbeat—a symphony of anxiety that had long held her captive.

"Imagine," Tanuja's voice echoed in the recesses of her mind, "successfully facing and overcoming this fear."

Taking a deep breath, Srishti closed her eyes for a moment and stepped forward. She visualized herself at the podium, not as the quivering reed she often felt herself to be, but as an oak, grounded and strong. She projected her voice, clear and resonant, into the hushed space.

"I am capable," she whispered to herself, opening her eyes to see the phantom audience before her nodding, their expressions alight with respect and understanding.

In this imagined triumph, the colours of the room were brighter, the sounds around her—footsteps, the rustle of paper, the gentle hum of the air conditioner—were affirmations of life and presence. The spotlight warmed her skin, a comforting embrace rather than the scorching scrutiny she feared.

"Feel the power you hold," Tanuja's words from past sessions resounded within her, "the power to command this space."

Srishti's heart swelled with a buoyant hope, her pulse now a steady drumbeat of courage. Her fears, once monstrous shadows looming over her, shrank back into the corners of her mind, overshadowed by a new-found light.

"Your ideas matter," she assured herself, her internal monologue kinder now, echoing Tanuja's empathetic tone. "Your words have value."

She saw herself gesturing with confidence, her movements fluid and sure. The audience was captivated, leaning in, hanging onto her every word. A smile graced her lips, genuine and unforced—a stark contrast to the tight-lipped mask of trepidation she had worn so many times before.

"Listen," she urged herself, "to the sound of your success."

The applause rang out, not thunderous or overwhelming, but steady and encouraging—the sound of barriers breaking and perspectives shifting. She could hear her name being called out with admiration, could see colleagues approaching with genuine smiles and outstretched hands.

"Thank you," they said, their voices a choir of validation. "That was inspiring."

Srishti savoured the warmth of acceptance, the quiet pride blossoming within her chest. This visualization, this detailed rehearsal of victory, was more than mere fantasy—it was a blueprint for reality, a guide toward the person she was becoming.

"Every step forward," she reminded herself, "is a step away from fear."

Her eyes still closed, Srishti knew that the real challenge lay ahead. But the scene she had just enacted with such vivid clarity was not an illusion; it was a promise—a promise etched into the fabric of her being.

"Remember," she could hear Tanuja's gentle affirmation, "courage is not the absence of fear, but the decision to act despite it."

And with that, Srishti opened her eyes. Today, she had rehearsed her success; tomorrow, she would live it.

The door to Tanuja Maben's office clicked shut, leaving Srishti alone with her thoughts and the task at hand. She settled into the comforting embrace of the plush chair, a soft sigh escaping her lips as she reached for the notebook that had become her constant companion.

"Set realistic goals," Tanuja's voice echoed in her mind, "for facing your fears and gradually reducing their impact on your life."

Srishti uncapped her pen with purpose, her almond-shaped eyes focusing intently on the blank page before her. The first goal seemed to write itself, a natural extension of her newfound understanding:

"Speak up in meetings at least once a week, regardless of certainty."

This was tangible; it was achievable. It wasn't about dismantling her fear overnight but rather chipping away at it, like a sculptor revealing the form within the marble.

"Attend networking events monthly," she wrote next, her script steady despite the flutter in her stomach. Each letter was a commitment, each word a stepping stone toward the future she envisioned.

"Ask for feedback regularly," Srishti continued, aware that growth often sprouted from the soil of constructive criticism.

Her heart rhythm matched the cadence of her pen—each beat a drumroll to courage, each breath a rehearsal for resilience. With every goal set down, the spectre of her anxieties seemed less formidable, shrinking under the light of clarity and resolve.

"Volunteer to lead a project by the end of the quarter." This one was a stretch, pushing the boundaries of her comfort zone. But wasn't that the point? To reach beyond the familiar into the realm of possibility?

"Record and listen to positive affirmations daily." A simple practice, perhaps, but one that would weave threads of self- belief into the fabric of her everyday life.

"Reframe negative outcomes as learning experiences." Srishti knew that failure was an inevitable companion on the journey to success. Embracing it as a teacher rather than a tormentor would be key to her progress.

"Share personal achievements with friends or family weekly." Pride need not be boastful; it could be a quiet acknowledgment of the steps she was taking, no matter how small.

"Begin each day with five minutes of focused breathing." In doing so, she would remind herself of her power over the present moment, over the rise and fall of her own chest, over the tide of her thoughts.

"Read one book on personal development each month." Knowledge was armour, and she intended to fortify herself with every resource available.

"Practice saying 'no' when necessary to honour personal boundaries." Self-care was not selfishness; it was the sustenance for her spirit.

"Remember," she whispered to herself, echoing Tanuja's affirmations, "fear is a reaction, courage is a decision."

With each goal etched onto the paper, Srishti felt the weight of dread lifting, replaced by the buoyancy of hope. She wasn't just planning; she was planting seeds in the garden of her future—one where fear would not dictate the harvest.

"Small steps," she reminded herself, "lead to great journeys."

The determined set of her jaw and the light in her eyes spoke of battles yet to be fought and victories waiting to be claimed. The scene around her remained unchanged—the same four walls, the bookshelves, the same gentle hum of the air conditioner—but within Srishti, a transformation was underway, one goal at a time.

The afternoon sun cast a golden hue over the room as Srishti faced her reflection in the mirror. It was time for action, and she knew it. With Tanuja's words echoing in her mind, she took a deep breath and began to outline small, conquerable steps on the path laid out before her.

"Speak up once in every meeting," she jotted down, her hand steady but her heart racing. "Even if it's just to agree with a point already made." This, she decided, was a manageable challenge—one that would require her to edge out of her comfort zone inch by incremental inch.

"Join a social group," came next, the pen pressing harder into the paper as if to embolden her resolve. A book club, perhaps, or a local community class—environments where the risk felt lower but the reward of connection remained high.

"Ask for feedback," she continued, acknowledging the tightness in her throat even as she wrote. To ask was to open herself to criticism, yes, but also to growth—and wasn't that what she sought?

As each step took shape on the page, Srishti allowed herself a moment of pride. Here she was, mapping out her own journey through the very fears that had once seemed insurmountable.

Srishti nodded, taking in those words like a sacred mantra. She turned back to the list, adding one more item: "Celebrate every small victory." For every step she took, no matter how insignificant it might seem, deserved recognition.

"Self-compassion," she whispered, allowing herself to feel the weight of the term. She had been too harsh on herself, too unforgiving. It was time to change the narrative.

"Each day, I will remind myself that I am learning," she promised herself. "I am growing. And it is okay to falter."

"Exactly," Tanuja affirmed, her voice soft yet assured. "Perfection isn't the goal—progress is."

Their session ended with a sense of quiet triumph. Srishti gathered her things, her notebook now a treasure trove of plans and affirmations. As she stepped out into the waning light, her shoulders were squared, her gaze lifted—not free from fear, but filled with a newfound tenderness for herself and an unshakeable belief in her ability to face tomorrow.

*****

The pen trembled slightly in her hand, not out of fear this time but from the determination coursing through her veins. Srishti sat at her desk, the rays of the rising sun casting a gentle glow on the paper before her. She exhaled softly, grounding herself in the moment—the present where she was safe, where she was in control.

"Dear Self," she began, her script wavering as though testing the waters of self-kindness. The room was quiet, save for the distant hum of life outside her window and the rhythmic tapping of her foot—a dance of anticipation and readiness.

"It's okay to have fears; they're part of being human." She wrote slowly, deliberately, as if carving the words into her very soul. Her almond-shaped eyes scanned the line, a silent acknowledgment of her shared humanity.

"Today, I accept that my fears don't define me—they refine me." A small smile played on her lips, a whisper of pride for her newfound wisdom. She paused, allowing the idea to sink deep within her, planting roots of empowerment in fertile ground.

"Each fear I face is a step toward growth." Srishti continued, her grip on the pen easing as she grew more comfortable with this act of self-compassion. The words flowed more freely now, a gentle stream of hope spilling onto the page.

"Every challenge is an opportunity for me to prove that I am capable, that I have always been capable." She could feel Tanuja's influence in these words, the echoes of their sessions together weaving confidence into her narrative.

"I acknowledge my past, the falls and stumbles, but they are not my present. I stand tall amidst the echoes of doubt, a testament to my resilience." The reminder brought warmth to her chest, a soft glow that radiated through her being.

"Self, you have walked through fire and emerged not unscathed, but stronger, tempered by trials and tribulations." She let out a breath she hadn't realized she'd been holding, feeling the weight of old shackles beginning to lift.

"Forgive yourself for the times you believed you weren't enough. For you are more than enough; you are extraordinary in your persistence to rise each time you fall." Her hand moved with newfound conviction, etching self-forgiveness into the fabric of her journey.

"Remember, it's okay to rest, to seek comfort, and to ask for help." A single tear traced its way down her cheek, a silent testament to years of striving alone. But alone was not a word that defined her anymore.

"Embrace your fears, for they show you where your courage lies. And with each small step, each spoken word against the silence of anxiety, you will find that you are managing them. You are moving mountains within." She drew a deep, steadying breath, feeling the mountains shift, making way for paths yet to be travelled.

"Be gentle with yourself. You are doing the best you can, and your best is more than good enough." The sentence was a balm, soothing old wounds, wrapping her spirit in a blanket of acceptance.

"Love, Me." Srishti signed off, the two simple words a powerful incantation sealing the promise of a kinder, braver existence.

She set the pen down, folding the letter with care and placing it in the top drawer—a private treasure map marking the spot where she buried old ghosts and planted seeds of courage. As the rays of sunlight filled her room, Srishti stood up, her heart lighter, her resolve firmer, ready to greet her reflection with a compassionate smile and open arms.

9

SELF-ESTEEM – Embrace Your Worth

Srishti sat in Tanuja's cozy office, sunlight streaming through the window and casting a warm glow on the room. The scent of lavender wafted through the air, creating an atmosphere of tranquillity and safety. She fidgeted with a small, smooth stone in her hand, feeling its coolness ground her as she prepared to delve deeper into her emotions.

"Imagine, for a moment," Tanuja began, her voice soothing and gentle, "who you would like to be, without any limitations or expectations from others. What does that version of yourself look like?"

Srishti closed her eyes, her heart racing as she allowed herself to envision her ideal self. A confident woman, unburdened by insecurities and doubt, emerged in her mind's eye. This woman smiled effortlessly, her laughter infectious and genuine. She stood tall, surrounded by supportive friends and excelled in her career, unafraid to take risks or make mistakes.

"Okay," Srishti whispered, opening her eyes and meeting Tanuja's compassionate gaze. "I see her clearly. She's...happy, confident, and surrounded by love."

"Beautiful," Tanuja nodded approvingly. "Now, let's explore some of the factors that may have contributed to the gap between your current self-esteem and this vision of who you'd like to be." She paused, allowing Srishti to process her words before continuing. "Unhappy childhoods, critical parents or teachers, poor school performance, difficult relationships, and financial issues can all make our self-esteem low. Can you identify any experiences in your life that might have affected your self-image?"

Srishti took a deep breath, her mind racing with memories of her past. "My parents always had high expectations of me," she admitted, her voice wavering slightly. "I felt like I had to be perfect – academically, socially, and even physically. And when I didn't meet those expectations, I felt like a failure."

"Such experiences can certainly impact our self-esteem," Tanuja acknowledged empathetically. "It's important to recognize that our self-image is not solely shaped by external factors but also by the way we interpret and internalize them."

As Srishti listened to Tanuja's words, she felt a sense of clarity beginning to form within her. She realized that her self-worth was not solely dictated by others' perceptions, but also by how she perceived herself.

"Remember," Tanuja continued, "you have the power to change your self-image. By acknowledging and understanding these past experiences, you can begin to reshape the way you see yourself and ultimately become the person you'd like to be."

Srishti nodded, feeling both humbled and empowered by Tanuja's guidance. As they continued to explore the depths of her emotions, she found herself embracing the possibility of transformation, ready to embark on the journey towards self- love and acceptance.

*****

As the sun streamed through the window, casting a warm golden glow on the room, Tanuja gently guided Srishti to explore deeper layers of her emotions. The soft rustle of leaves outside provided a soothing backdrop to their conversation, as if nature itself was lending its support.

"Often, as we grow older, we tend to lose touch with our true selves," Tanuja began, her voice calm and reassuring. "We start wearing masks, pretending to be someone we're not, just to fit in or to avoid rejection."

Srishti's eyes widened, as she recognized this behaviour within herself. Her heart raced with the realization that she had been hiding her authentic self for years. "I've always felt like I needed to be perfect," she confessed, her voice barely above a whisper.

"So I'd put on this act, trying to be the person I thought others wanted me to be."

Tanuja nodded understandingly, her expressive eyes reflecting both empathy and encouragement. "It's common to feel that way when we're constantly bombarded with negative self-talk. But remember, it's just that – talk. It doesn't define your true identity or worth."

As they delved further into the discussion, Srishti found herself caught between the desire to let go of her false persona and the fear of being vulnerable. Her hands twisted nervously in her lap, betraying her inner turmoil.

"Think about the unique qualities that make you who you are," Tanuja suggested, as if sensing her apprehension. "Embrace them, and let go of the need to pretend."

Taking a deep breath, Srishti closed her eyes and began to focus on the positive aspects of her personality. She thought of her resilience, her intelligence, and her unwavering determination to overcome obstacles.

"By embracing our authentic selves, we build genuine self-esteem and find true happiness," Tanuja continued, her words flowing like a soothing balm over Srishti's frayed nerves. "It's a journey of self-discovery, and I'm here to support you every step of the way."

With each word, Srishti felt the weight of her mask starting to lift, revealing the person she had hidden for so long. As she opened her eyes, she met Tanuja's warm gaze, feeling a newfound sense of hope and empowerment.

Tanuja smiled reassuringly, her calm voice echoing gently in the quiet room. "Now let's explore how low self-esteem can make us feel powerless in our lives."

Srishti nodded, her hands clasped tightly in her lap. "I always see myself as a victim," she admitted, her voice barely audible. "I think I'm not good enough, can't do things on my own, and have something wrong with me."

Tanuja leaned forward, her eyes filled with empathy. "It's important to recognize that these thoughts are not your reality," she said. "If you realize you're dealing with low self-esteem, it's a sign that things need to change."

"Change feels so difficult when I'm trapped in this mindset," Srishti confessed, her gaze downcast.

"Let's try an exercise," Tanuja suggested, her tone optimistic. "Close your eyes and focus on one situation where you felt like a victim. Then, imagine how you would handle that situation differently, knowing your true worth and capabilities."

Srishti closed her eyes, picturing a recent work presentation where she had faltered under the critical gaze of her colleagues. She felt the familiar knot of anxiety tightening in her chest as she relived the moment.

"Remember your strengths," Tanuja encouraged softly. "You're intelligent, resilient, and capable. How would you approach the situation differently with that knowledge?"

Slowly, Srishti's mental image shifted. She saw herself standing tall at the front of the conference room, her voice clear and confident as she delivered her presentation. Her colleagues listened attentively, their expressions impressed rather than judgmental.

"Great job," Tanuja praised as Srishti opened her eyes, a faint smile playing on her lips. "By visualizing yourself in a more empowered light, you're taking the first step towards changing your self-perception."

"Thank you," Srishti replied, feeling a surge of hope and determination. "I'll keep practicing this exercise whenever I feel like a victim."

"Remember," Tanuja said, her voice filled with warmth, "realizing that you have low self-esteem is the beginning of change. With time and effort, you can transform your self-image and regain control over your life."

With each word, Srishti felt the seed of change take root within her. She knew that the journey ahead was fraught with challenges, but she also knew that she had the strength to persevere and overcome her doubts. Her heart swelled with pride as she acknowledged all the small victories that had led her to this moment.

"Great job, Srishti," she whispered to herself, a smile playing on her lips. "You're doing much better than you thought."

In the midst of her reflection, Tanuja's voice brought her to the present. "Srishti, it looks like you've been implementing the strategies we discussed during the past sessions. How do you feel about your progress?"

"Surprisingly good," Srishti admitted, her voice tinged with newfound confidence. "I didn't think I could accomplish so much in such a short time, but setting realistic goals has made all the difference."

" Excellent, "Tanuja said, nodding approvingly "Acknowledging your achievements, no matter how small, helps reinforce a positive self-image and boosts your confidence. It's important to celebrate those moments."

"Sometimes, though," Srishti hesitated, her gaze dropping to the floor, "I still catch myself focusing on my mistakes or shortcomings. I can't help but berate myself for things I did wrong in the past."

Tanuja leaned forward, her eyes conveying empathy and reassurance. "Srishti, remember that it's normal to have negative thoughts from time to time. The key is to challenge them and replace them with positive affirmations. When you catch yourself dwelling on the past, remind yourself of your worth and capability."

"Like saying 'I am capable' and 'I am worthy'?" Srishti asked, her eyes seeking confirmation.

"Exactly," Tanuja affirmed. "Repeating those phrases can help rewire your thinking patterns and cultivate a more positive self- image."

"Okay," Srishti nodded, taking a deep breath. "I'll try that next time I find myself slipping into negative self-talk."

"Remember, it's a process," Tanuja reminded her gently. "Be patient with yourself as you practice this new way of thinking. It will get easier over time."

"Thank you, Tanuja. Your guidance means so much to me. I feel like I'm finally starting to see the light at the end of the tunnel."

Tanuja smiled warmly, placing a hand on Srishti's shoulder. "You're well on your way, Srishti. Keep setting realistic goals, celebrating your achievements, and challenging those negative thoughts. You have the power within you to change your self- image and embrace your true potential."

"Tanuja," Srishti said, "I've been taking better care of my physical health, and it has made a significant difference in how I feel about myself."

"Excellent," Tanuja replied, her eyes twinkling with pride. "Now let's explore another technique to further boost your self-esteem: visualization. It's a powerful tool that can help you create positive mental images, which can lead to increased confidence and self-belief."

"First," Tanuja began, "Close your eyes and imagine yourself in a situation where you feel confident, happy, and empowered."

Srishti closed her eyes, taking a deep breath as she searched her mind for such a scene. Gradually, an image formed – she was standing on stage, delivering a speech to a captivated audience.

"Good," Tanuja encouraged. "Now, engage all your senses. What do you see, hear, smell, and feel?"

As Srishti delved deeper into her visualization, she felt the warmth of the stage lights, heard the applause of the audience, and smelled the faint scent of her perfume mingling with the air.

"Focus on the positive emotions this scene evokes," Tanuja instructed. "Feel the confidence, joy, and self-assurance radiating from within you."

Srishti's heart swelled with pride as she basked in the empowering emotions that surged through her body.

"Finally," Tanuja said, her voice a gentle whisper, "Repeat affirmations to yourself. For example, 'I am worthy', 'I am capable', 'I believe in myself'."

"I am worthy," Srishti whispered, feeling the truth of the words settle deep within her. "I am capable. I believe in myself."

"Keep practicing this visualization technique regularly," Tanuja advised. "It will reinforce your positive self-esteem and help cultivate a more confident and empowered mindset."

"Thank you, Tanuja," Srishti expressed, her eyes shining with newfound determination. "I can already feel the difference it's making."

"Whenever you're ready, Srishti, find a comfortable position," Tanuja suggested

Srishti settled amidst the cushions, her body sinking into their plush embrace. She closed her eyes, eager to continue her exploration of self-esteem and worth.

"Let's start with some deep breaths to relax your body and calm your mind," Tanuja instructed gently.

Inhaling deeply through her nose, Srishti filled her lungs with air, feeling the life-giving oxygen expand her chest. As she exhaled slowly through her mouth, she sensed the tension in her muscles dissipate, replaced by a wave of tranquillity.

"Good," Tanuja praised softly. "Now, take a few more deep breaths, allowing yourself to sink deeper into relaxation."

Srishti continued to breathe, each inhalation drawing her further from the chaos of everyday life and closer to the sanctuary within. The sounds of the bustling city outside her window faded away, leaving only the soothing rhythm of her breath.

"Remember, Srishti," Tanuja's voice was a warm, comforting presence, "as you practice this technique, you're cultivating self- awareness and compassion towards yourself. And that is a powerful tool for positive change."

Srishti nodded, her mind fully immersed in the experience. Each breath brought with it a growing sense of empowerment and clarity, a stark contrast to the feelings of inadequacy and self- doubt that had plagued her for so long.

"Before we begin this visualization exercise, Srishti, I want you to set an intention," Tanuja said, her voice soothing and steady. "Think about what you'd like to achieve with this practice. It could be boosting your self-esteem, cultivating self-love, or overcoming negative self-talk."

Srishti took a moment to consider her goal, her brow furrowing slightly as she weighed the possibilities. She felt a deep yearning to believe in herself, to feel capable and worthy. With resolve, she whispered, "I want to overcome negative self-talk."

"Excellent choice, Srishti," Tanuja nodded approvingly. "Now, close your eyes and imagine yourself in a scene where you feel confident, happy, and empowered. It could be a past memory, a future scenario, or even an entirely imaginary situation."

Srishti let out a slow breath, feeling the tension leave her body. She closed her eyes and pictured herself standing on a stage, confidently delivering a presentation to a large audience. They listened intently, her words resonating with each member of the crowd. The room was illuminated by their collective energy, and she basked in the warmth of their admiration.

As Srishti immersed herself in this empowering scene, she could feel her pulse quicken, her chest swelling with pride and accomplishment. I can do this, she thought, her heart brimming with newfound confidence. I am strong, capable, and deserving of success.

"Remember to stay present in this moment, Srishti," Tanuja reminded her gently. "Allow yourself to truly experience the feelings of empowerment and happiness that this visualization brings."

Srishti nodded, her face a picture of determination and hope. In this imagined scene, she was fearless, unencumbered by the weight of self-doubt that had held her back for so long. She revelled in the knowledge that she could overcome her negative self-talk and embrace her true potential.

"Thank you, Tanuja," Srishti whispered, her voice full of gratitude and wonder. "I feel...transformed."

"Keep practicing this visualization, Srishti," Tanuja encouraged. "In time, the positive feelings and beliefs you've cultivated here will seep into your everyday life, helping you to overcome your negative self-talk and flourish."

As Srishti opened her eyes to the sunlit room, the warmth of her imagined success still lingering in her chest, she knew that she had taken another crucial step on her journey toward self- discovery and emotional healing. And with each step, she felt herself drawing closer to the person she knew she was meant to be.

*****

Srishti sat on the plush cushioned chair, her eyes closed and her breathing steady. The soft murmur of a nearby fountain mingled with the scent of lavender in the air, creating an atmosphere of serenity as she delved deeper into her visualization exercise. Tanuja's soothing voice guided her through the process, encouraging her to engage all her senses to make the experience as vivid as possible.

"Feel the warmth of the sun on your skin, Srishti," Tanuja suggested gently. "Listen to the laughter of your friends surrounding you, celebrating your achievements."

Srishti's lips curved into a smile as she imagined herself standing on a stage, accepting an award for her accomplishments. The applause from the crowd felt like a warm embrace, validating her hard work and dedication. She could almost taste the sweet, bubbly champagne that she would share with her loved ones in celebration.

"Remember to focus on the positive emotions this scene evokes," Tanuja reminded her. "Allow yourself to truly feel the confidence, joy, and self-assurance that comes from embracing your success."

As Srishti revelled in the empowering scenario, she felt a surge of happiness and self-confidence rising within her. The weight of doubt and insecurity that had once shackled her seemed to dissolve, replaced by a newfound belief in her own abilities.

"I can feel it, Tanuja," Srishti whispered, her voice shaking with emotion. "I can feel the strength inside me, just waiting to be unleashed."

"Embrace those feelings, Srishti," Tanuja encouraged her. "Let them wash over you, permeating every cell of your being. Remember that you have always been capable of great things; you just need to believe in yourself."

Tears glistened in the corners of Srishti's eyes as she allowed herself to fully absorb the positive emotions that flowed through her. It was as if a dam had burst within her, releasing the pent-up energy of self-love and acceptance that she had long denied herself.

"Thank you," she whispered to Tanuja, her gratitude evident in her tear-streaked face. "I never thought I could feel this way about myself."

"Believing in yourself is a powerful thing, Srishti," Tanuja replied with a warm smile. "By engaging your senses and embracing the positive emotions this visualization brings, you will gradually rewire your mindset and transform your life."

Srishti nodded, her determination renewed. She knew that it would take time and practice to fully overcome her negative self-talk, but she was now armed with a potent weapon: the knowledge that she possessed the power to change her own reality. And with each visualization exercise, she would step closer to becoming her most authentic, empowered self.

*****

Srishti took a deep, calming breath as she continued to hold onto the positive image of herself standing confidently on a stage, basking in the applause from an appreciative audience. Her heart swelled with pride, and she felt a newfound sense of self-assurance coursing through her veins.

"Repeat these affirmations after me, Srishti," Tanuja instructed gently, her voice calm and soothing. "I am worthy. I am capable. I believe in myself."

With conviction and sincerity, Srishti echoed Tanuja's words, feeling their truth resonate deep within her being. "I am worthy," she whispered, her voice growing stronger with each repetition. "I am capable. I believe in myself."

As she spoke, she could feel the affirmations taking root in her subconscious mind, gradually replacing the negative thoughts that had plagued her for so long. It was as if she were planting the seeds of a beautiful garden, one that would eventually blossom into a vibrant landscape of self-love and acceptance.

But as she focused on her affirmations, her mind began to wander, drifting back to past experiences where she had felt inadequate or unworthy. She could feel the tendrils of self-doubt starting to creep in, threatening to choke the fragile blooms of positivity she had just planted.

"Stay present, Srishti," Tanuja reminded her softly, sensing her struggle. "Remember that you are in control of your thoughts, and you can choose to focus on the positive."

Srishti took another deep breath, feeling the tension in her body melt away as she brought her focus back to the visualization and the empowering emotions it evoked. She reminded herself that she was the architect of her own reality, and she had the power to shape her thoughts and beliefs.

"Thank you, Tanuja," Srishti said, her voice steady and filled with determination. "I won't let my mind wander. I'll keep focusing on the positive."

"Good," Tanuja replied, her warm smile providing encouragement and support. "Remember, Srishti, this is a journey, and with each step, you'll grow stronger and more confident in your ability to overcome negative self-talk and embrace your true potential."

Srishti nodded, grateful for Tanuja's guidance and wisdom. She knew that the road ahead would be challenging, but she was no longer walking it alone. With Tanuja by her side and the power of positive affirmations to light her way, she felt ready to face whatever obstacles lay ahead, one step at a time.

*****

Bathed in the warm glow of afternoon sunlight filtering through the window, Srishti took a final deep breath, allowing the empowering emotions she had experienced during her visualization to settle within her. She felt a newfound sense of clarity and self-assurance that seemed to radiate from her core.

"Before we end this session, Srishti," Tanuja suggested gently, "I want you to take a moment to express gratitude for this experience. Thank yourself for taking the time to nurture your self-esteem and acknowledge the power within you to create positive change."

Srishti closed her eyes once more, focusing on the feeling of gratitude swelling in her heart. "Thank you," she whispered to herself, acknowledging the strength and resilience that had carried her this far. "Thank you for allowing me to see my worth and for giving me the courage to face my fears."

"Beautifully said, Srishti," Tanuja commended, her voice filled with warmth and pride. "Now, when you're ready, slowly bring your awareness back to the present moment. Wiggle your fingers and toes, stretch your body gently, and open your eyes."

Following Tanuja's guidance, Srishti wiggled her fingers and toes, feeling a renewed connection to her physical body as she eased out of the visualization. She stretched her arms above her head, releasing any lingering tension, before finally opening her eyes to embrace the world around her.

"Take a moment to reflect on how you feel after the visualization," Tanuja encouraged, observing the transformation in Srishti's demeanour.

Srishti paused, considering the impact of the exercise on her emotional state. A small, genuine smile spread across her face as she realized the weight of her negative thoughts had lightened. "I feel...hopeful," she admitted, her voice tinged with surprise and gratitude. "For the first time in a long while, I believe that I can overcome my self-doubt and create a better future for myself."

Tanuja's eyes sparkled with joy at Srishti's revelation. "That's wonderful to hear, Srishti," she replied, her voice brimming with enthusiasm. "Remember, this journey may be challenging at times, but by nurturing your self-esteem and focusing on the positive, you'll continue to grow and flourish."

"Thank you, Tanuja," Srishti said sincerely, grateful for the support and guidance she had received. As she rose from her seat, feeling lighter and more confident than before, she knew that the path ahead would be filled with both challenges and victories. But with each step, she was determined to embrace her true potential and cultivate a life of self-love and acceptance.

*****

In the soft, golden light of sunset, Srishti sat cross-legged on her favourite cushion, her hands resting gently on her knees. The soothing scent of lavender incense filled the room as she prepared to engage in the visualization technique Tanuja had taught her.

"Remember, Srishti," Tanuja's gentle voice resonated in her mind, "repeat this visualization regularly to reinforce your positive self-esteem and cultivate a more confident and empowered mindset."

Taking a deep breath, Srishti closed her eyes and began her journey into the mental landscape she had been cultivating over the past few weeks. As she travelled deeper within herself, she could feel her self-confidence growing with each mindful step.

"Even though I face challenges," Srishti whispered softly, "I have the strength within me to overcome them and embrace my true potential."

With each repetition of the technique, she felt her doubts and fears receding further into the distance, replaced by a sense of hope and determination that grew stronger every day. She knew that this journey was one of self-discovery, filled with challenges and triumphs, but ultimately leading to a place of acceptance and self-love.

"Tanuja is right," Srishti thought to herself, her heart swelling with gratitude for the guidance she had received. "I can do this. I am capable, worthy, and deserving of love."

Srishti allowed herself to bask in the warmth of these newfound realizations, feeling the weight of her insecurities slowly lifting. She knew that there would be moments of doubt and fear along the way, but she was determined to keep moving forward, one step at a time.

"Every day, I'm growing stronger and more resilient," she affirmed, repeating the mantra until it echoed throughout her being. "I will continue to learn, grow, and thrive, embracing my authentic self and finding true happiness."

As the sun dipped below the horizon, casting its final rays of light into the room, Srishti opened her eyes, feeling grounded and empowered. With a renewed sense of purpose, she embraced the journey ahead, ready to face whatever challenges lay before her with courage, grace, and self-compassion.

*****

Srishti stepped out into the warm sunlight, her heart lighter than it had been in months. The scent of fresh flowers wafted through the air as she walked towards the park, eager to put Tanuja's advice into practice.

"Self-care," she murmured to herself, feeling the word roll off her tongue like a promise. "It's time to make myself a priority."

As she reached the park, she spotted her closest friends gathered around a picnic blanket, laughter ringing through the air. Srishti felt a surge of gratitude for their unwavering support and encouragement, knowing that they were instrumental in helping her change her self-image.

"Hey, Srishti!" called Ananya, waving her over with a bright smile. "Come join us!"

"First and foremost, it is important to practice self-care," Tanuja's soothing voice echoed in her mind. Srishti took a deep breath and approached her friends, resolved to engage in activities that brought joy and fulfilment.

"Did you bring your sketchbook?" Susan asked excitedly as Srishti settled onto the blanket. "I've been dying to see your latest work."

"Actually, I did," Srishti replied, unzipping her bag to reveal the sketchbook within. Her hands trembled slightly as she handed it over, but she reminded herself of Tanuja's words: surround yourself with positive and supportive individuals.

As her friends flipped through the pages, their eyes widening with awe and admiration, Srishti felt a warmth spread through her chest. Their genuine praise and encouragement washed away any lingering doubts, leaving her feeling empowered and appreciated.

"Your art is incredible, Srishti," Ananya gushed. "You're so talented!"

"Thank you," Srishti replied, allowing herself to bask in their kind words. She knew that by surrounding herself with such supportive people, she was taking a crucial step towards managing her self-esteem.

"Promise me you'll keep pursuing your passion," Susan implored, her eyes shining with sincerity. "You deserve to do what makes you happy."

"I promise," Srishti whispered, her voice filled with determination. As she spent the afternoon surrounded by love and laughter, she felt her self-image shift ever so slightly. She was no longer a victim of her own thoughts but a strong, capable woman on the path towards healing.

And as the sun began to set, casting a warm glow over the park, Srishti knew that she had taken the first steps towards embracing self-care and surrounding herself with positivity. With each passing day, she would continue to nurture her self-esteem, fuelled by the unwavering support of those who believed in her abilities and the power within herself to change.

10

CHILDHOOD TRAUMA – Reclaim The Innocence

The room was bathed in a soft glow, the kind that wraps around you like a warm embrace. Tanuja sat across from Srishti, her presence a steady anchor in the tide of emotions that ebbed and flowed between them.

"Consider," Tanuja began, her voice a gentle nudge, "that we all start as a pristine canvas. Our families, our teachers, everyone we meet... they each hold a brush. They paint upon us their beliefs, their fears, and sometimes, their unresolved pain."

Srishti nodded, her fingers tracing the armrest of the chair as if to draw comfort from its solidity. "And what if those brushes become tainted?" she asked, her voice barely louder than a whisper, yet it carried the weight of her burden.

"Ah," Tanuja replied, leaning forward slightly, her eyes locking onto Srishti's with an unwavering kindness. "That is when the canvas begins to believe it is flawed, perhaps even responsible for the heavy strokes and dark colours."

"Like when I was told I wasn't good enough," Srishti murmured, recalling the stinging comparisons, the shame that crept into her young heart and made a home there.

"Exactly," Tanuja confirmed, her tone imbued with empathy. "When we are small, our worlds are defined by those who care for us. If they, intentionally or not, become harbingers of pain, the child learns to blame herself. It's a defence, an attempt to make sense of the senseless."

"Defense..." Srishti echoed, her gaze falling to her hands clasped in her lap, a frown forming as she considered the idea. "It's strange, isn't it? That self-blame can feel safer than accepting that those who should've protected us... didn't."

"Safer, perhaps, but also a trap," Tanuja said softly. "Yet, here you are, recognizing it, questioning it. That's the first step towards rewriting your story, Srishti."

A moment passed, filled with nothing but the quiet hum of the world outside. Then, as if a dam had been breached, Srishti's words began to flow.

"Sometimes, at night, I hear their voices—criticizing, comparing." She paused, took a deep breath. "But I'm starting to realize, maybe the problem wasn't me. Maybe it was never about my flaws or failings."Tanuja agreed, her words a soothing balm. "You were just a child, doing her best to understand a world that often makes little sense. Now, as an adult, you have the chance to nurture that child, to tell her she is enough just as she is. And together, we'll peel away the layers of blame and shame that were never yours to carry."

Srishti looked up then, her eyes meeting Tanuja's once more, a spark of something like hope flickering within them.It was a small victory, a single brushstroke of many to come, but it was hers, and for now, that was a start.

*****

Tanuja watched as Srishti folded her hands in her lap, a silent gesture betraying an inner turmoil that had become all too familiar to them both. The room felt heavy with the weight of unspoken thoughts, and Tanuja chose her words with care, ever mindful of the delicate balance between acknowledgment and hope.

"Patterns," Tanuja began, "like threads woven into a tapestry, can be intricate and complex. They can add beauty or create a tangle that obscures the image beneath." She paused, allowing Srishti to absorb the metaphor. "Your experiences, the hurtful ones, they've woven a pattern of self-blame within you."

Srishti nodded slightly, her eyes downcast, tracing the outline of a stain on the carpet—another blemish she found herself drawn to. "I guess I've gotten used to blaming myself," she admitted.

"It's like I'm stuck with people who keep reminding me of my supposed faults."

"Those wounds," Tanuja said softly, "they're real and deep. But remember, wounds can heal. Scars may remain, but they also signify strength, resilience. You've been through storms that have battered against your spirit, yet here you are. Still standing, still fighting."

"Sometimes it doesn't feel like fighting," Srishti interjected. "More like... surviving."

"Surviving is a form of fighting, Srishti.Every day you choose to move forward, you are defying those patterns." Tanuja continued gently, guiding the conversation like a ship through troubled waters, "Trauma comes in many forms, and each leaves its mark. But those marks don't have to dictate your journey."

"Feels like they already have," Srishti said, a frown creasing her brow.

"Perhaps," Tanuja acknowledged, "But we are not static beings. We learn, we grow, we evolve. You have the ability to redefine the contours of your life, to smooth out the edges that have caused you pain. By understanding that self-blame is a voice from the past, not the present. It's a voice that doesn't recognize your worth, your capacity for change."

"Change," Srishti mused, her posture subtly shifting, as if the very notion stirred something within her."Exactly," Tanuja said, a note of encouragement threading through her tone. "And remember, in your heart lies a wellspring of courage. It's been there all along, even when you felt most helpless."

"Courage," Srishti repeated, and this time, her voice held a sliver of strength. "To heal."

"More than that," Tanuja pressed on, leaning forward, her eyes locking with Srishti's. "To transform pain into purpose, to turn your wounds into wisdom. But remember, transformation isn't immediate; it's a series of small steps, brave choices, moments of truth.

"Each step you take is a declaration," Tanuja concluded, her own heart swelling with pride for the woman before her. "A declaration that you are more than your past, more than the trauma—you are a being of immense potential, ready to write a new chapter."

"New chapter," Srishti said, her voice steadier now, infused with resolve. "I'm ready to start writing it."

*****

Srishti sat across from Tanuja, her hands clasped tightly in her lap as if to hold herself together. The sun filtered through the sheer curtains, casting a soft glow on the room that belied the gravity of their conversation.

"Physical trauma," Tanuja began, her voice steady and soothing, "is not just an assault on the body. It's an invasion of your personal space, a violation of safety."

Srishti nodded, her eyes reflecting a pool of memories she had kept submerged for far too long. She swallowed hard, finding her voice amidst the storm within. "It was... relentless," she admitted, the words tasting bitter on her tongue. "The bruises healed, but the fear... it stayed."

"Your body remembers, even when the mind tries to forget," Tanuja acknowledged. "It keeps score of every hit, every fall."

A shudder coursed through Srishti's petite frame as she recalled each instance where her boundaries were shattered, leaving her feeling exposed and fragile. "I started to believe I deserved it," she confessed, a lone tear tracing the contour of her cheek.

"Deserve?" Tanuja's tone was gentle but firm. "No one deserves harm, Srishti. Not you, not ever."

"And... sexual trauma?" Srishti hesitated, the weight of the unspoken pressing against her chest.

"Sexual trauma," Tanuja responded, maintaining eye contact with care, "strips away more than clothes; it tears at the very fabric of being. It's a crime against your soul."

Srishti drew a shaky breath, her past a shadowed landscape she had avoided for years. "I felt so... powerless," she whispered, her hands now trembling.

"Powerlessness is the thief of autonomy," Tanuja said, compassion etched in every syllable. "But you are reclaiming your power, here, now."

"By speaking it?" Srishti's voice was laced with scepticism, yet hopeful.

"By naming it," Tanuja corrected softly. "You take back control. You redefine the narrative. Your experiences, they don't define you. They are chapters in your book, but you are the author. You decide where the story goes from here."

"Where it goes..." Srishti considered the possibilities, her mind slowly opening to the idea that she could craft a future untethered from her past.

"Forward," Tanuja affirmed. "Toward healing, toward wholeness. You are not alone in this journey."

"Thank you," Srishti murmured, gratitude mingling with newfound determination. "For believing in my strength."

"Believing," Tanuja echoed warmly, "and knowing. You have an inner resilience, Srishti. Let's harness it together."

"Resilience," Srishti said, the word rolling off her tongue like a promise. A promise to herself that she would embrace her scars as marks of survival, as signs of a battle won.

"Exactly," Tanuja smiled, her eyes glowing with pride. "Each step forward is a testament to your courage, a dance of defiance against the darkness. A dance that you are learning the steps to, gracefully, with each day, with each session, you'll find the rhythm"

"Gracefully," Srishti agreed, a sense of empowerment blossoming within her, and the corners of her mouth lifting slightly. Today, she had taken another step, small but significant. Tomorrow, she would take another, and then another, until the dance became her own.

*****

Srishti inhaled deeply, her chest rising as she gathered the scattered threads of her emotions—an assortment of pain and resilience. She sat across from Tanuja, the room quiet except for the soft hum of the air conditioner. Her hands were clasped tightly in her lap, knuckles whitening with the effort to anchor herself in the now.

"Emotional wounds," Tanuja began, her voice gentle as a lullaby, "they're like hidden currents beneath calm waters, aren't they? Invisible, yet powerful enough to steer the ship of our lives off course."

Her words hung in the air, weighty with truth. Srishti nodded, feeling the recognition stir within her. She had always been adept at navigating the academic rigors and social mazes, but her own emotional landscape was often uncharted territory.

"Sometimes," Srishti voiced, hesitant yet eager to uncover the layers, "it feels like I'm blindly trusting the currents to lead me somewhere safe."

"Understandable," Tanuja replied, her eyes holding Srishti's gaze with an unwavering steadiness. "But what if you could map these currents, understand their origin, and gently redirect them? Let's explore the emotional terrain," Tanuja suggested further, her tone imbued with hope. "The beliefs that were etched into your slate by those you trusted."

Beliefs that I thought defined me," Srishti added softly, acknowledging the past's grip on her present.

"Past tense," Tanuja pointed out with a reassuring smile. "Thought. You are beginning to see beyond them, to question their validity."

"Questioning," Srishti contemplated aloud, "leads to understanding, doesn't it?"

"Exactly," Tanuja affirmed. "And understanding paves the way to healing. Your destiny isn't set in stone, Srishti. It's written in sand, and you hold the quill."

"Imagine," Tanuja continued, her words painting a picture of potential, "a future where each step is not predetermined but chosen... by you, for you. Each day, you have the chance to write a new page, to craft a story that reflects who you truly are."

"Who I am," Srishti mused, her voice stronger, surer. She was more than her scars, more than the sum of her past experiences. She was the author of her tale, one that could be filled with healing and growth.

"Your story," Tanuja encouraged, "is one of overcoming, of transformation. Remember, emotional landscapes can be remodelled, gardens waiting to bloom anew."

"Remodelled landscapes," Srishti uttered, imagining her internal world flourishing with vibrant colors of self- compassion and strength.

"Your journey is unique," Tanuja concluded, her expression warm with pride. "And I believe in your ability to navigate it, to find peace amidst once turbulent waters."

"Navigate," Srishti repeated, a newfound determination lighting up her eyes. "To peace, to wholeness."

"Wholeness," Tanuja echoed, standing now, a silent sentinel of support. "It's a beautiful destination, and you're well on your way. Thank yourself for this, it's your courage that has brought you here, and it's your courage that will carry you forward. A compass guiding you home, to the heart, to the self."

"Home," Srishti agreed, her steps light as she left the session, her spirit buoyed by the therapeutic voyage she had just embarked upon.

*****

Srishti perched on the edge of the plush couch in Tanuja's office, her hands clasped together as if to hold herself steady amidst a sea of tumultuous thoughts. The room was tranquil, the soft hum of the air conditioner a gentle reminder of the world outside, but within Srishti, there raged a silent storm.

"Imagine," Tanuja began, her voice a soothing balm, "a child's world, vast and full of wonder. Each day brims with potential, each moment ripe with the promise of joy."

Srishti nodded, her eyes distant as they delved into the recesses of her own childhood memories—those days when she'd spun around until the world blurred into a kaleidoscope of colours, laughter bubbling from her lips, the grass beneath her feet a tickling comfort.

"But sometimes," Tanuja continued, drawing Srishti back to the present, "that same world can be a battleground. A place where a child learns too soon about the weight of words and the sharpness of tones."

A flicker of recognition crossed Srishti's face. She remembered the scolding voices that had once dwarfed her giggles, the stern looks that had stifled her innocent curiosity. How quickly she had learned to read the room, to sense the tension, to adapt.

"Children are observant," Tanuja said, leaning forward, her gaze locked onto Srishti's. "They see more than we think. They learn to play parts not meant for them, to become little adults in a play of life they barely understand. Yet, this mimicry, this survival dance, is not who you are. It's simply a pattern, learned and practiced."

"Patterns," Srishti echoed, the concept rolling over her tongue, familiar yet newly understood. "They can be unlearned, can't they?"

"Absolutely, you are not bound by the scripts handed down to you. You possess the power to author a new narrative, to embrace your true self. Your innocence, your joy, they are still a part of you," Tanuja said, her voice a melody of conviction. "Allow them to emerge, to guide you back to the playground of life, where every day holds a new adventure."

"New adventures," Srishti mused, a smile breaking through the clouds of her contemplation. She imagined herself reclaiming those carefree days, laughter once again a language she could speak fluently.

"Embrace the lessons," Tanuja encouraged, standing as if to end their session, "but also the freedom to choose, to grow, to heal beyond the battles. Towards a future where you write the rules, where your inner child's laughter is the sweetest melody. Your melody, your healing song. And may it play on, brave and beautiful"

"Brave and beautiful," Srishti carried those words with her as she stepped out, the world no longer daunting but inviting, a playground awaiting her return.

*****

Srishti sat across from Tanuja, her hands fidgeting with the hem of her sleeve—a small, unconscious testament to the unease that had brought her here. The room was quiet, a soothing backdrop to the charged atmosphere between therapist and client.

"Sometimes," Srishti began, her voice barely above a whisper, "it feels like I'm watching my life through a foggy lens. I can't connect... Can't fully feel. Joys seem so distant now, it's as if they belong to someone else's story, not mine."

Tanuja nodded, her presence a pillar of calm in the storm of Srishti's inner turmoil. "Disassociation," she said gently, "a buffer against pain. But it can also obscure the joys, the connections that make life worth living. Your story is still being written. Trauma may have set the tone, but each day offers a new sentence, a chance to change the narrative."

"Change the narrative," Srishti repeated, the concept foreign yet tantalizing. She pondered the possibility of seizing the pen, reclaiming authorship of her life's tale.

"Imagine," Tanuja continued, leaning forward, bridging the space between them with her conviction, "removing those glasses, seeing the world with fresh eyes. What might you discover?"

"Clarity, perhaps," Srishti mused, allowing herself a small smile at the thought. "A world where problems are just challenges waiting to be solved."

"Exactly," Tanuja affirmed. "Challenges, not insurmountable walls. You've scaled walls before, haven't you? Your resilience is evident. Let's explore these feelings, acknowledge them, understand them, without letting them define you. In the process you will redefine yourself – stronger, clearer and ever hopeful"

"Hopeful," Srishti whispered, embracing the word as if it were a lifeline. She stood, feeling the weight of her defences begin to unravel, the wounds starting to breathe and heal.

"Hope is the light that guides us through the fog," Tanuja offered, her words a beacon in the shadowy recesses of Srishti's mind.

"Through the fog," Srishti agreed, stepping into the light of her newfound perspective, ready to see her world—and herself—in vivid, unfettered detail.

"Perception," Tanuja said, her voice a gentle anchor, "is not a fixed lens. It evolves, adapts. Imagine your perception as clay, mouldable. With time and effort, you can shape it to reveal new horizons."

"New horizons..." Srishti let the words linger, a faint smile touching her lips. Possibilities. They were there, weren't they? Just beyond the tunnel's confines.

"Your trauma," Tanuja continued, "has been like a shadow, dimming the light of opportunities. But shadows shift, they don't remain still. You're not confined to this tunnel. Fatigue and sleeplessness, they are chains forged by unresolved feelings, aren't they?"

"Chains," Srishti acknowledged, closing her eyes. They felt heavy, those chains, wrought from years of self-blame and unrecognized grief.

"Yet, deep inside, you know," Tanuja assured her, reaching out to cover one of Srishti's hands with her own, "you know it's more than just thoughts. There's something tangible blocking your path to healing."

"Something... tangible," Srishti murmured, opening her eyes. Tanuja's touch grounded her, reminded her that her experiences were real, not imagined figments designed to torment her.

"Can we try to talk to that something?" Tanuja proposed, her question wrapped in the safety of her therapeutic space.

"Talk to it..." Srishti hesitated, then nodded. It was time to confront the barriers, to acknowledge their presence before she could dismantle them.

"Tell me about these chains," Tanuja prompted. "Describe them to me."

Srishti inhaled deeply, searching for words. "They're like... like vines," she began, her voice gaining strength. "Vines that have grown around my legs, anchoring me to a spot filled with doubts and what-ifs."

"Vines can be cut," Tanuja pointed out simply, yet profoundly.

"Cut," Srishti whispered, daring to believe. Yes, the vines could be severed. One by one, with patience and persistence.

"Let's start by identifying the sharpest shears you possess—your strengths," Tanuja suggested, her tone imbued with hope.

"My strengths," Srishti repeated, considering the tools she had at her disposal. Her intellect, her empathy, her drive. She could use them all to prune away the overgrowth.

"Exactly," Tanuja smiled, releasing Srishti's hand, confident in her ability to begin the process of untangling herself.

"Untangling..." Srishti held onto the word like a promise. She would unravel the vines, slowly, carefully, until she could step forward freely, leaving the chains behind.

"Step by step," Tanuja encouraged. "And I'll be here, walking alongside you."

Srishti's heart raced as the familiar sensation crept up on her—the tightening of her chest, the quickening pulse, the sudden chill that cascaded down her spine. It was happening again: a trigger had been sprung, unbidden and ferocious.

"Can you feel it? The surge within you?" Tanuja's voice was a gentle nudge in the dimly lit room.

"Yes," Srishti admitted, her eyes fixed on a point in the distance, a place only she could see. "It's like... a tiger, ready to attack."

"Good," said Tanuja, nodding slowly. "Now hold that image. Don't push it away. What if this tiger is not here to harm you but to lead you somewhere important?"

"Lead me?" Srishti's breath came out in short bursts. The idea seemed counterintuitive, almost alien.

Imagine facing the tiger," Tanuja continued, her words painting a picture of courage in the face of fear. "See its power, but look beyond it. There's wisdom in your fear, knowledge in your body's response."

Srishti closed her eyes, envisioning the daunting creature before her. With every thud of her heartbeat, the tiger's presence grew less menacing, more instructive. She inhaled deeply, allowing her lungs to expand with newfound resolve.

"Good, Srishti. Now, what truth is it guarding? What has it come to teach you?" Tanuja's inquiry was soft yet insistent, prompting exploration.

The shadows in Srishti's mind began to clear, revealing glimpses of insight. "It's... showing me where I'm stuck. The memories I've tried to forget," she murmured, connecting with a deep-seated realization.

"Exactly," Tanuja affirmed, a smile touching the corners of her mouth. "Your triggers are not obstacles; they are signposts, guiding you to heal parts of yourself that still need attention."

"Signposts..." The word resonated within Srishti, transforming her perception of the past from one of victimhood to a path of learning.

"Every time you face them, you reclaim a piece of yourself," Tanuja explained, her tone imbued with hope. "Strength lies in confrontation, not avoidance." Tanuja's eyes locked with Srishti's, conveying belief in her capacity to grow. "Remember, healing is a journey," Tanuja reminded her gently. "Each step you take is progress, no matter how small it may seem."

"Progress," Srishti acknowledged, a soft smile beginning to form. Her journey was hers alone, but with Tanuja's guidance, she felt less alone.

"Let's keep walking together," Tanuja offered, her hand extended across the space between them.

"Thank you," Srishti whispered, grasping the lifeline. Together, they would traverse the once-terrifying landscape of her mind, finding strength and solace in the light of understanding.

*****

Srishti inhaled deeply, the air cool and soothing as it filled her lungs. She sat across from Tanuja, her gaze steady though her heart thrummed with a nervous energy. The office, bathed in soft light, felt safe—a cocoon where she could unfold the delicate layers of her past.

"Validation," Tanuja began, her voice smooth and even, "is often sought from others. But true safety, Srishti, comes from within."

"From within?" Srishti's fingers traced the armrests of her chair, seeking comfort in the solid wood beneath them.

"Indeed," Tanuja affirmed. "From recognizing that you are enough, just as you are. That you are worthy of love and respect, regardless of external approval."

The words settled over Srishti like a warm blanket, heavy with truth yet soothing to her soul. She nodded, considering the weight of her need for validation—how it had always been tied to someone else's opinion.

"And what if those opinions were... not kind?" Srishti asked, her voice a whisper of vulnerability.

"Then," Tanuja said, leaning forward, her eyes locking onto Srishti's, "we learn the art of re-parenting."

"Re-parenting?" The concept was unfamiliar, a new seed planted in the fertile soil of her mind.

"Imagine," Tanuja instructed gently, "activating an inner mother or father. One who nurtures you, believes in you, and helps rewrite the old stories that no longer serve you. It's about embracing your flaws, understanding they are part of your unique tapestry. Especially the broken threads, they add depth, strength and beauty to the weave."

"Strength," Srishti mused, a smile playing on her lips. "I've never seen my flaws that way."

"Yet, here you are," Tanuja spread her hands wide, encompassing the journey laid out before them, "ready to forge a new path. Your very own, independent of the shadows cast by others' expectations."

"Shadows..." Srishti's brow furrowed, contemplating the metaphor. "I've lived in them for too long."

"Then let's step into the light," Tanuja suggested, her tone imbued with encouragement. "You will discover the vibrant colours of your spirit, untainted by the grey of past judgments."

"Into the light," Srishti agreed, her voice firmer now. There was work to be done, but she felt ready, armed with newfound insights and the support of her compassionate guide.

"Remember," Tanuja offered as they wrapped up their session, "each day is an opportunity to practice loving yourself, just a little more."

"Practice," Srishti acknowledged, standing to leave. She felt taller somehow, bolstered by the simple yet profound truths unearthed today.

"Until next time," Tanuja said, her farewell a gentle benediction.

"Until then," Srishti replied, stepping out of the office with a sense of purpose. She carried the seeds of validation and re-parenting within her, ready to nurture them to life.

Outside, the world awaited—not as a judge, but as a canvas upon which she could paint her own story, one stroke of self-love at a time.

*****

Srishti took a deep breath, the crisp air of early morning filling her lungs with a sense of renewal. She stood at the edge of the park, gazing at the joggers weaving through the paths and the tai chi practitioners moving with an effortless grace. It was here, amidst the symphony of life unfurling around her, that she felt the truth of Tanuja's words settle into her bones.

"Trauma," Srishti whispered to herself, "you are but a chapter in my book, not the entire story."

With each step forward, she felt the weight of her past loosening its grip. The chains of old memories clinked faintly, growing more distant as she walked. Each stride was an affirmation, a silent declaration of her right to heal, to move beyond the invisible barriers that once hemmed her in.

She paused to watch a leaf, golden and crisp, break free from its branch and spiral to the ground. There was beauty in its descent, a natural letting go that Srishti yearned to emulate.

"Letting go is not giving up," she reminded herself. "It's choosing to rise."

Turning her gaze towards the horizon, Srishti envisioned her future stretching out before her—unwritten, unbound, and beckoning with promise. She allowed herself a small smile, a glimmer of hope igniting in her chest.

"Survivor," she said, testing the word on her tongue, feeling its power. "Warrior. Champion."

With renewed determination, she began to walk again, her pace steady and sure. Her thoughts turned to the journey ahead, to the healing that awaited her like the dawn after the long night.

"Embrace it," she murmured, taking comfort in the familiar rhythm of her heart—a drumbeat propelling her onward. "Embrace the journey, with all its twists and turns."

The path unwound before her, dappled with sunlight filtering through the trees. With each step, the light grew stronger, bolder, until it enveloped her in warmth.

"Promise," she breathed, the sun's rays caressing her face. "Possibility."

A laugh bubbled up from within, surprising and bright, as Srishti realized something profound: she was no longer walking towards the light; she was part of it, radiant and alive.

"Here I am," she declared to the world, her voice ringing clear. "Not a victim, but a creator of my destiny."

She knew there would be challenges, moments of doubt and shadows of the past. But armed with self-compassion and the wisdom shared by Tanuja, Srishti felt equipped to face them head-on. For she was a warrior of her own making, and her story was hers to write—one hopeful, healing step at a time.

****

Srishti sat across from Tanuja, her eyes reflecting a cautious hope. The room was quiet, save for the gentle ticking of a clock on the wall, marking the passage of time—a silent reminder that each moment held the potential for change.

"Attachment styles," Tanuja began, her voice soft yet clear, "they're like blueprints, guiding how we connect with others." She leaned forward slightly, a gesture inviting trust. "Especially after trauma, understanding your own attachment style can be transformative."

"Secure attachment," she continued, watching Srishti absorb the words, "is the foundation for healthy relationships. It's where we all aim to be."

Srishti nodded, her mind racing with questions. She had always felt the pull of connection, yet there was a hesitance within her, a lingering doubt seeded by past pains.

"Imagine a child," Tanuja said, painting the picture with her hands, "who is consistently nurtured, their emotions respected and understood. They grow up feeling safe to express themselves, to seek support."

"Is it possible," Srishti asked, her voice barely above a whisper, "to find that security, even if you didn't start there?"

"Absolutely," Tanuja affirmed, her eyes warm with conviction. "It's not about where you begin, but the journey you take and the work you put into it. Journeys are more like spirals, bringing us back to lessons until we've gathered what we need from them."

Srishti took a deep breath, letting the idea of spirals, of returning and progressing, settle in her chest. There was comfort in knowing that healing wasn't linear—that she could circle back, armed with new tools and perspectives each time.

"Every step you take toward understanding yourself," Tanuja said, her tone encouraging, "is a step toward secure attachment, toward building the relationships you desire and deserve. Nurture those seeds of self-worth, Srishti. Water them with compassion and watch them grow."

"Anxious-preoccupied attachment," Tanuja continued, her voice a gentle nudge, "often arises from inconsistency in childhood. When love felt like a question mark, not an exclamation."

Srishti nodded, memories surfacing like raindrops on still water. "Always seeking approval," she whispered, "fearing... abandonment."

"Exactly," Tanuja affirmed, her eyes soft with understanding. "But fear does not have to be the compass by which you navigate your world."

"Is it possible," Srishti asked, her voice barely above a murmur, "to change the pattern?"

"More than possible," Tanuja responded, her certainty a warm blanket around Srishti's shoulders. "It begins with recognizing your worth apart from others' presence or praise."

A pause followed as Srishti let the words settle in her chest, their weight less heavy than she anticipated. She exhaled slowly, releasing years of held breath.

Tanuja shifted the conversation with the practiced ease of a mind therapist steering her client toward self-discovery. "Then there's dismissive-avoidant attachment," she said, watching Srishti closely.

"Keeping distance," Srishti reflected, her insight quickening. "To protect myself from... what? Being seen?"

"Being vulnerable," Tanuja corrected gently. "You learned to equate solitude with strength. But true strength lies in allowing yourself to connect, to depend, to feel."

"Even if it scares me?" The question hung between them, fragile as glass.

"Especially then," Tanuja affirmed. "Bravery is facing the fear, not avoiding it."

Their eyes met, two souls reaching across a divide built by years of misconceived protection. Srishti's heart thrummed with the possibility of change, the allure of healing.

"Remember," Tanuja said as their session neared its end, "your past may have mapped out a certain path, but you are the cartographer now. You chart your own course."

"Charting a new course," Srishti repeated, feeling the truth of it resonate within her. Her journey was hers to claim, each step a testament to her evolving story—a story no longer written in the shadow of anxious tethers or dismissive walls, but in the light of self-compassion and newfound courage.

"Time can be our ally in healing," Tanuja said, arranging her notes. "Now, I think we're ready to explore another attachment style: fearful-avoidant."

"Sounds ominous," Srishti murmured, a ripple of tension crossing her features.

"Perhaps," Tanuja nodded. "But understanding is the first step toward change." She leaned forward, her gaze steady. "Fearful-avoidant—rooted in ambivalence. A push and pull between the need for closeness and the fear of it. Driven by past hurts, it's the child who craved affection yet feared the pain it might bring. The adult who longs to be understood but distrusts intimacy."

"Caught between wanting to reach out and wanting to run away." Srishti's words were a mirror, reflecting her inner chaos.

"Exactly," Tanuja affirmed. "And this tug-of-war within you can manifest in relationships as mixed signals—drawing people in, then pushing them away."

"Unsettling," Srishti admitted, her eyes closing briefly as if to shutter the truth.

"Yet," Tanuja continued, the hope in her tone undiminished, "acknowledging this is powerful. It means you can start to nurture trust in yourself, to balance those opposing forces."

"Balance..." Srishti pondered the word as though tasting it for the first time. "How do I find it?"

"Through acceptance and gentle exploration," Tanuja replied. "By validating your fears without letting them define your actions."

"Validating, not capitulating," Srishti corrected herself, a small smile playing on her lips.

"Indeed," Tanuja chuckled. "And from there, cultivating self-compassion, creating a space where you feel safe to express vulnerability."

"Self-compassion," Srishti echoed, rolling the concept around her mind like a puzzle piece waiting to fit. "That's new territory for me."

"New, yes, but not unreachable," Tanuja encouraged. "Consider this: you have survived every challenge life has thrown at you. That resilience speaks volumes."

"Survived, but not unscathed," Srishti countered, her voice tinged with both pride and sorrow.

"Scars are evidence of healing," Tanuja gently pointed out. "They show where you've been and also how far you've come."

"Scars as milestones..." Srishti contemplated, a shift in her perspective dawning like the first light of morning. "Markers on the path to somewhere better."

"Somewhere better, indeed." Tanuja's voice held the promise of a journey not yet finished but embarked upon with courage. "And along this path, you'll find tools to help you build the secure connections you deserve. Building blocks forged by your own hands. Crafted with care, patience, and an unwavering belief in your capacity to love and be loved."

"Love..." The word hung in the air, fragile yet filled with potential. Srishti met Tanuja's gaze, her own alight with nascent understanding. "I'm ready to learn how."

"Then let's begin," Tanuja said, her smile as warm as the afternoon sun streaming through the window. "Together, we'll transform fear into freedom, avoidance into acceptance."

"Freedom," Srishti repeated, allowing the word to settle over her like a comforting shawl. She leaned back, the contours of the chair no longer confining but supportive, as if cradling her newfound determination.

"Acceptance," she added, her heart lighter, her path clearer. "I am more than my fears."

"Much more," Tanuja agreed, her nod an affirmation of the strength residing within Srishti—the strength that would carry her forward into a future of her own making.

*****

Srishti unfolded her legs and sat up straighter, a conscious mimicry of Tanuja's poised composure across from her. The room was quiet except for the gentle hum of air flowing through the vent—an undercurrent to the symphony of their shared silences and spoken truths.

"Secure attachment," she began, her voice a tentative whisper testing the strength of the words. "It sounds so... grounded."

"Indeed," Tanuja responded, her hands resting calmly in her lap. "Think of it as the roots of a tree—deeply embedded, providing stability and nourishment."

Srishti pondered this, her gaze drifting to the potted fern on the windowsill, its green leaves vibrant against the sunlit glass. "Roots that were planted in trust, watered with consistency."

"Exactly." Tanuja inclined her head. "Securely attached individuals usually had caregivers who responded to their needs predictably and affectionately. They learned that the world is a safe place where support is given and emotions are valued."

"Valued..." Srishti echoed, rolling the word around like a smooth pebble in her mouth. "That's so different from fear or avoidance."

Tanuja nodded. "When you're secure in your attachments, you're more likely to be open about your feelings. You're also more adept at seeking help when faced with challenges."

"Seeking help isn't a sign of weakness, then?" Srishti asked, hope threading through her tone.

"Far from it," Tanuja assured her. "It's an act of courage. It means you understand your own worth and the value of your emotional well-being."

"Understanding your worth," Srishti mused, absorbing the concept like a parched plant soaking in rainwater. "So, in times of trauma..."

"Those with secure attachments often have better tools for coping," Tanuja explained. "They're able to process their emotions in healthier ways and are skilled at setting boundaries that protect their mental space."

"Boundaries..." Srishti let the idea linger, visualizing them as soft but firm barriers, cocooning her from old patterns of self-doubt.

"Healthy boundaries," Tanuja continued, "allow you to distinguish where you end and another begins. They enable you to give and receive love without losing yourself."

"Without losing myself," Srishti repeated, the phrase a buoyant melody amidst the cacophony of her past fears. She felt a smile touch the corners of her lips, a rare visitor eager to become a friend.

"Remember," Tanuja said gently, reaching for a pen and notepad, "the journey towards secure attachment begins with small steps. It's about reinforcing the foundation you've already laid down. Acceptance of your needs, your emotions, and the validity of your experiences. And above all, the unwavering belief that you deserve to give and receive love freely."

"Freely," Srishti whispered, the word a tender promise to herself. She imagined her roots growing deeper, spreading outwards, finding hold in fertile soil—a testament to her resilience and her capacity for growth.

"Shall we explore how to cultivate this secure attachment within you?" Tanuja asked, eyes alight with compassionate resolve.

"Yes," Srishti answered, her voice stronger now, bolstered by the vision of who she could become. "Let's grow these roots."

"Craving closeness," she began, her voice unsteady like the flicker of a candle flame, "I've always longed for it, yet I'm haunted by the fear that those I love might leave." Tanuja nodded, understandingly, her pen poised above the notepad. "It's a difficult space to be in," she acknowledged, "constantly seeking assurance."

"Yes," Srishti agreed, her fingers nervously tracing the hem of her sleeve. "Always on edge, as if one misstep might shatter everything."

"Your feelings are valid," Tanuja reassured her, her voice a soothing balm. "They stem from experiences that were beyond your control."

"Beyond my control," Srishti repeated, letting the words sink in. She felt a weight lift ever so slightly, a burden she'd carried for so long beginning to ease.

"Dismissive-avoidant attachment," Tanuja transitioned, touching upon the next point with deliberate care, "is often marked by emotional distancing. Does this resonate with you?"

"Emotional distance..." Srishti contemplated, her gaze drifting. Memories surfaced, times when she'd retreated into herself, building walls where bridges should have been.

"Minimizing your pain," Tanuja continued, "can be a defense mechanism. It keeps the hurt at bay, but it also keeps healing at arm's length."

"Keeping hurt at bay," Srishti echoed, realizing how often she'd denied her own need for comfort.

"Let's work on acknowledging your emotions," Tanuja suggested, her tone imbued with hope. "Accepting them without judgment."

"Without judgment," Srishti mused, considering the idea like a new seed planted in fertile ground.

"Can we try an exercise?" Tanuja proposed, her expression encouraging. "Express something you've kept hidden, just here, between us."

"Something hidden..." Srishti hesitated, then found her resolve. "I'm tired," she confessed, her voice barely above a whisper, "of always being the strong one."

"Being strong doesn't mean you can't seek help or express vulnerability," Tanuja gently corrected. "On the contrary, it takes courage to do so."

"Courage," Srishti tasted the word, finding an unfamiliar strength within its syllables. "To be vulnerable, to seek help."

"Exactly," Tanuja affirmed, her eyes warm with pride. "And in doing so, you create opportunities for deeper connections."

"Deeper connections," Srishti considered, a flicker of anticipation stirring within. "Not just with others, but with myself too."

"Indeed," Tanuja smiled. "With yourself first and foremost."

"First and foremost," Srishti repeated, her heart lighter, as though she had shed a layer of armor she no longer needed.

"Remember," Tanuja concluded, the session drawing to a close, "you have the power to change these attachment styles. They are not your destiny."

"Not my destiny," Srishti declared, standing a little taller. She felt a newfound determination, ready to embark on this journey of transformation.

"Positive self-talk," Tanuja reminded her, "will be a beacon for you. Use it to navigate through the complexities of your emotions."

"Sometimes," Srishti said, her voice barely above a whisper, "I feel like I'm at war with myself. Wanting someone close... but then, it's as if I'm pushing them away with both hands."

Tanuja nodded, her eyes reflecting a pool of understanding.

"That push and pull can be exhausting," she acknowledged. "It's the hallmark of fearful-avoidant attachment – craving intimacy yet fearing it at the same time."

"Exactly," Srishti affirmed, her fingers tracing the edge of the cushion, finding solace in the texture. "And when I do let someone in, it's like... there's this alarm bell inside me, ringing non-stop, telling me to run."

"Because closeness once equalled chaos," Tanuja offered gently. "Your alarm bell was a necessary tool once, designed to protect you."

Srishti's eyes met Tanuja's, a silent question flickering within them. "But now?" she asked.

"Now," Tanuja said, leaning forward slightly, "understanding your attachment style is your new tool. It shines light on these patterns, doesn't it?"

"Patterns," Srishti echoed, considering the word. "Like threads in a tapestry, each one woven by experiences."

"Indeed," Tanuja smiled. "And like any weaver, you have the power to choose which threads to use moving forward."

"Choice," Srishti tasted the concept, feeling its weight. "It means responsibility, doesn't it? To pick... healthier threads."

"Responsibility and opportunity," Tanuja corrected softly. "You're not just choosing threads. You're creating a new pattern, one that serves you better."

"Creating... not just reacting," Srishti mused, a sliver of empowerment threading through her uncertainty.

"Reacting is instinct," Tanuja agreed. "Creating is intentional. It's positive self-talk, it's recognizing triggers, it's reaching out when the fear feels too great."

"Intentional," Srishti repeated, the word settling into her like a puzzle piece clicking into place. "So, what now? How do I... practice this intention?"

"Start small," Tanuja advised, her voice a lighthouse guiding through fog. "When you notice the urge to retreat, pause. Ask yourself, 'What am I afraid of?'"

"Pause," Srishti whispered, locking the advice away like a treasure. "I can do that. I can ask questions."

"Questions open doors," Tanuja confirmed. "They lead to insight, healing, and eventually, to a sense of security within yourself."

"Security," Srishti pondered, the word foreign yet alluring. "It sounds peaceful."

"Peace is possible, Srishti," Tanuja's assurance was firm, unwavering. "Through understanding, through patience with yourself, through embracing the journey."

"Embracing," Srishti allowed herself a small smile, a seed of hope unfurling. "Not enduring."

"Exactly," Tanuja's eyes sparkled with shared triumph. "Embrace the journey, Srishti. Step by step, day by day. Remember, healing isn't just possible—it's within your reach."

Srishti nodded, absorbing the words as if they were sunlight breaking through clouds. "It starts with me, doesn't it?" she asked, a newfound determination flickering in her eyes.

"Yes," Tanuja affirmed. "With acknowledging that the pain you endured was never your fault. It's about courage now—courage to face what was, so you can embrace what will be."

"Courage," Srishti echoed, letting the word linger on her lips, feeling its weight and power. She imagined herself shedding the heavy cloak of self-blame, piece by frayed piece, revealing the resilient woman beneath.

"Attachment-based therapy," Tanuja explained, her hands gesturing as if weaving a tapestry of understanding, "can be a path to redefining how you relate to yourself and others. It helps to explore and reshape those patterns etched into you during childhood."

"Reshape," Srishti contemplated aloud. "Like sculpting a new form from old clay."

"Exactly," Tanuja replied, a smile touching the corners of her mouth. "And trauma-focused approaches help to address the wounds directly, to heal them with the precision they need."

"Precision," Srishti repeated. "Focusing on the wound... not just the symptoms it causes." She pictured herself under a microscope, the intricate design of her past experiences coming into sharp focus.

"Self-awareness is your tool," Tanuja continued, her expressive eyes locking onto Srishti's. "Empathy, your guide. And support, your scaffolding as you rebuild trust in yourself."

"Rebuild..." Srishti's voice wavered but did not break. "I'm learning to trust again—not just in others, but in myself."

Tanuja leaned forward slightly, a silent gesture of encouragement. "You're on a journey, Srishti. One step at a time, each day a page in a new chapter you're writing for yourself."

Srishti felt the truth of Tanuja's words settle around her like a protective shroud. "A journey," she said, a smile beginning to curve her lips. "One where I learn, where I grow, where I heal."

"Where you heal," Tanuja responded, her presence a steady beacon. "Keep moving forward, Srishti. Embrace your future, filled with hope and healing."

"Hope and healing," Srishti said, her voice stronger now. She stepped towards the door, pausing to glance back at Tanuja with gratitude shining in her eyes. "Until next time," she said, stepping out into the world, a warrior ready to claim her destiny.

*****

Srishti slid the bolt across her apartment door and exhaled, the metallic click a signal to the world that she was carving out a sanctuary for herself. The city's din faded as she padded across the room to her favourite chair, an old, overstuffed armchair that seemed to hug her back whenever she nestled into it.

Closing her eyes, she inhaled deeply, drawing the cool air of solitude into her lungs. With each breath, the tightness in her chest loosened, threads of tension unwinding until her shoulders dropped and her body felt anchored in the present.

She envisioned her mind as a vast sky, clouds of thoughts drifting by. Some were dark with the weight of rain, others wispy and fleeting. Today, she would not chase them or hide from them—she would simply observe.

"Safe," she whispered to the empty room. "Here, now, I am safe."

With the stage set, Srishti allowed her mind to drift back to her childhood home in Mangalore, where the monsoons were fierce and the pressure to excel was fiercer still. She could almost hear the echo of her parents' expectations bouncing off the walls, the silent demands that she be more, do more.

An image surfaced—a younger Srishti, hunched over textbooks at the dining table, her parents' figures looming in the periphery. The memory brought a familiar ache, a cocktail of sadness and anger brewing in the pit of her stomach.

"Hello, emotions," she acknowledged softly, granting them permission to exist. "You are the children of my past, and you have a place here."

The sadness spoke of lost moments, of laughter drowned out by the relentless pursuit of perfection. The anger flared from injustices, from every scolding that suggested she was not enough.

"Anger, you protected me," she said, finding strength in naming her guardian. "Sadness, you kept my hope alive. You both have served me."

Her heart fluttered, a bird testing its wings after too long in the cage of her ribcage. Fear peeked around the corner, the familiar spectre of doubt, but Srishti held her ground.

"Even you, fear," she continued, her voice a gentle caress. "You taught me caution, showed me how to navigate the storms."

Confusion spun its delicate web, a reminder of times when love and pain walked hand in hand, leaving a child to wonder which was which.

"Confusion, you were the puzzle I learned to solve," she reasoned, a note of pride threading through her words. "And now, clarity is born from your chaos."

As the emotions swirled within her, Srishti remained still, a lighthouse amidst the tempest of her own making. She recognized each feeling, honoured its origin, and understood that they were signposts on her path to healing.

"Thank you," she breathed out, gratitude replacing the heaviness. "For guiding me here."

Tears pricked the corners of her eyes, not of sorrow but of release. They traced warm paths down her cheeks, each one a testament to her journey.

"See, Srishti?" Tanuja's voice echoed in her memory, soft yet resolute. "Embrace every part of you. Your feelings are valid. Your experiences matter. And they lead you to growth, to understanding, to peace."

"Peace," Srishti repeated, the word a promise. "In understanding myself, I find peace."

The chair embraced her, the air around her buzzed with the energy of transformation, and within her, a deep well of calm reassured her that this space, this moment, was exactly where she needed to be.

Srishti settled into the softness of her armchair, a sense of serenity enveloping her as she clutched a pen with purpose. The pages before her lay blank, pristine and inviting. She closed her eyes for a moment, taking in a deep, steadying breath. In the quietude of her own space, she reached back through years, past the tumult and the tears, to touch the tender memories of her childhood self.

"Dear Little Srishti," she began, her hand moving with newfound confidence.

Words tumbled onto the page, each one soaked with the love and understanding that had been absent in moments when she needed them most. With every stroke of the pen, she painted a picture of compassion, a tapestry woven from the threads of her grown wisdom and the undying innocence of the child within.

"I see you, with your wide, hopeful eyes, and I know the hurt you've carried," she wrote, acknowledging the weight that her younger self had borne in silence.

She paused, her gaze drifting to the window where the sun dipped low, casting a warm glow that seemed to dance across her words. A gentle breeze stirred in the room, as if carrying the echoes of laughter from playgrounds and schoolyards long forgotten.

"Your pain is real, and it's not your fault," she continued, her pen resolute against the paper.

The scent of jasmine from the garden crept in, mingling with the ink and paper, a sensory bridge between past and present. Srishti felt her heart swell, a tide of empathy rising within her for the girl she once was—a girl who deserved nothing less than to be held, heard, and healed.

"Know this, my dear: you were always worthy of love," she whispered to herself, her voice a soft melody in the stillness.

Tears no longer threatened; they were unnecessary companions on this journey of reconnection. Instead, a smile graced Srishti's lips, a silent ovation to her strength and the unwavering spirit of the child who survived it all.

"Love, Compassion, Understanding," she signed off, a trinity of promises from her present self to her past.

The letter sat complete, a testament to her resilience. It was more than mere words on paper—it was an act of healing, a bridge across time, crafted by hands that learned to build rather than break.

"Little Srishti," she murmured, tracing the loops and lines of her name, "we've come so far."

And in that quiet room, as dusk embraced the day, Srishti found solace in the knowledge that the child she once was and the woman she had become were now allies in a world they were learning to navigate together—with courage, with hope, and an unshakeable belief in their shared future.

*****

Srishti's hand hovered over the paper, her fingers trembling slightly with the weight of unspoken truths. With a deep breath that filled her lungs with resolve, she let the pen touch down, staining the page with ink and intention.

"Dear Little Srishti," she began, the words flowing like a gentle stream, "I've learned so much since the days we shared. Life has taught me lessons only time could reveal."

She paused, memories cascading through her mind, each one a stepping stone to the wisdom she now possessed. She wrote of compassion, not just for others but for oneself; of resilience, the quiet strength that emerges from adversity; and mostimportantly, she wrote of hope—the golden thread weaving through the fabric of life.

"Please know, you are not alone in your journey," she inscribed earnestly, "Your feelings, as deep and vast as the ocean, are valid. The pain you felt was real, and it mattered."

The room around her faded into a blur as she poured out reassurances to her younger self, affirmations that stitched together the fragmented pieces of her past. "Healing is not only possible, it is within your grasp."

Srishti felt a release with each word, a shedding of the old skins of doubt and fear. Her thoughts, once caged birds, now took flight on the page, soaring high on the winds of liberation.

"Your tears have watered the garden of your soul, where now resilience blooms," she penned, a smile touching her lips. "Trust in your journey, for it has equipped you with the courage to face tomorrow and the grace to embrace each new dawn."

With each sentence, the rhythm of her writing became more confident, a symphony of self-love that resonated within the walls of her heart. She ended the letter with a promise—a vow of unwavering support to the child who still lived within her.

"Walk forward with your head held high, dear one, for the world awaits your unique light. And remember, I am here, always cheering you on."

Laying down the pen, Srishti folded the letter gently, a ritualistic conclusion to her sacred dialogue. She tucked it away, a treasure map to the heart of her inner child, marking the path to healing and wholeness.

In that moment, surrounded by the quiet affirmation of her own words, Srishti felt a profound connection to the essence of her being—whole, healed, and hopeful.

*****

The letter, now a tangible testament to her journey, lay beside her. Srishti traced the edges of the paper, each crease a line in the chronicle of her soul's evolution. She closed her eyes, inhaling deeply, and exhaled the lingering shadows of doubt that once clouded her mind.

"Look at you," Tanuja's voice was a gentle nudge, pulling Srishti back into the present. "You're not the same person who walked into my office all those months ago."

Srishti nodded, a quiet acknowledgment of the truth in Tanuja's observation. The room around them felt like a cocoon, a safe haven where metamorphosis was not only possible but encouraged.

"Every challenge, every tear, every moment I thought I couldn't go on... they were forming me, weren't they?" Srishti's voice was barely above a whisper, yet it carried the weight of realization. "My experiences, they've sculpted me into someone stronger, more resilient."

"Indeed," Tanuja affirmed, her eyes reflecting pride. "It is through our struggles that we uncover the depths of our strength."

Srishti considered the mosaic of her life, each piece a fragment of experience that contributed to the intricate design of who she was. With a slight tremor of awe in her voice, she confessed, "I never knew how much courage I had until I had no choice but to face my fears."

"Courage isn't the absence of fear," Tanuja said, her tone both empathetic and hopeful. "It's the determination to move forward despite it."

"Even in the darkest times," Srishti continued, "when I felt lost and alone, something within me fought to see the light of day." She paused, her heart swelling with a newfound respect for the resilience that had been her silent companion all along.

"Your resilience is a beacon," Tanuja added, "guiding you out of the darkness. It's an inner strength that has always been part of you."

"Sometimes I faltered," Srishti confessed, "but I never broke."

"Resilience isn't about never falling," Tanuja responded, her words painting pictures of hope in Srishti's mind. "It's about rising every time you do."

"Each scar is a lesson," Srishti said, a tentative smile playing on her lips. "A reminder that I've survived, that I've grown, and that I can keep going, no matter what."

"Exactly," Tanuja replied, her voice soft yet firm. "Every scar is a story of survival, a testimony to your unyielding spirit."

In the stillness that followed, Srishti felt the threads of her past weaving together with the fabric of her present, creating a result rich with the colours of perseverance and hope. She was no longer just a survivor; she was a warrior, armed with the knowledge of her own strength and the certainty that she could conquer whatever lay ahead.

*****

Pen poised above the paper, Srishti drew in a deep breath and let it out slowly, ready to seal the letter with words of power. She wrote with deliberate strokes, addressing the child she once was.

"Always remember," Srishti penned, "you possess an inherent worth that time cannot tarnish nor trials diminish. Within you is a wellspring of potential, boundless and pure, waiting to be tapped."

She paused, nodding slightly to herself, as if to affirm the truth of her own words.

"Your journey will be marked by growth," she continued, "a path that only you can tread, leading to heights yet unseen and achievements yet unclaimed."

Lowering her pen, Srishti folded the letter with care, the creases sharp and decisive. She then held it in her hands, its weight light but its significance immense. With reverence, she read over her own encouragement, each sentence infusing her spirit with warmth and strength.

"May you always know the courage that beats in your heart," she whispered to the quiet room, "and may you step into your future with the certainty that you are capable of overcoming any obstacle."

The words resonated within her, echoes of past struggles juxtaposed with the promise of healing. It was as if the very act of writing had loosed the shackles of old pains, now slipping away like shadows at dawn.

"Embrace your story," Srishti concluded, a final stroke of the pen underscoring the sentiment, "for it is uniquely yours, sculpted by resilience and graced with the capacity to inspire."

Closing her eyes, Srishti allowed the love and compassion from the letter to envelop her. A profound sense of closure washed over her, gentle waves carrying away remnants of doubt and fear. In their place, a feeling of release unfurled, blossoming into freedom—a newfound liberty to live unbound by the narratives of the past.

"Thank you," she murmured, a simple expression of gratitude to herself, to Tanuja, to the therapeutic process that had led her here. The words hung in the air, a testament to the transformative power of self-compassion and the enduring hope that propels us forward.

*****

Srishti's fingers trembled slightly as she folded the letter, its creases holding the weight of her journey. With deliberate care, she slid the envelope into the back of a leather-bound journal—a silent sentinel to guard her words. The journal, a mosaic of thoughts and dreams, now cradled a new treasure within its pages. It was a small act, but it filled the room with a sense of sanctity.

"Here," she thought, "it will be safe."

She placed the journal in the top drawer of her desk, a personal alcove where sunlight filtered through curtains and danced upon the wood. The letter was more than paper and ink; it was a beacon of resilience, a tangible reminder that the echoes of the past did not have to define the symphony of her future.

"Whenever I need strength," Srishti promised herself, "I'll find it here, among my own words."

"Writing Release: Letting Go of the Past" Tanuja had called it—an exercise in healing, a way to unburden the soul. Srishti picked up a fresh sheet of paper, this one blank and inviting. She poised her pen above it, taking a deep breath as if to draw courage from the very air around her.

"Let the pain flow out," Tanuja had encouraged, her voice a gentle nudge toward freedom. "Let your words carry it away."

And so, Srishti began, each word a step on the path to letting go. She wrote of shadows and light, of tears shed in silence, and of laughter that bubbled up in unexpected moments. Her hand moved with a rhythm born of hope, tracing the contours of old wounds with a touch that sought to soothe rather than probe.

With every sentence, the grip of old ghosts grew weaker, their whispers fading into the background. In their place, a chorus of new voices emerged—whispers of possibility, chants of strength, hymns of self-love.

"Goodbye to the chains," she wrote, her pulse steady, "and hello to the wings."

The final period was an exhalation, a release of all that had been pent up for years. Srishti leaned back, feeling the space inside her open up, making room for something expansive and bright. The simple act of writing had become a rite of passage, a crossing from the tangled brambles of yesterday into the clear skies of tomorrow.

"May these words be the wind beneath your wings," she said aloud, a smile curving her lips. It was a blessing for herself, a spell cast in the language of self-compassion.

Gazing at the page, now filled with the essence of her release, Srishti knew what needed to be done. She stood and walked to the fireplace, the paper held gently between her fingers. With reverence, she placed it among the kindling, struck a match, and watched as flames leapt up to embrace her offering.

As the paper turned to ash, her heart felt lighter, as if she had just laid down a heavy burden at the side of a road she no longer needed to travel. She imagined the ashes rising with the smoke, carrying away the remnants of her pain, dispersing them to the four winds.

"From these ashes," Srishti whispered, "new growth begins."

She returned to her desk, to the life that awaited her beyond the window, to the future she would now write with her own hand. There was work to be done, healing to nurture, and love to rediscover—especially the love she held for herself.

"Step by step," she reminded herself. "One word at a time."

****

Srishti slipped into the small alcove of her apartment that she had transformed into a sanctuary. The soft hum of the city outside faded as she closed her eyes, inhaling the quietness. She settled onto the plush cushion, her body sinking into the embrace of its comfort. With each deep breath, the tension in her shoulders eased, and the clamour of her thoughts grew distant.

"Find your centre," Tanuja's gentle voice echoed in her mind—a mantra that now felt like an anchor in Srishti's quest for serenity. She imagined her breath as a wave, washing over her, clearing away the debris of distress, leaving behind a shore of serenity.

Her heart began to speak, its whispers loud in the silence. Memories long obscured by the bustle of daily life surfaced, timid as forest creatures in the half-light. Childhood laughter mingled with moments where expectations loomed large and words of criticism cut deep. Srishti let them come, watching them float up like leaves on a stream, acknowledging their presence without reaching to pluck them from the current.

"It's okay," she murmured to herself, a soothing balm to the sting of old wounds. "It's okay to feel." She pictured herself as a child again—the eager eyes, the earnest smile, the seeking heart. In this sacred space, there was no judgment, only acceptance.

"Your emotions are valid," Tanuja would often remind her. Srishti drew upon that wisdom now, allowing herself the grace to honour each emotion that arose—sorrow for the little girl who tried so hard, anger at the unfair comparisons, a twinge of fear from the shadows of doubt. But there was also love, a fierce, protective love for that child who still lived within her.

"Every feeling has a place," she whispered. It was a new creed, one she was learning to live by, a testament to her journey through the landscape of healing. In this quiet corner of her world, Srishti faced the echoes of her past, not as Specters to flee from, but as fragments of the mosaic that was herself—imperfect yet beautiful in its wholeness.

"Thank you," she said softly, gratitude colouring her tone. Thank you for the lessons, for the strength, for the resilience that blossomed from the cracks of broken dreams. Her past no longer a chain, but a chrysalis from which she emerged, day by day, into the fullness of her own being.

"Peace," she breathed out, opening her eyes to the golden light that filtered through the curtains. The room was the same, yet she was transformed, her spirit a little lighter, her resolve a little stronger. There was hope here, nestled among the threads of pain, a promise woven into the fabric of her soul.

*****

The pen hovered over the page, trembling slightly in Srishti's grasp. With a steadying breath, she let the tip touch down on the surface, the ink bleeding a small dot before it began to slide across the paper. Words emerged hesitantly at first, like the first drops of a long-awaited rain.

"I remember," she wrote, her handwriting a mirror of her inner turmoil—jagged at times, then looping gracefully as if finding brief moments of peace. "I remember the tightness in my chest, the way my heart seemed to pound against its cage."

She paused, her eyes closing briefly as she summoned the courage to continue. The room was silent, save for the soft scratch of pen on paper, a sacred symphony that filled the spaces between her thoughts.

"Anger," the next word came stronger, bolder. It was a declaration, a release of emotions pent-up and pushed aside. "Anger for the words that stung sharper than any slap, for the silence that spoke volumes of neglect."

With each sentence, the dam within her cracked, the waters of unshed tears flowing through ink and imagery. She described the cold fear that clutched her during nights spent under a blanket of uncertainty, the sadness that settled like dew upon her dreams, drenching them with doubt.

"Yet," she continued, the narrative shifting, "within me, there was fire, a flickering flame refusing to be snuffed out." It was the story of her resilience, the tale of a spirit unbowed despite the buffets of fate.

"From pain, I learned compassion...for myself," she confessed to the page, the words an intimate whisper of self-discovery.

"From fear, came the wisdom to seek light even when shadows loomed large."

She explored the landscape of her emotions with newfound

bravery, each memory plucked from the depths and laid bare upon the page. Her story was not one of simple sorrow, but a complex tapestry woven from threads of loss and love, hurt and healing.

"Today," she wrote, her hand steady now, "I stand amidst the ruins of what was and the foundation of what will be." The past had been acknowledged, its power over her challenged by the act of claiming her own narrative.

"Through the storm, I walk, not alone, but with the strength of my own heart to guide me." It was a vow, a promise etched into the fibres of the paper, a testament to the journey she was on—a path that led toward the warm glow of hope on the horizon.

Srishti set down the pen, her chest rising and falling with a rhythm that spoke of battles fought and still to be won. She read over her words, each one a step towards understanding, a bridge built from the darkness to the dawn of self-compassion.

"Your story matters," Tanuja would often say, her voice a gentle nudge towards self-acceptance. And as Srishti folded the pages, tucking them close to her heart, she believed it. Her story did matter, and with every beat of her heart, she penned its next chapter.

*****

Srishti's fingers trembled as she picked up the pages, her eyes grazing over the words that poured from the deepest parts of her soul. There was a quiet bravery in acknowledging the darkness, and she felt it now—raw and real—in the pulse of her veins. She breathed in the musty scent of ink, letting the weight of her own narrative settle within her chest.

"Look at what you've written," she whispered to herself, "the truths you've dared to face." The room around her felt still, almost sacred, as if bearing witness to the emergence of someone new.

With a deep breath that seemed to draw courage from the very air, she began to fold the paper, her hands steady. Each crease was a marker of resilience, each line a map of the journey she had traversed—a latticework of pain transformed into strength.

"Letting go doesn't mean forgetting," Tanuja had told her many times, "it means choosing not to carry the burdens that aren't yours to bear." Srishti clung to those words now as she took the folded story between her fingers and slowly, deliberately, tore it down the middle.

The sound was crisp, a declaration of intent. She continued, each tear an act of liberation, each piece a fragment of a past that would no longer define her. With every rip, she imagined releasing the tendrils of fear that had clung to her for so long, watching them drift away like leaves on an autumn wind.

"Goodbye, old ghosts," she murmured, her voice a melodic resolve. "Thank you for the lessons, but your time has passed." The pieces lay scattered before her, a mosaic of memories freed from their hold.

A sense of lightness enveloped her, the beginning of a space within where healing could take root. Srishti closed her eyes, a smile touching her lips as she pictured the open skies of her future, unclouded and vast with possibility. She was more than the sum of her scars; she was the author of her destiny, writing her way toward a horizon filled with the gentle hues of hope.

*****

Srishti knelt beside the fire pit, her heart pulsing with a quiet rhythm of courage. With hands that trembled not from fear but from the weight of what they released, she placed the torn pieces of her story into the cold embrace of the pit. She inhaled deeply, the crisp air filling her lungs like a promise, steadying her resolve.

"Letting go is an act of strength," she whispered to herself, echoing Tanuja's gentle affirmations. Her fingers brushed against the rough edges of the paper, each piece a silent testimony to the past she was ready to transform.

She struck a match, the tiny flame quivering at the end of the stick, a beacon in the dimming light. The fire caught quickly, eager and hungry, consuming the paper as it turned to ash. Srishti watched, her gaze unflinching, as the flames danced across her words, her pain, her memories. It was a ritual of renewal, a sacred moment where every flicker spoke of healing.

"From these ashes, new life," she affirmed, the warmth of the fire caressing her face. She envisioned the pain lifting, dissolving into the heat, forging a path toward wholeness. The crackling sound of paper turning to cinders was a symphony of rebirth, each note a step away from the shadows of yesterday.

"Be gone, darkness," Srishti murmured, the corners of her mouth curving upward in a tender smile. "Welcome, light." She could almost feel the tightness in her chest loosening, making room for a peace that glimmered like the first rays of dawn.

The flames waned, leaving a soft glow of embers, a testament to the power of letting go. Srishti sat back on her heels, a sense of accomplishment blooming within her. For the first time in a long while, the future beckoned with open arms, inviting her to step forward into a life crafted by her own hands—a life rich with possibility and crowned with the strength of her own resilient spirit.

The crackle of the dwindling fire was a gentle whisper in the stillness, the last word in a long and arduous conversation. Srishti watched the embers glow, their orange light dimming to a soft, comforting hue. She wrapped her arms around herself, feeling the cool night air against her skin. The heat from the fire had dissipated, but a different kind of warmth spread within her—a warmth that came from an inner sanctuary she'd only just discovered.

"Let it go," she told herself, the words floating out on a breath that seemed to carry the weight of years. The fire's warmth had been replaced by the cool touch of the evening, as though nature itself were soothing her, acknowledging her release.

Her heart felt lighter, unburdened by the sorrow that had once filled it so completely. It was a sensation unfamiliar yet welcome, like the first step into a new home. With every trace of paper that turned to ash, a piece of her past settled into quiet slumber, no longer a haunting shadow but a memory laid to rest with reverence.

"New beginnings," she whispered to the stars peeking through the dark canopy above. A smile tugged at her lips, the corners lifting in a spontaneous embrace of the moment. In this sacred space, she found the courage to face tomorrow, not as a continuation of past hurts, but as a canvas awaiting her touch.

Srishti stood up, her movements slow and deliberate. She stretched her arms toward the sky, reaching for the dreams that had once seemed so distant. The cool ground beneath her feet reminded her of where she stood—firmly rooted in the present, ready to grow toward the light.

"Clarity," she realized, the word tasting sweet on her tongue. The heaviness in her eyes had lifted, revealing a clarity that shone like a beacon in the darkness. For the first time, she could see the path ahead not as a road marred by obstacles, but as a journey illuminated by self-compassion and the promise of healing.

"Peace," she acknowledged, closing her eyes and taking a deep, grounding breath. The serenity that enveloped her was a gentle caress, a silent affirmation of her resilience. She held onto this feeling, a treasure to carry with her into the days and nights ahead.

"Thank you," she offered to the night, to the fire, to herself. Her words were a vow, a declaration of acceptance and self-love. She had walked through the flames of her own fears and emerged transformed, not by the fire, but by her own enduring spirit.

"Welcome," she said finally, turning her gaze upward, "to a future crafted by me."

Srishti knelt by the remnants of her past, now reduced to a mound of grey ash under the moonlit sky. The air was still, expectant of the ritual she was about to complete, a rite of passage that marked the end of an era and the beginning of another. In her hands, she cradled a small spade, its metal surface cool against her skin. With a steady hand, she scooped a portion of the ashes, feeling their weightless finality.

"Here's to planting new seeds," she whispered to herself, her voice a soft murmur in the hush of the night. She chose a spot beneath the old mango tree, where memories of laughter mingled with whispers of wisdom from years gone by. Gently, she dug into the earth, each turn of the soil a step towards healing.

As the hole grew deeper, so did Srishti's awareness of her transformation. This was not merely burying the ashes; it was an act of honouring her journey, acknowledging the pain that had once consumed her and choosing to let it nourish the ground beneath her feet.

"Grow strong, grow wild," she encouraged, imagining the roots of her future self-taking hold in the fertile ground of her present. With care, she deposited the ashes into the earth, their descent slow and deliberate. They settled into their new home, a testament to her resilience.

"From this," Tanuja's words echoed in her mind, "you will rise anew, grounded and free." Srishti could almost feel the warmth of her therapist's smile, a beacon guiding her through the fog that had once clouded her vision.

Covering the ashes with the displaced earth, Srishti patted the ground gently, as if tucking in a child after a long day. Her actions were tender, purposeful, imbued with a newfound reverence for the life she was cultivating within and around her.

"May you find peace here," she said, her tone imbued with gratitude. A symphony of crickets accompanied her quiet declaration, nature itself bearing witness to her evolution.

Rising to her feet, Srishti stepped back and surveyed her work. The mango tree stood tall and strong above the freshly turned soil, its leaves rustling softly in agreement. It was done. The past, acknowledged and honoured, now lay beneath the earth, a foundation for the blossoming of her being.

"Thank you," she breathed out, her heart swelling with the hope of what was yet to come. "For everything."

The night wrapped around her like a comforting shawl as she made her way back inside, leaving behind the ashes, but carrying forward their lessons. In the darkness, Srishti found light; in silence, a song of renewal. And in herself, the unshakeable certainty that she was, indeed, the author of her own story.

11

REJECTION – Fuel For Resilience

Srishti sat across from Tanuja, her fingers knotting together in her lap. The room was quiet except for the soft hum of the air conditioner and Srishti's shallow breaths. She had spent so many years trying to fit in, to be the person she thought everyone wanted her to be. It was exhausting.

"Sometimes," Srishti started, her voice a mere whisper, "I feel like I'm running a marathon with no finish line. I help others, bend over backwards to fit in, and all for what? To end up feeling more alone than ever."

Tanuja nodded, her presence a steady beacon in the choppy sea of Srishti's emotions. "You're seeking acceptance through your actions," she said. "But when these efforts aren't met with the validation you hope for, it feels like rejection all over again."

"Exactly," Srishti agreed, her eyes reflecting the weariness of someone who had fought too many battles. "It's as if I'm trapped in this cycle where I can't stop trying, yet I'm always overlooked, always the afterthought."

"Rejection can lead us to act from a place of insecurity," Tanuja explained. Her tone was both hopeful and encouraging. "But remember, Srishti, you have the power to step out of this cycle."

"Power?" Srishti mused, sceptical. "What power do I have when every effort I make seems to push people further away?"

"The power of self-acceptance," Tanuja said firmly. "By embracing yourself fully, imperfections and all, you can begin to break free from the need for others' approval."

"Self-acceptance..." Srishti repeated the words slowly, as if tasting them for the first time. "How do I even start?"

"Start by confronting the past," Tanuja suggested. "Acknowledge your experiences without judgment. Understand that they shaped you but don't define you."

"Confronting the past..." Srishti considered this. "It's like facing a monster that's been chasing me for years."

"Perhaps," Tanuja offered a gentle smile, "but once you face it, you'll see it's not as monstrous as you think. You've grown since then, become stronger. And you're not facing it alone."

"Stronger," Srishti echoed, allowing the thought to settle within her. A flicker of determination sparked in her eyes.

"Every disappointment is a lesson, not a verdict on your worth," Tanuja continued. "With each step towards self-acceptance, you'll find the strength to overcome obstacles."

"Lessons, not verdicts," Srishti whispered, a mantra forming in her mind. She looked up at Tanuja, gratitude mingling with newfound resolve.

"Exactly," Tanuja affirmed. "And I will be here, each step of the way, as you learn to embrace the unique person you are."

Tanuja watched as Srishti fidgeted with the hem of her sleeve, a small but telling gesture that spoke volumes about the internal struggle she faced. The room was a sanctuary of sorts, a place where Srishti could peel back the layers of assumed identities to reveal the scared child within.

"Tell me, Srishti," Tanuja began, her voice a soft melody in the quiet room, "how do you see your childhood shaping the relationships you have now?"

Srishti's eyes flickered up, meeting Tanuja's gaze before retreating once more. "I... I guess I've always been afraid. Afraid that I'm not enough. My parents—they meant well—but their expectations... it was like walking on a tightrope."

"Ah, the tightrope." Tanuja nodded thoughtfully. "Always balancing, never sure if you'll fall into disapproval or manage to reach the other side, where acceptance awaits."

"Exactly," Srishti said, the word escaping like a sigh of relief.

"And now, I find myself overcompensating, trying to prove my worth to everyone, even when it hurts."

"Because as a child, your attachment to those around you was fraught with uncertainty," Tanuja said, guiding the conversation with care. "You learned to equate love and acceptance with perfection, something unattainable yet desperately sought after."

Srishti swallowed hard, her throat constricting with the truth of it. "So, what now? How do I change this pattern?"

"Now," Tanuja replied, leaning forward slightly, her eyes alight with empathy, "we begin the work of understanding how these childhood interactions have formed your attachment style. We look at how they've influenced your behaviours, your beliefs, and your expectations in relationships."

"By seeing the roots, we can nurture new growth," Srishti murmured, a spark of hope igniting within her.

"Indeed," Tanuja affirmed, a smile gracing her lips. "The journey isn't easy, but it's necessary. Slowly, you'll learn to develop healthier ways of connecting with others—ways that don't require you to earn acceptance, but to know that you are already worthy of it. Every step you take is a step towards healing, towards rewriting the narratives that no longer serve you."

"Rewriting narratives..." Srishti repeated, standing a bit taller as she spoke. It was more than just an affirmation; it was a commitment to herself, to the future she deserved—a future free from the chains of past rejections.

"Let's talk about your earliest memories of feeling supported," Tanuja began, her voice a gentle lullaby against the storm outside. "Can you recall a time when your needs were met with warmth and attentiveness?"

Srishti closed her eyes, breathing in the scent of rain mixed with the faint aroma of jasmine from the incense on Tanuja's desk.

She sifted through her childhood memories, searching for moments drenched in comfort and security.

"There was this one time," Srishti said slowly, "I remember falling off my bike. My knee was scraped, and I was trying so hard not to cry." Her voice caught, but she pressed on. "My father, he came rushing over. He didn't scold me for being careless; instead, he lifted me up and took care of my wound. He made sure I knew it was okay to be hurt."

Tanuja nodded, encouragingly. "How did his response make you feel?"

"Safe," Srishti whispered, a smile beginning to break through as she opened her eyes. "I felt safe, and like... like it was alright to explore, to make mistakes because he'd be there."

"Exactly," Tanuja affirmed. "That safety net is what we call secure attachment. Your father's consistent and sensitive response helped build trust. It allowed you to develop a belief that you were worthy of care and attention."

Srishti leaned forward, the realization lighting up her features. "So, what you're saying is, these early interactions—they shape how we connect with people even now?"

"Indeed," Tanuja confirmed, her hands folded in her lap. "They become the foundation from which we explore our world. When caregivers are emotionally present and supportive, we carry that sense of security into our adult relationships."

"Is it possible," Srishti asked tentatively, "to create that base for myself now, even if I sometimes missed it growing up?"

"Absolutely," Tanuja replied, her eyes warm and assuring. "You can cultivate that secure base within yourself. It starts with acknowledging and nurturing your own emotional needs—much like your father did for you when you were a child."

"By being my own source of comfort and reassurance," Srishti murmured, more to herself than to Tanuja.

"Exactly." Tanuja's voice held a promise of growth and healing. "And in doing so, you'll learn that your value doesn't hinge on others' approval or rejection. You are already enough."

"Already enough," Srishti repeated, the phrase settling in her chest like an anchor.

Rain pattered softly against the window, mirroring Srishti's internal tumult. The silence hung heavy before she finally spoke again, each word laced with a lifetime of uncertainty.

"Growing up, it wasn't that my parents weren't there... they were, but not always in the ways I needed." Srishti's voice was a whisper, almost drowned by the rain. "It was like walking on a tightrope—never knowing if I'd have a hand to hold or if I'd be left to fall."

Tanuja nodded, her presence a steady beacon in the dim room. "That inconsistency, it can lead to an anxious-preoccupied attachment," she explained gently. "You become ever-watchful, hypersensitive to the cues that might mean support—or its withdrawal."

"Like I'm forever reaching out, but also bracing for... nothingness." Srishti swallowed hard, her almond eyes reflecting a depth of pain.

"Exactly," Tanuja affirmed. She leaned forward, bridging the gap not just in space but in understanding. "And when caregivers are distant, emotionally unavailable... it can foster an avoidant attachment. Self-reliance becomes a shield, one that often hides a well of unmet needs."

Srishti nodded, her petite frame curling inward as if to protect herself from invisible blows. "You learn to rely on yourself because it's safer than expecting others to care."

"Safer, perhaps, but also lonelier," Tanuja added softly. "Traumatic experiences, whether it's loss, abuse, or severe neglect, further complicate these patterns."

"Disorganized, fearful," Srishti murmured, articulating the chaos that had too often been her inner landscape. "It's like... no matter how old I get, there's a part of me still trapped in those moments of helplessness."

"Those experiences shape your expectations of relationships, leaving you to navigate a world where trust feels like a double-edged sword," Tanuja said, her tone imbued with empathy.

"Trust... something so simple yet so complex," Srishti contemplated, her gaze losing focus as if sifting through memories. "How do I build that when it's been razed so many times before?"

"By acknowledging the past, but not letting it dictate your future," Tanuja advised, her words painting a picture of hope amidst the shadows. "By recognizing that while some caregivers may have faltered, you can still find security within yourself."

"Security within," Srishti echoed, testing the weight of the concept. "To trust myself first, so I can learn to trust others."

"Indeed," Tanuja smiled, the warmth in her eyes promising that growth lay ahead, even if the path was strewn with the debris of yesteryears. "You start small, step by careful step, rebuilding what was once fragile."

"Small steps toward... what? Not just acceptance from others, but from myself?" Srishti asked, a flicker of determination passing across her features.

"Self-acceptance, yes," Tanuja confirmed. "It's there, Srishti, within you. A strength that's survived every inconsistent touch, every emotional distance. It's time to embrace it."

"Embrace it," Srishti repeated, a mantra forming from the fragments of her resolve. Outside, the rain had ceased; inside, a shift as subtle and profound as the breaking of clouds began to take root.

"Your mind has built a blueprint of expectations based on those early years," Tanuja's voice broke through Srishti's contemplation. "It's like an architect who designed your approach to every relationship you've encountered."

"Blueprints can be redrawn, though, right?" Srishti ventured, her gaze rising to meet Tanuja's steady presence.

"Absolutely," the therapist nodded with a gentle certainty that made the room seem warmer. "Redrawing begins with understanding the original plans—your internal working models. Imagine these models as filters through which you see yourself and others." Tanuja leaned forward, bridging the gap between theory and practice. "They colour your interactions, shaping how you respond to closeness, intimacy, and even conflict."

"Mine are probably all shades of grey," Srishti said with a faint smile, finding a shard of humour in her self-reflection.

"Perhaps," Tanuja conceded, "but we can introduce new colours, Srishti. With self-awareness, you begin to discern which hues belong to the past and which you'll choose for your future."

"Introspection," Srishti mulled over the word. It wasn't merely thinking; it was excavating, examining, and ultimately, evolving.

"More than that," Tanuja corrected softly, "it's about being intentional in your efforts. Notice when old patterns emerge. Pause, reflect, then gently guide yourself towards more secure and healthy ways of relating."

"Sounds daunting," Srishti admitted, her shoulders tensing at the thought of confronting entrenched habits.

"Yet entirely achievable," Tanuja assured her. "You're not rewriting your story from scratch. You're editing, improving, and sometimes, yes, erasing. But always, you're the author. Every day, you make choices that either reinforce your old narrative or create a new chapter. One where trust isn't a scarce resource but something you cultivate within yourself first."

"Trust myself," Srishti repeated, her voice steadier than before. A small step, she recognized, but one in the right direction—a step away from the shadows of doubt and toward the light of self-compassion.

"Exactly," Tanuja affirmed, her eyes reflecting the pride she felt for Srishti's progress. "And as you build that trust internally, your external relationships will start to mirror it. Secure, healthy, fulfilling.It's time to draw a new blueprint, Srishti—one that includes the resilience and wisdom you've acquired along the way."

Tanuja watched Srishti clasp her hands tightly in her lap, her fingers woven together like the intricate roots of an ancient tree. "It's about understanding yourself," Tanuja said gently, her voice a soft beacon in the quiet room.

Srishti nodded, her gaze fixed on the patterned rug beneath their feet. She seemed to be tracing the lines and shapes, seeking order in the chaos of threads. It was a metaphor not lost on either of them—this quest for clarity amid the tangles of past experiences

.

"Reflect on your relationships," Tanuja prompted, her tone imbued with both empathy and encouragement. "What patterns do you notice?"

There was a long pause before Srishti spoke. "I... I always seem to put others first. To the point where I forget myself," she confessed, her voice barely above a whisper.

"Go on," Tanuja urged, sensing the walls around Srishti's heart beginning to crumble.

"Whenever there's conflict, I retreat. I'm afraid if I assert myself, they'll leave." Srishti's eyes brimmed with the realization of her words. The room filled with the weight of unspoken truths and the silent strength of vulnerability.

"Your awareness is the first step towards change," Tanuja assured her, her eyes holding Srishti's steady gaze. "You recognize the pattern. Now, we can work on altering it."

"By being self-aware?" Srishti asked, seeking confirmation.

"Exactly," Tanuja affirmed with a nod. "Identify where these behaviours stem from, understand why you cling to them, and then we can gently reshape them into something healthier, more balanced."

"Balanced," Srishti repeated, rolling the word around in her mind like a smooth stone. A balance between giving and receiving, between holding on and letting go.

"Think back to when these feelings first started," Tanuja suggested. "Can you remember any specific moments?"

"Sure," Srishti replied after a moment's thought, her expression pensive. "It was often when expectations were high, and I felt I couldn't meet them." Her shoulders slumped slightly, the weight of years of self-imposed standards pressing down.

"See, by acknowledging this, you're already taking control of your narrative," Tanuja pointed out, her voice warm and reassuring. "You're no longer that child striving for perfection. You are capable, worthy, and deserving of equal footing in your relationships."

"Capable, worthy, deserving," Srishti echoed, the words feeling foreign yet comforting as they left her lips.

"Let's set some intentions," Tanuja said, encouraging a slight smile. "Positive affirmations that celebrate Srishti, not just for what she does but for who she is."

Srishti took a deep breath, her chest rising and falling rhythmically—a dance of life and hope. "I am enough," she began, her voice growing stronger. "I deserve love and respect, just as I give it."

"Beautiful," Tanuja praised, her eyes shining with pride. "Remember, Srishti, you are the architect of your future. Brick by brick, you have the power to build a foundation of security and joy."

"Security and joy," Srishti whispered, allowing herself to feel the promise of those words. For the first time in a long while, she felt a spark of anticipation for what lay ahead, a future designed with self-awareness and painted with the colours of self-love.

*****

Tanuja observed Srishti as she practiced her breathing, each inhale deeper than the last, each exhale a release of pent-up emotions.

"Focus on your breath," Tanuja instructed gently. "Let it anchor you in the present moment."

Srishti's eyes were closed, but her furrowed brow spoke volumes. She was wrestling with the storm within, trying to calm the waves of emotion that threatened to overwhelm her once more.

"Mindfulness is about noticing what's happening right now, without judgement," Tanuja continued. Her voice was a beacon in Srishti's tempestuous sea of thoughts. "It's about recognizing your feelings, acknowledging them, and allowing them to be without letting them control you."

"Sometimes, I feel like my emotions are a tangled mess," Srishti confessed, her words punctuated by a sigh.

"Imagine each emotion as a thread," Tanuja suggested. "Observe each one as it arises, then gently unravel it from the knot. This way, you can address them one by one, calmly and effectively."

Srishti nodded, picturing her anger, her sadness, each forming its own distinct strand. She could feel her body responding to the visualization, her muscles relaxing, her heart rate slowing down

"Now, let's talk about expressing these emotions," Tanuja shifted the topic smoothly. "Clear communication is key. It's important to articulate your feelings without blame or criticism."

"Even when I'm hurt?" Srishti asked, opening her eyes to meet Tanuja's steady gaze.

"Especially then," Tanuja affirmed. "Use 'I' statements. Say 'I feel hurt' rather than 'You hurt me.' It allows you to own your emotions and opens up a space for understanding."

"I see," Srishti pondered this approach. "That sounds less confrontational."

"Exactly," Tanuja smiled encouragingly. "And remember, setting boundaries is not just okay; it's necessary. It's how you teach others to respect your needs."

"Boundaries..." Srishti repeated thoughtfully. The concept felt both foreign and empowering to her. "I need to practice that."

"Let's try it now," Tanuja suggested. "Think of a recent situation where your boundaries were crossed. How could you express your needs clearly and assertively?"

Srishti recalled an incident at work where her ideas were dismissed. She took a deep breath and began, "I felt overlooked when my suggestions weren't considered. In the future, I would appreciate if we could discuss my proposals more thoroughly."

"Very good," Tanuja's praise was warm. "See how you've communicated your feelings and set an expectation for next time? That's effective communication in action."

Srishti felt a glimmer of hope. For too long, her emotions had been a whirlwind, her voice lost in the chaos. But now, armed with mindfulness and the tools of clear expression, she sensed the dawn of a new chapter—one where she could navigate the waters of emotion with confidence and speak her truth without fear.

"Thank you, Tanuja," Srishti said sincerely, gratitude shining in her eyes. "I feel... lighter somehow."

"Progress often feels that way," Tanuja replied. "Like setting down a heavy load you've been carrying for too long."

As the session drew to a close, Srishti stood up, her posture straighter, her steps surer. She carried within her a newfound sense of calm and a commitment to harnessing the power of her voice.

*****

Srishti arrived early for her session with Tanuja, her steps deliberate and paced, a testament to the reflective journey she had undertaken. The waiting room was empty; the calm before the daily therapeutic storm of unravelling emotions and mending psyches.

"Surround yourself with supportive and trustworthy individuals," Tanuja often advised, her voice echoing in Srishti's mind as she sat down, crossing her legs. "They are your secure base."

The concept wasn't foreign to Srishti, yet it felt like an uncharted territory she was now willing to explore. She pondered over the relationships in her life, sifting through them like precious gems under a jeweller's loupe. It was time to invest in connections that fortified her spirit rather than those that left her feeling drained.

"Good morning, Srishti," Tanuja greeted, her smile warm and familiar. "How are you today?"

"Good morning, Tanuja." Srishti matched her smile. "I've been thinking about what we discussed last time—about secure relationships."

"Ah, yes," Tanuja nodded, gesturing for Srishti to follow her into the therapy room. "Tell me more."

Srishti settled into the chair, a soft exhalation escaping her lips. "I realized I've been holding on to certain friendships out of habit, even when they don't serve me well. It's scary, but I want to make space for healthier ones."

"Letting go can be freeing," Tanuja affirmed, her tone encouraging. "Creating a support system is vital for emotional growth."

As they delved deeper into conversation, Srishti's resolve solidified. She would foster connections that resonated with her current values, not just with nostalgia.

"Self-care," Tanuja shifted gears, "is equally important. What have you done for yourself lately?"

A faint blush coloured Srishti's cheeks. "I started a yoga class. And I've been reading more—just for pleasure."

"Beautiful steps, Srishti." Tanuja's eyes sparkled with approval. "Nurturing your body and your mind is key to strengthening your self-esteem."

"Sometimes, I feel guilty for taking time for myself," Srishti confessed, her gaze faltering.

"Self-care isn't selfish," Tanuja reassured her. "It's essential. It helps you become more resilient in facing life's challenges."

Srishti absorbed her words, allowing the truth in them to wash over her doubts. Yoga brought her calmness; books, a sense of adventure. They were small acts, but they whispered to her soul, reminding her that she was worthy of care and affection.

"Thank you for helping me see that," Srishti said, a genuine smile gracing her features.

"Always remember," Tanuja concluded, "the relationship you have with yourself sets the tone for every other relationship in your life."

"Let's explore those thought patterns you mentioned last time," Tanuja said, her voice gentle as she opened her notebook.

"Okay," Srishti replied, taking a deep breath. "I've always had this belief... that I'm not quite good enough, especially when it comes to relationships."

"Where do you think that comes from?" Tanuja prodded softly.

"Childhood, maybe? My parents were... are perfectionists. They always pointed out what I did wrong, rarely what I did right," Srishti admitted, her eyes tracing the pattern on the carpet.

"Those experiences shaped your beliefs about yourself," Tanuja acknowledged. "Now, let's challenge them. What are some positive qualities you bring to a relationship?"

Srishti hesitated, then started tentatively, "I'm... loyal. And caring. I listen well."

"Excellent!" Tanuja beamed. "See? You have valuable traits that anyone would be lucky to find in a friend or partner."

"Feels odd to say that about myself," Srishti confessed, a small smile tugging at her lips.

"Positive self-talk is a skill, like any other," Tanuja explained. "It takes practice. Replace those old, negative beliefs with these new, affirmative ones."

"Small steps, right?" Srishti mused.

"Exactly," Tanuja affirmed. "Celebrate each step. Every positive thought is progress."

"Like planting a garden," Srishti visualized, "cultivating little seeds of positivity until they grow."

"Beautiful analogy," Tanuja agreed. "And remember, gardens don't bloom overnight. Patience and consistent care are key."

"Patience," Srishti repeated, letting the word settle in her heart. "I can do that."

"Shall we identify a few small steps to take before our next session?" Tanuja suggested, her pen poised.

"Sure." Srishti nodded, feeling a spark of hope. "I'll start a journal. Write down three positive things about my day, every day."

"An excellent practice," Tanuja praised. "You're laying the groundwork for a more secure and loving attachment to yourself."

"Thank you, Tanuja," Srishti said, rising at the end of the session. "For helping me see that the most important acceptance... is my own."

As she walked out into the evening, Srishti felt the weight of years of self-doubt begin to lift, replaced by a newfound determination to nurture her garden of self-worth—one small, hopeful step at a time.

*****

The sunlight filtered through the blinds, casting a warm glow over Tanuja's office as Srishti settled into the familiar comforting space for her session. She had been practicing self-awareness, and with each passing day, she felt a shift—a gentle unfurling of the tightly wound strings of her past.

"Commitment," Tanuja began, her voice soft yet resonant, "is a powerful force. It's your promise to yourself to persist in this journey toward a more secure attachment."

Srishti nodded, her hands clasped together in her lap. "I've realized I need support, and I'm here to accept it—not just from you but from myself too."

"Embracing that support," Tanuja said, "is a sign of strength. It's how we build healthier relationships, starting with the one we have with ourselves."

"Healthier relationships..." Srishti echoed, rolling the words around like tasting something new. "It's a hopeful thought."

"Let's talk about cognitive reframing," Tanuja suggested, leaning forward. "Tell me about a recent stressful situation and how you perceived it."

Srishti took a deep breath, recalling an incident at work where her ideas were overlooked. "I felt invisible, like nothing I do is ever enough," she admitted, her voice tinged with frustration.

"Understandable," Tanuja acknowledged. "Now, can we look at that situation from a different perspective? Perhaps one that acknowledges your effort and values your contribution?"

"Maybe... maybe my ideas weren't right for that project," Srishti pondered. "But that doesn't mean they're not valuable. It could be an opportunity to refine them or find where they fit better."

"Exactly," Tanuja affirmed with a smile. "By changing how you think about the situation, you reduce the negative emotions tied to it. How does this new perspective make you feel?"

"Lighter," Srishti replied, surprised by the ease of the tension within her. "And less critical of myself."

"Progress," Tanuja said, her eyes reflecting pride. "You're learning to cope by focusing on positive and adaptive perspectives."

"Like reprogramming the way I think," Srishti mused, a spark igniting in her eyes. "I never knew I had that power."

"Power," Tanuja echoed, "and potential. And with time, these new thought patterns will become second nature, leading to improved emotional well-being."

"Recognizing effective coping strategies is crucial," Tanuja said, her voice a soothing balm to Srishti's frayed nerves. "It's about finding balance, using both problem-focused and emotion- focused approaches. Professional guidance can support you in learning healthier skills to manage stress," Tanuja added, offering a roadmap to a stronger, more resilient self.

Srishti glanced down at the worksheet titled 'Exploring Feelings of Rejection'. It seemed like a mirror, reflecting back parts of herself she had long tried to ignore.

"Let's walk through this together," Tanuja said gently. "It may help you understand your feelings and how to cope with them more effectively."

With a tentative hand, Srishti picked up her pen. The worksheet asked her to delve into the patterns of rejection she had experienced—those insidious whispers of self-doubt that stemmed from years of striving for an elusive standard of perfection.

"Rejection... it feels like a cold shadow that never quite leaves my side," Srishti confessed, her words tumbling out in a rush.

"Describe that shadow," Tanuja encouraged. "What does it look like? How does it make you feel?"

"It's dark, looming," Srishti replied, her hand trembling slightly as she wrote. "It makes me feel small, unworthy."

"Those are powerful emotions," Tanuja acknowledged. "Now let's identify triggers—situations that bring these feelings to the surface."

"Unmet expectations," Srishti murmured, recalling the sting of criticism over trivial imperfections. "The fear of not being good enough."

"Understanding triggers helps us prepare and respond differently," Tanuja explained. "It's a step towards regaining control."

"Control..." Srishti pondered the word as if tasting it for the first time. A sense of agency, perhaps a way out of the cycle of self-rejection.

"Remember, coping mechanisms vary. Some retreat, others seek validation. What's important is recognizing which ones serve you well," Tanuja said.

"Serve me well..." Srishti echoed, feeling a shift within her. It wasn't just about surviving the storm; it was about learning to dance in the rain.

"Positive affirmations can help," Tanuja suggested. "They counteract negative self-talk."

Srishti wrote down an affirmation, her script firm and hopeful: "I am deserving of love and acceptance."

"See," Tanuja smiled, "you're already taking steps toward self-care, nurturing resilience."

"Self-care," Srishti whispered, a concept once foreign now taking root. She imagined it as a garden where she tended to her own needs, a sanctuary from the harshness of the world.

"Reflect on this exercise," Tanuja said as their session drew to a close. "Consider how understanding rejection can guide your responses in the future."

"Guide my responses..." Srishti mused, standing up, feeling less burdened than when she arrived.

"Exploring these feelings is tough," Tanuja reminded her, "but it's a vital part of your journey."

As she walked, Srishti clutched the worksheet, a tangible reminder of the progress she'd made and the path that lay ahead. With every positive affirmation, every moment of self-care, she was rewriting her story—one where she was the protagonist, no longer overshadowed by rejection but illuminated by self- acceptance.

*****

Srishti sat at her desk, the worksheet from Tanuja spread out before her. The room was quiet, save for the soft tick of the clock on the wall and the distant hum of city life beyond her window. She took a deep breath, her fingers poised above the paper, ready to write.

"Identify the situation," Srishti whispered to herself, echoing Tanuja's instructions. Her mind drifted back to a recent team meeting at work. She had presented an idea she was passionate about, only to be met with dismissive glances and noncommittal murmurs. Her proposal was overshadowed by another colleague's project, which was immediately embraced.

She wrote down the details, each word a tiny echo of that moment—the cool conference room, the long table separating her from her peers, the sinking feeling as her excitement turned into invisibility.

"Emotional response," she continued, recalling the sting of rejection. Sadness enveloped her like a heavy cloak, its weight familiar yet unbearable. Anger simmered beneath the surface, anger at being overlooked again. Loneliness crept in, whispering doubts about her place in the team, her worthiness of acknowledgment.

Srishti listed the emotions, acknowledging their presence. "Sadness, anger, loneliness," she recited, giving voice to her silent companions. As she did, she felt a shift within—a gentle loosening of the knot of emotions that had tightened around her heart.

"Anything else?" she asked herself, probing deeper. There was disappointment too —the bitter taste of unmet expectations—and frustration at her own vulnerability. But alongside these, she also found something new: a flicker of determination. It was small, but it was there, a sign that even in the midst of emotional turmoil, she was beginning to see her own strength.

"Disappointment, frustration, determination," she added to the list, her handwriting steady.

"Good," she imagined Tanuja saying, her voice a warm embrace in Srishti's mind. "You're recognizing your feelings, not letting them control you."

Srishti nodded, feeling a surge of gratitude for the journey she was on, for the guidance of her therapist, and for the resilience she was slowly uncovering within herself—a resilience that promised hope and healing, one word at a time.

*****

Srishti sat at her desk, the room's silence enveloping her like a shroud. Her fingers hovered over the keyboard, still and uncertain. The task was simple: reflect on the thoughts that had assailed her during that stinging moment of rejection when her contributions were ignored, her presence seemingly invisible to those around her.

"Am I not good enough?" The question echoed in her mind, a merciless drumbeat. "They don't value me. They never will."

With each internal accusation, her self-esteem withered. She scribbled frantically in her journal, the pen scratching against the paper as if to etch out her insecurities permanently. Each word was a testament to the negative self-talk that plagued her:

"Useless. Inadequate. Invisible."

The words formed a mantra of self-rejection, a chorus that had become all too familiar.

Srishti paused, her breath catching in her throat. She noticed her body's reaction to these harsh judgments. There was a tightness in her shoulders—a coiled tension, as if bracing for impact. Her heart raced, an unsteady rhythm betraying her inner turmoil. Shallow breaths came in rapid succession, as though she couldn't draw enough air to steady the storm within.

"Focus on your breathing," she whispered to herself, recalling Tanuja's advice. "Deep breath in, slow breath out."

As she inhaled slowly, Srishti tried to picture her breath reaching every tense muscle, coaxing them to relax. With each exhale, she envisioned releasing the pent-up emotions that clenched her body tight.

"Your worth is not defined by others," she reminded herself, the words a gentle balm to soothe the raw edges of her psyche.

She closed her eyes and took another deep breath, allowing the simplicity of the action to anchor her to the present. Gradually, the physical sensations eased—the tension ebbed away, the heart found its natural cadence, and her breathing deepened into a tranquil tide.

In this quiet space, Srishti sought the glimmer of hope that had surfaced amid her listed emotions. That flicker of determination grew brighter with each calming breath, a beacon guiding her towards a future where self-acceptance awaited.

"Progress, not perfection," Srishti affirmed, her voice steadier now. It was a step forward, a promise to herself that she would continue to heal, learn, and ultimately thrive.

*****

Srishti sat in her usual chair, the soft fabric now familiar under her fingertips. Across from her, Tanuja's presence was a steady beacon of calm. The room was quiet except for the occasional shuffle of Srishti's feet on the plush carpet as she worked through the labyrinth of her emotions.

"Let's explore what might trigger these intense feelings," Tanuja suggested gently. Her voice carried the weight of kindness, guiding Srishti to confront her vulnerabilities.

"Sometimes... it's just a word, or even a look," Srishti began, hesitance lacing her words. "Like when someone raises an eyebrow at my ideas, or when there's a pause before they respond. It's as if I'm back there again, trying to prove I'm worthy."

"Back where, Srishti?" Tanuja probed softly, encouraging her to dig deeper.

"Childhood," she whispered, feeling the sting of old wounds. "When perfection was expected, and anything less was met with disappointment."

"Those early experiences helped shape your reactions today," Tanuja acknowledged, validating her feelings. "Recognizing them is a brave step toward change."

Srishti nodded, memories flooding back—the biting remarks about untidiness, the disapproving glances over a less-than-perfect grade. Each memory was a brick in the wall she built around herself, a wall meant to protect but instead isolated her from the very acceptance she craved.

"Do you see how past experiences influence your present?" Tanuja asked, her eyes locked onto Srishti's with unwavering support.

"I do," Srishti replied, the realization dawning on her like the first light of morning. "I've been so afraid of being rejected that I've rejected myself first."

"Understanding this pattern is a powerful insight," said Tanuja, a smile touching her lips. "It's from here we can start rebuilding, laying down new foundations based on self-compassion rather than fear."

Srishti felt something shift within her—a loosening grip on old narratives. For the first time, she glimpsed a path forward, one where her triggers were not roadblocks but signposts, guiding her toward healing and self-acceptance. With Tanuja's guidance, she would learn to walk that path—one hopeful, determined step at a time.

"Thank you," Srishti murmured, gratitude mingling with newfound resolve. "I'm ready to begin."

Srishti sat, legs crossed, on the plush carpet of Tanuja's office, a notepad balanced on her knees. She drew a deep breath, her pen poised above the paper. The room was silent except for the steady tick of the wall clock—a metronome to her thoughts.

"Let's explore how you cope with rejection," Tanuja suggested, her voice soft yet clear. "Understanding your strategies can reveal a lot about your emotional needs."

"Most times... I withdraw," Srishti confessed, her script wavering slightly as she wrote. "I curl up with books or lose myself in work—anything to avoid facing those feelings head- on."

"Isolation can be a double-edged sword," Tanuja observed gently. "It gives you space, but it can also magnify the loneliness."

"Exactly." Srishti nodded, adding a bullet point to her list:
Withdraw into solitude.

"Other times," she continued, "I seek validation, fishing for compliments or reassurance from friends, even if it feels hollow."

"Seeking connection is human," Tanuja reassured her. "But it's important that it comes from a place of self-worth, not just a need to fill a void."

Srishti scribbled another note: *Seek external approval.* She looked up, her eyes meeting Tanuja's. "How do I change these patterns?"

"By beginning a new dialogue with yourself," Tanuja said, prompting a small smile from Srishti. "Positive affirmations can be powerful tools. They're like seeds of self-belief that, with care, can grow into a garden of confidence."

"Affirmations..." Srishti repeated, considering the word. She then began to write, each statement a proclamation:

I am deserving of love and acceptance.
I am strong enough to overcome rejection.

"Good," Tanuja praised. "Feel those words as you say them, believe in their truth."

Srishti recited the affirmations silently, a warmth spreading through her chest. She added another, her hand steadier now:

I am valuable, not because of what others think, but because of who I am.

"Can you see the difference?" Tanuja asked, her eyes gleaming with pride.

"Yes, I feel it," Srishti replied. The tight knot of anxiety in her stomach loosened. "It's like I'm breathing life into a part of me that's been ignored for too long."

"Keep nurturing that part," Tanuja encouraged. "With time and practice, these affirmations will become part of your inner voice, guiding you towards healing and self-acceptance."

Srishti closed her notepad, a sense of resolve etched onto her features. For the first time in a long while, she felt equipped with the right tools—a map to navigate the labyrinth of her emotions and a light to shine on the shadows of her doubts.

*****

Srishti unfolded her notepad, the creases worn from constant handling. For a moment, she held her pen poised above the paper, collecting her thoughts like pebbles along a shore. Tanuja watched silently, a patient sentinel in Srishti's journey of self-discovery.

"Self-care," Srishti murmured, finally pressing ink to page. "Journaling has always helped...but maybe, it's time to expand that."

"Go on," Tanuja prompted gently.

"Spending time with friends who uplift me," Srishti continued, her list taking shape. "Family dinners that remind me I'm loved. And hobbies..." A smile touched her lips. "Painting brings me peace. It's like each stroke on the canvas is a stroke of healing."

"Beautiful," Tanuja affirmed. "And don't forget, seeking professional support is also an act of self-love."

"Right," Srishti nodded, a newfound determination in her eyes. "Therapy sessions are a safe haven—a place where I'm heard and understood."

"Exactly." Tanuja's voice was soft, yet it carried the weight of truth.

Srishti set the pen down, her gaze lingering on the plans she'd laid out before her. She leaned back, allowing the silence to envelop them both as she contemplated the patterns etched into her life's tapestry.

"Patterns," she said at last. "There's this thread of...expectation. And fear. The fear of falling short." She looked up at Tanuja, her almond-shaped eyes seeking affirmation.

"Insightful observation," Tanuja acknowledged. "Now, how do you think you can use this awareness?"

"By recognizing when I'm setting unrealistic standards for myself," Srishti replied. "And instead of spiralling into self-criticism, I'll pause and practice kindness—towards myself."

"Self-compassion," Tanuja echoed, nodding. "That's the key to navigating through rejection."

"Instead of searching for external validation," Srishti added, a spark igniting within her, "I'll validate myself."

"Empowerment," Tanuja smiled, proud of the growth unfolding before her. "You're learning to rewrite the narrative of your life."

Srishti closed her eyes, breathing in the truth of her own worth. When she opened them again, they shone with the light of realizations hard-won but deeply cherished.

Tanuja watched as Srishti's hands trembled slightly, the pen she held was more than just an instrument—it was a tool of self-rediscovery. The worksheet before her, a canvas painted with the hues of her emotional journey.

"Remember," Tanuja began, her tone a gentle caress in the quiet room, "exploring feelings of rejection can be challenging." She paused, letting the words sink in, "but it's an important step towards understanding yourself better and fostering resilience."

Srishti exhaled slowly, a visible release of tension from her petite frame. Her eyes, once clouded with uncertainty, now held a glimmer of determination. With each word she wrote, the rhythm of her thoughts echoed a newfound clarity.

"Take your time with this," Tanuja encouraged, her voice a beacon guiding Srishti through the fog of past hurts. "And be gentle with yourself throughout the process."

The walls around them seemed to absorb Tanuja's wisdom, standing witness to countless tales of healing. There was a sacredness in the air, a testament to the power of vulnerability and growth.

"Being gentle," Srishti whispered, more to herself than to Tanuja. Her meticulous nature often led her to be her own harshest critic. But here, in this moment, she allowed herself grace.

"Exactly," Tanuja nodded approvingly. "Gentleness is the soil in which the seeds of self-compassion take root."

As Srishti navigated the worksheet, her initial hesitation transformed into thoughtful introspection. Each question prompted a deeper dive into her psyche, unravelling layers of emotional armour she had built over the years.

"Patterns of thought... they're like well-trodden paths in our minds, aren't they?" Srishti pondered aloud, her earnest voice seeking confirmation.

"They are," Tanuja affirmed, her expressive eyes reflecting the depth of her understanding. "And just as paths can be redirected, so too can our thoughts."

"Redirected towards... positivity?" Srishti asked, tilting her head slightly as she considered the possibility.

"Towards truth," Tanuja clarified. "Towards acceptance of the full spectrum of who you are."

With each line Srishti penned, the weight of self-imposed judgment lifted. The simple act of writing became a silent conversation between her present self and the child within who still longed for validation.

"Self-acceptance," she said, the words feeling foreign yet familiar on her tongue. "It's like learning a new language."

"And with practice," Tanuja added, "it becomes your mother tongue."

Srishti set the pen down once more, this time with a sense of completion. She looked up at Tanuja, her gaze steady and clear.

"Today," Srishti declared, standing taller than when she first walked in, "I choose resilience."

"Today, and every day after," Tanuja echoed, her voice imbued with hope.

The session concluded, not with an ending, but with a continuation—a story still being written, with Srishti as both the protagonist and the author.

12

SELF TALK – Shaping Self

The morning light spilled into the therapy room, casting a soft glow on Tanuja's face as she observed Srishti sitting across from her. The therapist's eyes, pools of gentle understanding, watched as Srishti fidgeted with the hem of her sleeve, a nervous habit that surfaced whenever the young woman grappled with the storm within.

"Think of your self-talk as a river," Tanuja began, her voice a soothing balm to Srishti's frayed nerves. "It flows through you, constant and persistent. It can either nourish or erode the landscape of your mind."

Srishti's gaze lifted, meeting Tanuja's steady presence. "But my river seems to be in a perpetual flood," she confessed, a tremor in her words mirroring the uncertainty she felt inside.

"Rivers can indeed overflow," Tanuja acknowledged, a nod affirming Srishti's feelings. "Yet every river has banks that can be strengthened. Your thoughts are the banks of your river. They shape its course."

"Sometimes I feel like I'm drowning in my own thoughts," Srishti admitted, her voice barely above a whisper.

"Let's explore those thoughts together," Tanuja suggested, inviting trust with a warm smile. "What they say about you, your actions, your experiences."

Srishti took a deep breath, as if drawing strength from the air itself. "They tell me I'm not doing enough, that I'm falling behind," she shared, her almond-shaped eyes reflecting vulnerability.

"Those are powerful currents," Tanuja said, leaning slightly forward. "But remember, you are the one who can direct their flow."

"How?" The question hung between them, heavy with the weight of years of self-doubt.

"By choosing which thoughts to let float by and which to hold onto," the therapist explained, her hands gesturing like leaves on the surface of water.

"Can I really change the way I talk to myself?" Srishti's words were tinged with hope, a flicker of possibility in her tone.

"Absolutely." Tanuja's confirmation was firm, unequivocal. "Every thought is an opportunity. You have the power to cultivate a positive dialogue with yourself."

"Positive..." Srishti repeated, tasting the word as if it were new.

"Think of a recent success, no matter how small," Tanuja encouraged, her voice coaxing out confidence.

"I... I finished a project at work ahead of schedule." A hint of pride surfaced in Srishti's posture, straightening her spine.

"See? That's the nourishment your river needs," Tanuja said, her eyes sparkling. "Acknowledge your capabilities, celebrate your achievements."

"Even the little ones?" Srishti asked, a tentative smile beginning to form.

"Especially the little ones," Tanuja affirmed. "They add up, building resilience against the negative currents."

"Maybe my river isn't so destructive," Srishti mused, a sense of self-compassion slowly rising within her.

"Exactly." Tanuja's smile broadened. "Your self-talk shapes the river of your life. Choose thoughts that support you, that recognize your strengths. And when the waters rise," Tanuja added, her expression kind yet earnest, "remember you have the tools to reinforce your banks."

"Tools..." Srishti pondered, her mind embracing the metaphor.

Affirmations, reflections, memories of success," Tanuja listed, each suggestion a stepping stone towards healing. "Use them to construct a nurturing environment for yourself."

"An environment where I can thrive." For the first time that morning, Srishti's self-talk whispered words of encouragement, a gentle reminder that she held the power to shape her inner narrative.

"Exactly," Tanuja said, her heart swelling with pride for her client's breakthrough. "A river teeming with life, guided by the compassion and understanding you give yourself."

As the session drew to a close, the room seemed brighter, the air lighter. Srishti stood, not just physically but emotionally taller, ready to tend to the river of her thoughts with newfound respect and care.

*****

Tanuja watched as Srishti folded her hands in her lap, her knuckles whitening with the grip. The room was still, save for the soft hum of the air conditioner. Outside, the city thrummed with life, but within these walls, a quieter battle was being waged.

"Positive self-talk," Tanuja began, breaking the silence with her measured tone, "is like nurturing seeds in a garden. It requires patience, care, and sometimes, a change in the environment."

Srishti nodded slowly, absorbing the words. A hint of determination flickered across her features, a silent acknowledgment of the work ahead.

"Negative self-talk," Tanuja continued, "is the frost that threatens to stifle growth. It's fed by those critical voices we've heard since childhood." Her eyes held empathy, knowing well the weight of such echoes.

"Voices that weren't always kind," Srishti whispered, her voice barely audible. She was staring down at her own thoughts, seeing them for what they were—internalized shadows of past judgments.

"Exactly," Tanuja agreed softly. "But remember, Srishti, you're not a child anymore. You have the power to cultivate your inner voice, to choose which seeds to water."

"Choose... how?" There was a tremble in Srishti's question, a vulnerability that spoke volumes.

"Start by recognizing those moments when the frost sets in," Tanuja suggested. "What does it say? And more importantly, is it true?"

"Most times, it isn't," Srishti confessed, her admission a brave step into the light. "It exaggerates... criticizes..."

"Then let's find the warmth," Tanuja said, her own voice a beacon. "Counter each cold thought with one that's supportive. Tell me, what are your strengths, Srishti?"

A pause lingered before Srishti spoke again, her words a cautious trail. "I'm resourceful... adaptable." The corners of her mouth twitched upwards, a small victory against the chill.

"See?" Tanuja's smile encouraged her further. "You're already rewriting the script. What else?"

"I'm caring... dedicated." With each word, Srishti's posture straightened, as if shedding an invisible burden.

"Those are voices that will help your garden flourish." Tanuja's praise was genuine, her belief in Srishti unwavering. "Nurture them, and watch as confidence takes root."

"Confidence," Srishti echoed, tasting the word like a newfound delicacy. "That sounds... possible."

"More than possible," Tanuja assured her. "It's within you, waiting for the spring."

As they spoke, the dance of self-talk played out within Srishti—a waltz of doubts and affirmations, each step a choice. Today, she had chosen to listen to the melody of hope, the rhythm of resilience.

"Remember, Srishti," Tanuja said as their time neared its end, "the voices from our past don't have to dictate our future. We can create new harmonies, ones that uplift and inspire."

The air felt lighter now, charged with potential. Srishti stood, a soft resolve in her eyes. She had begun to hear her own voice amid the cacophony, a soothing whisper promising that she was indeed enough.

"Thank you, Tanuja," Srishti said, gratitude shaping her words. "For helping me tune into... me."

With a nod of mutual respect, they parted, both aware that the session was another step on a longer journey—one where each positive affirmation would be a note in the symphony of Srishti's reclaimed self-talk.

*****

Srishti fumbled with the hem of her sleeve, a habit that surfaced whenever the storm inside her brewed—a tempest of self- criticism. Across from her, Tanuja sat patiently, the room between them filled with unspoken thoughts and the faint hum of a clock ticking towards clarity.

"Tell me about the moments you feel most challenged," Tanuja prompted gently, anchoring the session back to the present.

"Whenever I try something new... or when there's a chance of failing." Srishti's voice was a mere whisper, a fragile thread in the vast tapestry of her inner turmoil. "It's like there's this voice inside me, insisting that I must excel, or else I'm worthless."

Tanuja nodded, her eyes reflecting understanding. "That voice, the one demanding perfection—do you recall when you first heard it?"

Srishti closed her eyes, delving into a sea of memories. "Childhood," she started, the word heavy with significance. "My parents praised every A, every top score. 'You're our little genius,' they'd say. But it wasn't just affection—it was expectation."

"Expectation can be a double-edged sword," Tanuja observed. "It can motivate but also confine. How did it shape your inner talk as you grew older?"

"Perfection became my benchmark for everything." Srishti opened her eyes, finding strength in vulnerability. "Anything less felt like... failure."

"Yet here you are," Tanuja offered a gentle smile, "brave enough to confront these voices. That takes immense courage. Recognizing the roots of our self-talk is the first step toward change. And remember, perfection isn't the absence of flaws but embracing them as part of your unique journey."

"Embracing," Srishti repeated, rolling the concept around her mind like a puzzle piece looking for its place. "I've never allowed myself that."

"Perhaps it's time to start." Tanuja leaned forward slightly, bridging the gap with warmth. "Your emotions, the deep ones that react and feel, they don't need to be silenced by unrealistic demands. They can be acknowledged, understood."

"Understood," Srishti echoed, feeling the weight of years lifting ever so slightly. "Not criticized or neglected."

"Exactly." Tanuja's voice was soft yet powerful, a beacon guiding Srishti's wayward ship. "Let's work on creating a space where those emotions can exist without judgment. Where success isn't defined by a grade or an accolade, but by the growth you experience along the way."

"Success in growth..." Srishti let the concept settle in her heart, a seed of change taking root amidst the weeds of self-doubt.

"Every step you take is progress," Tanuja affirmed. "Every time you challenge the old voices, you're cultivating a garden of self- compassion."

Srishti looked up, her gaze meeting Tanuja's, a spark of determination flickering within. "Then let's begin gardening," she said, a tentative smile forming as she envisioned herself tending to the blossoms of her own well-being.

*****

Srishti's hands trembled as she arranged the papers on Tanuja's desk, a perfect right angle to the edge. Her breath came in short bursts, a silent symphony of stress that hummed beneath her skin. She could feel the familiar surge of anxiety, a tide that rose with every thought of imperfection.

"Perfect alignment doesn't equate to control over outcomes," Tanuja observed gently, her voice a grounded chord in the dissonance of Srishti's mind.

Srishti paused, the truth in Tanuja's words piercing through the haze of her anxiety. "But it feels like if I don't get everything just right," she confessed, voice laced with fear, "everything will fall apart."

Tanuja nodded, her expression mirroring understanding. "That voice urging you to be cautious, to avoid any potential fault—it's trying to protect you. But it's also keeping you from living freely, isn't it?"

Srishti let out a shaky sigh, nodding. It was as though Tanuja had read the pages of her soul. "Yes, and it's exhausting. The dependence on others' approval... it paralyzes me."

"Let's explore that," Tanuja encouraged, leaning back in her chair, creating space for Srishti's thoughts to unfold. "When did you last make a decision purely for yourself, without seeking validation?"

A pensive silence filled the room as Srishti searched her memory. She found only a collage of moments where her choices were audience-driven performances, each step measured, each word weighed for its worthiness.

"I can't remember," Srishti admitted, her voice barely above a whisper. "It's always about being enough for someone else."

"Imagine," Tanuja prompted softly, "a day where your choices are yours alone. Where the voice of fear is quiet, and you trust your abilities. How does that feel?"

"Scary," Srishti answered after a moment, "but... liberating."

"Trust is a muscle," Tanuja said, her tone infused with hope. "And like all muscles, it strengthens with use. Start small. Listen to your own desires, give them space alongside the fear."

"Small steps," Srishti repeated, the concept taking root. "Maybe then, I won't need to cling to perfection or approval."

"Exactly." Tanuja smiled warmly. "Each step is a victory. And remember, growth is never in vain, even when it's invisible to others."

"Victory in growth," Srishti mused, a subtle shift occurring within her. She envisioned herself standing at a crossroads, paths untrodden and inviting, her heart lighter with the possibility of choosing for herself.

"Would you like to try an exercise?" Tanuja suggested, her eyes encouraging.

Srishti nodded, ready to test the waters of self-reliance.

"Close your eyes," Tanuja directed. "Think of something small you've wanted to do but hesitated because of doubt."

Srishti closed her eyes, inhaling deeply. A simple desire surfaced—one that always seemed trivial under the weight of expectations.

"I've wanted to paint my room lavender," she murmured, a soft smile curving her lips.

"Good," Tanuja responded. "Now, affirm your decision. Tell yourself it's okay to want this."

Srishti took another breath, steadier this time. "It's okay to want this," she affirmed, her own voice surprising her with its conviction.

"See?" Tanuja's voice was a beacon. "You're learning to nurture your inner garden, one seed of self-trust at a time."

Opening her eyes, Srishti met Tanuja's gaze, a newfound strength blossoming within. "One seed at a time," she agreed, her spirit buoyed by the promise of a garden blooming with self-compassion and vibrant hues of lavender.

*****

Srishti sat stiffly on the edge of her seat, her fingers interlaced tightly in her lap. The room felt still, save for the occasional chirp from a bird outside the window. Tanuja observed her carefully, noting the subtle tension in her posture.

"Tell me about your week," Tanuja prompted gently.

Srishti's breath hitched slightly before she began. "I've been...overwhelmed," she admitted. "The voices—they're relentless. Always saying I'm not enough, that I'll fail."

Tanuja nodded, her eyes warm with understanding. "And how does this constant self-criticism make you feel?"

"Exhausted," Srishti exhaled wearily. "Hopeless at times. I lie awake worrying about everything I might do wrong."

"Chronic stress can be debilitating," Tanuja acknowledged. "It wears on the mind and body, leaving little room for peace or health."

Srishti looked down, her shoulders slumping. "I know," she whispered. "I can feel it draining me."

"Have you noticed any impact on your relationships?" Tanuja inquired, steering the conversation toward social connections.

"Definitely." Srishti's voice was tinged with sadness. "I push people away, expecting them to be disappointed in me. Or I become too demanding, seeking constant validation."

"Isolation and conflict are often byproducts of our own inner turmoil," Tanuja explained. "But remember, Srishti, these patterns can change."

"Can they?" Srishti's eyes searched Tanuja's face for hope.

"Yes," Tanuja affirmed confidently. "By fostering a kinder inner dialogue, you can reduce anxiety and rebuild your relationships."

"Sounds impossible," Srishti murmured.

"Let's try something," Tanuja suggested. "Think of one person you've pushed away recently."

"My brother," Srishti said after a moment.

"Imagine reaching out to him, without the burden of perfectionism. What would you say?"

Srishti took a deep breath, closing her eyes to envision the scenario. "I'd tell him I miss him. That I'm sorry for being so critical."

"Good," Tanuja smiled. "That's a start. You're acknowledging the need for connection over criticism."

"Connection over criticism," Srishti repeated softly, letting the words sink into her consciousness.

"Exactly," Tanuja encouraged. "Now, let's practice some affirmations to help quiet the negative voices. Repeat after me: 'I am learning and growing.'"

"I am learning and growing," Srishti echoed, a trace of strength returning to her voice.

"Excellent," Tanuja beamed. "Let's add another: 'I am worthy of love and understanding.'"

"I am worthy of love and understanding," Srishti continued, her voice steadier.

"See how these simple words can soothe the soul?" Tanuja asked, her expression inviting belief.

Srishti nodded, a glimmer of optimism lighting her eyes. "They're like a balm," she agreed.

"Indeed, they are," Tanuja confirmed. "With practice, they can transform the way you interact with yourself and others."

"Transform..." Srishti pondered the word, its weight and promise. She stood up, feeling a sense of purpose. "I have work to do," she declared, not as a burden but as a hopeful journey toward healing.

"Remember, Srishti," Tanuja called out as Srishti reached for the door, "be gentle with yourself. Healing takes time."

Srishti paused, hand on the doorknob, and turned back to Tanuja with a smile. "Thank you," she said, her gratitude genuine. "For reminding me there's light beyond the shadows."

"Always," Tanuja replied, her voice a soft echo as Srishti stepped out into the world, carrying with her the seeds of self-compassion and the courage to nurture them.

*****

Tanuja adjusted the sunlight-filtering curtains, casting a soft glow around the cozy office. Srishti sat across from her, her fingers intertwined in her lap, a silent testament to the war within.

"Understanding these voices," Tanuja began, her voice a lullaby against the clatter of self-doubt, "is like learning to navigate a hidden map of your mind."

Srishti's eyes met Tanuja's, a flicker of curiosity breaking through. "How do you mean?"

"Every thought," explained Tanuja, gesturing as if plucking words from the air, "shapes the path we walk on. Negative self-talk is like thorns on that path."

"Thorns..." Srishti murmured, picturing her thoughts as a bramble, scratching and ensnaring.

"Indeed," Tanuja continued, "they can prick at your confidence, increase your stress, even change how you grow."

"Like saying I'm not enough or I'll never succeed?" Srishti's voice was a whisper, vulnerable yet seeking.

"Exactly," Tanuja affirmed. "These are the common types of negative self-talk. They are powerful but not invincible."

"Feels invincible," Srishti confessed, a wry smile touching her lips.

"Let's disarm them, then," Tanuja proposed, her eyes gleaming with conviction. She leaned forward, bridging the space between doubt and hope. "Replace 'I'm not enough' with..."

Srishti took in a deep breath, her chest rising with the tide of a new challenge. "'I am growing stronger every day.'"

"Perfect," Tanuja praised. "And instead of 'I'll never succeed,' try..."

A pause as Srishti searched for the words, finding them nestled in newfound strength. "'My efforts will lead me to success.'"

"Words have power, Srishti," Tanuja said softly. "They can be your armour or your anchor."

"Armour," Srishti decided, her heart syncing with the rhythm of positive truths.

"Whenever the thorns of negative talk appear," Tanuja instructed, "visualize yourself cutting them away. You hold the shears."

"Cutting away," Srishti repeated, imagining each snip releasing her from the entangled vines.

"Remember," Tanuja's hand reached out, resting gently on Srishti's, "these inner voices are not the whole of you. You're the gardener here."

"Can I really?" Doubt shadowed Srishti's features, but hope was there too, peeking through.

"Absolutely," asserted Tanuja, her voice unwavering. "With time and practice, your garden will flourish."

"Thank you," Srishti whispered, standing up as the session ended. Her posture was straighter, her steps surer than before.

"Be kind to yourself," Tanuja called after her, her words an invisible cloak around Srishti's shoulders as she walked out, ready to tend to her inner landscape, one positive word at a time.

*****

Srishti sat across from Tanuja, her fingers tracing the edges of her notebook, a habit she developed when her thoughts ran in circles. The room was serene—a sanctuary of soft hues and comforting stillness, yet Srishti's mind was a battleground of extremes.

"Last week," Srishti began, her voice a tremor, "I missed a deadline at work. It felt like... like I'd fallen off a cliff."

Tanuja nodded, her presence a balm to Srishti's frayed nerves. "And what did that moment tell you about yourself?"

"That I'm a failure," Srishti confessed, her words heavy, laden with a lifetime of self-imposed verdicts.

"Is missing one deadline equal to being a complete failure?" Tanuja's question was light, a feather on the scales of Srishti's judgment.

"I know it shouldn't mean that," Srishti sighed, "but it feels like everything I do just proves that point."

"Let's explore that," Tanuja suggested. "We often take one event and let it colour all our experiences. That's extreme thinking. Can you think of something you've succeeded at recently?"

Srishti's brow furrowed, her mind sifting through the dark to find a glimmer. "I... helped a coworker the other day. She thanked me." A small smile dared to touch her lips.

"See? There's balance. Successes and setbacks," Tanuja smiled. "You're looking at the whole picture now."

"Balance," Srishti echoed, feeling the weight of her extremes lessen slightly.

"And when you focus solely on the negatives, what happens to the positives?" Tanuja's eyes held an invitation to see beyond the fog.

"They... get lost, I guess," Srishti admitted, her gaze lifting.

"Exactly," said Tanuja. "By acknowledging both, you give yourself a fair chance. And what about blame? Who truly owns that missed deadline?"

"Partly me," Srishti conceded, "but the project was delayed before it even reached me."

"Then why carry all the blame?" Tanuja's question was gentle, yet it pierced the heart of Srishti's self-blame.

"Because it's easier to blame myself than to accept that sometimes things are out of my control," Srishti said, a realization dawning within her.

"Control can be an illusion," Tanuja offered. "Acknowledge your part, but also recognize the factors beyond you."

"Beyond me," Srishti repeated, considering the liberation in those two words.

"Let's replace some of that negative self-talk," Tanuja proposed. "Instead of 'I'm a failure,' try..."

"Try..." Srishti paused, searching for the antidote to her poison. "'I learn from my mistakes.'"

"Good," Tanuja encouraged. "And replace 'Everything always goes wrong' with..."

"Something more grounded," Srishti thought aloud. "'Sometimes I face challenges, but I also find solutions.'"

"Brilliant," Tanuja affirmed. "You're recalibrating your inner dialogue, Srishti. Bit by bit."

"Bit by bit," Srishti agreed, feeling the shift within her. Her extreme thinking was not her destiny; it was a pattern she could unravel.

"Remember, every step counts," Tanuja said, as their time together neared its end. "You're not alone on this journey."

"Thank you," Srishti spoke, her gratitude sincere. As she left the room, her steps carried a new rhythm—one of hope, balance, and the quiet strength of a woman learning to silence her harshest critic: herself.

*****

The soft patter of rain against the window accompanied Srishti's shallow breaths as she settled deeper into the plush chair, her fingers nervously tracing the armrest. Tanuja watched her, understanding in her eyes.

"Sometimes," Srishti began, voice barely above a whisper, "I'm convinced that one mistake at work will ruin my entire career."

"Ah, catastrophizing," Tanuja said, her tone neither dismissive nor alarmed. "Tell me, what evidence supports this belief?"

Srishti's gaze fell to her lap, her mind scrambling for an answer. "There isn't any... It just feels like it could all come crashing down."

"Feelings can be powerful," Tanuja acknowledged, "but they aren't always reality. What might a more balanced perspective look like?"

"Maybe..." Srishti faltered, trying to push through the fog of anxiety. "Maybe that people understand that everyone makes mistakes?"

"Exactly," Tanuja encouraged warmly. "Mistakes are universal, not catastrophic."

Srishti nodded, a tentative smile tugging at her lips. She took in a deep breath, letting it out slowly, feeling the weight of doomsday scenarios lift ever so slightly.

"And what about assumptions?" Tanuja inquired, guiding her to the next hurdle. "Do you often find yourself guessing others' thoughts about you?"

"Always," Srishti confessed. "I walk into a room and I just know they're thinking I don't belong."

"Know or assume?" Tanuja probed gently.

"Assume," Srishti corrected, a painful admission. "It's like I decide for them that they're judging me."

"Can we truly know another's thoughts?" Tanuja posed the question with a soft tilt of her head.

"No, we can't," Srishti murmured, the realization brightening the dark corners of her mind.

"Then perhaps," Tanuja suggested, "it's time to offer yourself compassion instead of conjecture."

"Compassion," Srishti repeated, rolling the word around like a soothing balm. "I'd never treat a friend the way I treat myself."

"Exactly," Tanuja affirmed. "You deserve your own kindness."

"Kindness," Srishti whispered, embracing the concept like a lifeline.

"Next time," Tanuja offered a parting thought as the session came to a close, "when the voice of catastrophe or assumption whispers, challenge it with kindness and seek the truth."

"Challenge with kindness," Srishti echoed, her heart lighter than when she'd arrived. As she stepped into the drizzle outside, she felt each droplet reminding her — gentleness, not judgment; curiosity, not conclusions. The path ahead was less daunting now, each step a testament to the resilience she was building within.

*****

Srishti perched on the edge of the plush chair, her hands clasped tightly in her lap. The office around her was a cocoon of peace, Tanuja's presence an anchor in the quiet space.

"Let's talk about the 'shoulds'," Tanuja began, her voice as gentle as the morning rays filtering through the blinds.

"Shoulds?" Srishti echoed, her brow furrowing slightly.

"The pressure you place on yourself with statements like 'I should be perfect' or 'I must always please everyone.' Can you think of a recent time when this type of thinking emerged?"

Srishti nodded, the memory surfacing like a stone skipped across water. "Just yesterday, I made a small mistake in my report and immediately thought, 'I'm so stupid.'"

"Stupid," Tanuja repeated, allowing the word to hang in the air for a moment. "That's quite a harsh label for a simple error, isn't it?"

"It is," Srishti admitted, her voice tinged with sadness. "But it feels automatic, like I can't stop it."

"Automatic, but not accurate." Tanuja's eyes held Srishti's gaze, steady and unwavering. "What might happen if instead of 'stupid,' you said 'human'?"

"Human," Srishti tested the word, feeling its weight and warmth. "It doesn't sting the same way."

"Exactly." Tanuja leaned forward, bridging the gap between them with her intent. "Mistakes don't define you. They are simply moments of learning, part of being human."

"Moments of learning," Srishti repeated, the idea settling into her thoughts, softening edges sharpened by years of self-criticism.

"Let's practice turning these 'shoulds' into something more compassionate. What could you say instead of 'I should be perfect'?"

Srishti paused, searching for the words that eluded her for so long. Finally, she whispered, "I am doing my best."

"Beautiful," Tanuja smiled, her voice imbued with hopeful sincerity. "Your best is enough, Srishti. Perfection is an illusion. Effort and progress, those are real."

"Effort and progress," Srishti repeated, feeling the shift within her, a loosening of the chains of perfectionism.

"Whenever you catch yourself using 'should' statements," Tanuja offered, "pause and ask yourself if they're serving you. Replace them with kinder, more realistic affirmations."

"Kinder affirmations," Srishti nodded, already feeling the weight of expectations begin to lift off her shoulders. "I can do that."

"As you practice," Tanuja concluded, "you'll find the voice inside growing gentler, your self-talk more encouraging. And you'll see how capable and deserving you truly are."

"Capable and deserving," Srishti echoed, her heart brimming with newfound hope. She stood up, ready to face the world outside, armed with kindness for the one person she'd often forgotten to nurture—herself.

*****

As the morning light filtered through the sheer curtains, casting a soft glow across the room, Srishti sat on the edge of her chair, hunched over her journal. She was scribbling furiously, her pen racing to keep up with the whirlwind of thoughts that had ambushed her upon waking.

"Everyone else seems to have it all figured out," she whispered to herself, frustration lacing her tone as she compared her own perceived failures to the accomplishments of her peers.

Tanuja, seated in her customary armchair, watched Srishti with a gentle gaze. "It's easy to look at others and feel like we're falling behind," she said, her voice steady and soothing. "But everyone's journey is different."

Srishti looked up, her eyes brimming with uncertainty. "I know, but..." she hesitated, biting her lip. "I can't help feeling inadequate when I see someone succeeding where I struggle."

"Those feelings are valid," Tanuja acknowledged, nodding slowly. "But remember, comparison often omits the full story. Successes and struggles alike."

"Full story," Srishti echoed, considering the words. "I guess I only see the highlight reel."

"Exactly," Tanuja affirmed. "And what about your own highlights, Srishti? Your intelligence, your resilience?"

"Sometimes, they feel overshadowed by doubt," Srishti confessed, her shoulders slumping. "I question if I'm really capable."

"Capable," Tanuja repeated, leaning forward. "That's a word you should hold onto. Tell me, what does self-doubt whisper to you?"

"It tells me I'm not enough, that I'll never match up to others," Srishti admitted, her voice barely above a murmur.

"Let's challenge that," Tanuja suggested gently. "For every comparison, let's find an affirmation. Shall we try?"

Srishti nodded, taking a deep breath as she prepared to face her inner critic.

"Someone might be thriving in their career," she started tentatively, "but I am dedicated and making progress in my own."

"Good," Tanuja encouraged. "More."

"Others may have more friends," Srishti continued, gaining confidence, "but I am cultivating meaningful relationships."

"Excellent," Tanuja smiled. "And self-doubt, what do you say to it?"

"I tell it that I am learning and growing," Srishti declared, her voice stronger now. "I am charting my own path and trusting my journey."

"Trusting your journey," Tanuja echoed. "That's the spirit. Remember, you don't need to be anyone else but yourself."

"Be myself," Srishti mused, letting the idea resonate within her. "That's the only person I need to be."

"Exactly," Tanuja said, standing up as their session drew to a close. "Carry this truth with you, Srishti. Let it guide your self-talk from shadows of doubt into the light of self-acceptance."

"From doubt to acceptance," Srishti said, standing alongside Tanuja. A smile began to form on her lips. Today, she would walk in the world not as a mirror to others, but as the unique embodiment of her own aspirations and dreams.

*****

Srishti perched on the edge of the plush chair, her hands clasped tightly in her lap. The silence of the room wrapped around her like a comforting blanket, punctuated only by the soft ticking of the clock on the wall. Tanuja observed her with a gentle gaze, patiently waiting for the words to surface.

"Growing up," Srishti began, her voice barely above a whisper, "it was never quite enough. 'You can do better,' they'd say, or 'Why can't you be more like...?' It starts to echo, you know?"

Tanuja nodded, her expression one of understanding. "That echo becomes a voice, doesn't it? One that follows you."

"Yes," Srishti exhaled, the admission freeing yet heavy with memories. "It whispers doubts, especially when I'm about to take a step forward."

"Tell me, Srishti, what does it whisper?" Tanuja's question hung in the air, inviting a confession.

"It says..." She paused, bracing herself to vocalize the haunting refrain of her upbringing. "'You never do anything right.' Over and over."

"Ah," Tanuja acknowledged the weight of those words. "And when you hear it, how do you feel?"

"Small. Trapped in this belief that I'll fail before I even begin." Srishti's eyes flickered down, a frown creasing her brow.

"Let's challenge that voice," Tanuja suggested softly. "What if you could speak back to it? What would you say?"

Srishti hesitated, her mind grappling with the unfamiliar concept of confronting the critical chorus. Slowly, she lifted her head, a spark of defiance igniting within her eyes.

"I would say... I have done things right. Many times." Her voice gained steadiness with each word. "I've succeeded and overcome challenges."

"Beautiful," Tanuja encouraged. "Keep going."

"Every mistake has taught me something valuable," Srishti continued, her self-doubt yielding to a burgeoning confidence. "I am not my failures. I am the resilience and learning that comes from them."

"Resilience and learning," echoed Tanuja, her praise genuine. "Feel the power in those truths, Srishti."

The room felt warmer somehow, as if Srishti's newfound declarations were a light dispelling the shadows. She sat taller, the grip on her hands loosening.

"Look at you," Tanuja smiled. "You are more than good enough. You are capable, and you are worthy."

"Capable and worthy," Srishti repeated, the words tasting sweet on her tongue. She had not just spoken; she had spoken back. And in doing so, she sensed the oppressive voice losing its grip, its whispers fading into insignificance against the strength of her own affirmations.

"Today, let's set an intention," Tanuja proposed, her tone imbued with hope. "To recognize that voice for what it is – an old script that no longer serves you."

"An old script," Srishti affirmed, her heart lighter. "I'm ready to write a new one."

"Then let's begin." Tanuja's smile was the promise of a new chapter, one where Srishti would author her own narrative, guided by compassion and illuminated by the truth of her worth.

*****

Srishti traced her finger along the varnished wood of the armrest, each grain a testament to growth, despite imperfections. She exhaled slowly, matching the cadence of Tanuja's calm breathing from across the room.

"Growing up," Srishti began, her voice soft but steady, "comparison was the yardstick by which I measured myself. My brother, always the top of his class. Me, not so much. It's like... I'm always running a race I can never win."

Tanuja nodded, her gaze gentle yet unwavering. "And when we're constantly looking at the person ahead, we miss our own progress, don't we?" she asked, guiding Srishti towards self- reflection.

"Exactly." Srishti's fingers paused on the armrest, her realization dawning like morning light. "My teacher once said my brother set the bar high. All I heard was that I wasn't reaching it. 'I can't do anything right,' became my mantra."

"Mantras are powerful," Tanuja affirmed, "but they can also be rewritten. What if you chose one that celebrated your journey instead of diminishing it?"

A flicker of curiosity sparked in Srishti's eyes. "I've never thought about it that way," she confessed.

"Let's explore further," Tanuja suggested with an encouraging tilt of her head. "How has fear influenced your inner dialogue?"

"Ah, fear," Srishti murmured, a wry smile touching her lips. "It's always there, whispering, 'You're going to mess this up.' It keeps me from taking chances."

"And what about success?" Tanuja probed gently.

"Success," Srishti hesitated, "it's double-edged. If I succeed once, the pressure mounts. 'Now everyone will expect more from me, and I can't handle that.' It's paralyzing."

"Paralysis isn't permanent," Tanuja assured her, leaning forward slightly. "Every step forward is movement. Success isn't a burden; it's proof of your capability."

"Capability," Srishti repeated, tasting the word, feeling its weight and its wings.

"Your achievements aren't demands for more; they are evidence of what you've already accomplished," Tanuja explained, her voice a soothing melody.

"Accomplishments... not demands," Srishti echoed, letting the idea seep into her consciousness, challenging years of conditioned fear.

"Consider this," Tanuja offered, a warm invitation in her tone, "each success, each stumble—they're all part of learning. You don't have to carry the weight of expectations, just the willingness to grow."

Srishti nodded, the corners of her mouth curving upward ever so slightly. "Willingness to grow," she said, embracing the phrase like a lifeline thrown into turbulent waters.

"Indeed," Tanuja smiled, her presence a beacon of hope. "Shall we work on crafting a new mantra together? One that celebrates you as you are, right here, right now?"

"Yes," Srishti affirmed, strength burgeoning within her voice. "I'm ready to set my own pace."

"Then let's begin," Tanuja said. "With words that build, not break."

"Words that build," Srishti declared, her spirit lifting with the promise of change. "Not break."

*****

Tanuja watched Srishti trace the outline of a water stain on the wooden table, her finger moving in slow circles as if trying to smooth away the edges of her own self-imposed limits. The air between them was thick with revelations, each one a thread weaving into the fabric of understanding.

"Math," Srishti said abruptly, her voice barely above a whisper, yet it cut through the silence with the sharpness of a knife. "I've always told myself I'm not good at it. Ever since I was little."

"Ah," Tanuja responded, her tone acknowledging the weight of those words. "Those messages we hear, they can set roots deep within us."

Srishti nodded, eyes lingering on the darkened wood grain, seeing beyond it to a past riddled with red marks on schoolwork and the stern look of disappointment in her teacher's eyes. "I remember this one time, I failed a math test... It felt like a confirmation. Like my fears had substance."

"Failures can feel like anchors sometimes," Tanuja agreed, leaning forward, her presence enveloping Srishti in an invisible embrace of empathy. "But what if we saw them instead as buoys, marking the spots where we need to navigate differently?"

"Buoy..." Srishti repeated, considering the metaphor. Her shoulders relaxed, the tension seeping out of them gradually, as if the thought had loosened something constricted inside her.

"Exactly. A marker for growth, not inadequacy," Tanuja continued, her words painting possibilities over the landscape of Srishti's doubts.

"Nobody ever told me that," Srishti admitted, meeting Tanuja's gaze. There was a flicker of something new in her eyes—perhaps the beginnings of belief.

"Then let me be the first," Tanuja said with a gentle finality. "Your ability to learn and improve is boundless. Math, or any challenge, is just another language you haven't become fluent in yet."

"Another language..." The corner of Srishti's mouth twitched into the semblance of a smile, a soft chuckle escaping her lips. "I like that. It doesn't sound so scary when you put it that way."

"Good," Tanuja smiled back, warmth radiating from her. "Replace 'I can't do more' with 'I am learning more every day.' Let that be your new equation."

"I am learning more every day," Srishti echoed, testing out the words. They felt foreign but hopeful on her tongue, like a promise she could choose to keep.

"Remember, Srishti," Tanuja added, her voice carrying the strength of conviction, "you are not defined by the failures of yesterday but by the lessons you take into tomorrow."

"Lessons for tomorrow," Srishti murmured, a mantra taking root. She straightened up, a newfound resolve lifting her posture. "Thank you, Tanuja."

"Whenever you're ready, we will tackle the next sum together," Tanuja assured her, her expressive eyes holding a vision of the future where Srishti stood tall, unencumbered by doubt.

"Ready," Srishti affirmed, the word no longer an echo but a declaration, filled with the potential of all the tomorrows stretching out before her.

*****

Srishti sat across from Tanuja, her fingers nervously tracing the pattern on the fabric of the couch. The room was quiet except for the soft hum of the air conditioner, a reassuring white noise in the background. She had always found comfort in Tanuja's office; it was a sanctuary of sorts, where her fragmented thoughts could be pieced together under the gentle guidance of her therapist.

"Let's dig a little," Tanuja suggested with a calm and steady voice. "Think back to your childhood. What messages did you receive about yourself?"

Memories flickered through Srishti's mind. Her parents' praise when she aced a test, the frowns that creased their brows during piano recitals gone wrong. Their voices echoed in her head, a mixture of encouragement and disappointment.

"I was told I could do anything if I put my mind to it," Srishti began hesitantly. "But also that I should always strive to do better."

"And how did those messages make you feel?" Tanuja probed gently.

"Driven, but never quite satisfied," Srishti admitted, her voice a whisper. "Like nothing I did was ever enough."

"Those experiences shaped your self-talk," Tanuja nodded, understandingly. "Now, let's challenge those old tapes. Are they really true?"

Srishti paused, considering the weight of her inner critic against the evidence of her life. An internal battle ensued, one where truth sought to dethrone long-held beliefs.

"Maybe not," she conceded after a moment. "I've achieved a lot despite setbacks. But it's hard to remember that when I'm caught in the spiral of negative thoughts."

"Exactly," replied Tanuja, her eyes reflecting pride. "Now, let's shift the focus. Tell me about your strengths, your achievements."

A hesitant smile tugged at the edges of Srishti's lips. She drew a deep breath, emboldened by Tanuja's belief in her. One by one, she recounted her successes: the scholarships she'd won, the projects she'd spearheaded at work, the friends who turned to her for advice.

"Write them down," Tanuja instructed, pushing a notepad and pen across the table. "Keep the list close and read it often. It's your armour against the negative barrage."

Pen to paper, Srishti started listing, each word a testament to her resilience. 'Organized,' 'resourceful,' 'compassionate'—the words flowed, forming an anthology of her worth.

"See?" Tanuja's voice was soft yet triumphant. "You are much more than your inner critic allows you to believe."

Srishti looked down at the list, her personal narrative rewritten in ink. It was tangible proof, something to hold onto when doubts arose like unwelcome shadows.

"Thank you," she said sincerely. "This... it helps to see it all laid out."

"Remember, you control the narrative," Tanuja reminded her, the sentence punctuated with conviction. "Positive self-talk is a powerful tool. Use it to pave the way forward."

Srishti folded the paper carefully and tucked it into her journal. A small but significant act of reclaiming her story.

"I will," Srishti promised, her voice no longer shaky but steady, like the resolve that now sparked within her. "I'll start with this list. And I'll add to it, day by day."

"Exactly, day by day," Tanuja echoed, her smile an echo of hope as the session drew to a close. "And remember, the strength you seek is already within you."

*****

Srishti hesitated at the door of her colleague's office, the weight of vulnerability heavy in her chest. She raised a hand, knocked lightly, and waited. Inside, she knew, was an opportunity to break the cycle of self-criticism that often held her captive.

"Come in," called a familiar voice, tinged with warmth.

She entered, finding solace in the inviting space. Books lined the shelves, plants added a touch of life, and there, behind a tidy desk, sat Meera, her colleague, whose insight Srishti valued.

"Hey, Srishti, what brings you here?" Meera asked, her eyes kind and attentive.

"I..." Srishti started, then paused, gathering her thoughts. "I've been working on silencing my negative self-talk. I could use some feedback—constructive feedback," she clarified, unsure but hopeful.

"Of course," Meera said, gesturing to the chair across from her. "Let's talk through it."

As Srishti recounted her recent challenges, Meera listened intently, nodding at intervals, her presence a comforting anchor. When Srishti finished, Meera leaned forward, her words measured and sincere.

"Firstly, your work ethic is unmatched, and your contributions are invaluable," Meera began, her praise not just empty words but reflections of truth. "Your ability to empathize with clients is remarkable. But remember, you're also human, and perfection isn't the goal—it's about progress."

"Progress, not perfection," Srishti repeated softly, the phrase a balm to her anxious thoughts.

"Exactly," Meera affirmed. "And don't forget, we all stumble sometimes. It's part of learning and growing."

"Thank you, Meera," Srishti said, feeling a lightness she hadn't felt in days. The conversation was a mirror, reflecting not the distortions of her inner critic but the reality of her strengths and efforts.

Later, alone in the quiet of her apartment, Srishti's mind buzzed with the day's revelations. A pang of self-doubt surfaced as she replayed a minor mistake made during a presentation. She closed her eyes, took a deep breath, and imagined what she would say to a friend in the same situation.

"Everyone makes mistakes," she whispered to herself, the words soft but firm. "What matters is what you learn from them."

Her heart eased, the harsh edges of criticism softened by kindness. This was self-compassion in practice, a gentle reminder that she deserved the same patience and understanding she so freely gave others.

"Tomorrow is another day," she thought, a smile tugging at the corners of her lips. "Another chance to grow, to be kind to myself, and to keep moving forward."

With this newfound resolve, Srishti reached for her journal, the list of her strengths tucked safely within its pages. She penned down the insights from her talk with Meera, each sentence a commitment to nurture her mind with grace and encouragement.

"Seek feedback. Practice self-compassion," she wrote, her hand steady, her spirit buoyed by the powerful simplicity of these actions. "You are more than enough."

The room hummed with the promise of change as Srishti prepared for rest, her journey towards healing illuminated by the soft glow of self-acceptance.

*****

Srishti sat at her desk, sunlight filtering through the window and casting a warm glow on the array of achievements lining her wall. Her gaze lingered on each one, a silent testament to her journey. Yet, in the quiet of her room, she felt the familiar tug of comparison pulling her into the shadowy depths of inadequacy.

"Tanuja always says to honour my own path," she murmured, tracing the edge of a photograph from her last trek—a challenge she had conquered alone. It was a tangible reminder, not just of reaching the summit, but of the individual steps that carried her there, each one significant.

She could almost hear Tanuja's soothing voice, "Srishti, your path is yours alone—unique, incomparable. Revel in it."

With a deep inhale, Srishti released the breath slowly, as if exhaling the weight of comparisons that clouded her mind. She turned to the open journal before her, the pages a canvas for her thoughts.

"Today, I choose to celebrate me," she wrote with deliberate strokes, the words a personal declaration of freedom from the trap of measuring herself against others.

The doorbell rang, a cheerful interruption to her introspection. Srishti rose to answer, finding a small package at her doorstep. Inside was a custom-made bookmark, a gift from an old friend adorned with an inscription: 'Celebrate every victory, no matter how small.'

Her lips curved into a smile, a genuine reflection of appreciation for the thoughtfulness behind the gesture—and for the milestone it represented. It wasn't about grand successes; it was about acknowledging the steps she took each day, the growth within them.

"Every little progress is worth celebrating," she said aloud, feeling the truth of those words settling in her heart.

She returned to her desk, placing the bookmark between the pages of her journal, a symbol of her commitment to value her own pace and progress. The comparison that once loomed over her now seemed distant, its power diminished by her newfound resolve.

"Small steps lead to big changes," Srishti whispered, her voice brimming with hope. The affirmation was a seed planted in fertile ground, ready to sprout with each act of self-recognition.

As the afternoon waned, the light in her room softened, casting long shadows that danced upon the walls. Srishti leaned back in her chair, allowing herself to bask in the quiet triumphs of her personal journey.

"Thank you, Tanuja, for reminding me to cherish my own way," she thought, a serene sense of gratitude enveloping her. With each passing moment, the tendrils of doubt receded, replaced by an empowering certainty that her path was hers alone—worthy, valid, and full of potential.

*****

Srishti sat across from Tanuja, her hands wrapped tightly around a steaming mug of masala tea. The scent wafted up, mingling with the calm serenity of the therapist's office—a contrast to the storm that had been raging in Srishti's thoughts.

"Sometimes," Srishti began, her voice steady but low, "the voices in my head aren't kind. They echo doubts and fears louder than I can fight."

Tanuja offered a gentle nod, a subtle invitation for Srishti to continue unravelling her worries. She waited patiently, knowing the value of silence when it came to coaxing out the shadows lurking in the corners of one's mind.

"Have you considered seeking help is not a sign of defeat, but a step towards healing?" Tanuja asked, her tone imbued with warmth and understanding.

Srishti pondered the question, letting the simplicity of the idea sink in. It resonated within her, disrupting the pattern of negative whispers that so often filled her consciousness.

"Maybe," she replied hesitantly, "maybe it's time I did."

"Therapists and counsellors can be allies," Tanuja explained. "Together, you can find strategies to quiet those harsh voices and replace them with ones that uplift and support you."

The thought unfurled like a delicate bloom within Srishti's chest—hopeful, bright. The possibility of change, of transformation, seemed less like a distant dream and more like an achievable reality.

"Understanding the root of these thoughts is like turning on a light in a dark room," Tanuja continued. "It doesn't erase what's there, but it helps you see things clearly."

Srishti felt a shift, a subtle lifting of the weight that had clung to her spirit. She imagined herself standing in that illuminated room, the shadows retreating before the glow of her own awareness.

"Addressing negative self-talk isn't just about silencing it," Tanuja said, her eyes reflecting the conviction in her words. "It's about learning to speak to yourself with the same compassion you offer others."

With each syllable, the rhythm of Tanuja's speech wove a tapestry of strength and confidence around Srishti. She could almost touch the threads, each one a promise of a future where she was her own ally, not her own enemy.

"By nurturing this inner dialogue, you cultivate a garden where self-doubt withers and self-assurance blossoms," Tanuja concluded, the metaphor painting vivid images in Srishti's mind.

"Could I really learn to talk to myself like that?" Srishti asked, daring to clutch at the tendrils of optimism that spiralled through her thoughts.

"Absolutely," Tanuja affirmed with a smile that seemed to cradle Srishti's fragile hope. "And with practice, your confidence will grow, empowering you to chase after your dreams."

The room hummed with the power of possibility. Srishti took a deep breath, exhaling slowly as she allowed herself to believe in the journey ahead. She would learn to navigate her mental landscape with a kinder internal compass—one that pointed towards self-compassion and fulfilment.

"Thank you, Tanuja," Srishti murmured, the gratitude genuine and profound. "For shining a light on the path I've been searching for."

"Always remember, Srishti," Tanuja said as their session drew to a close, "you have the strength within you to transform your life."

As Srishti stepped out into the world, the light from Tanuja's office lingered in her eyes. She carried it with her, a beacon against the darkness of doubt, guiding her towards a horizon filled with the hues of hope and the promise of a more fulfilling life.

*****

Srishti stood before the bathroom mirror, her eyes locking with her own reflection. The fluorescent light flickered briefly, casting a wavering glow over her delicate features. She inhaled deeply, steadying her breath as she prepared to voice the thoughts that Tanuja had gently planted within her.

"Positive affirmations," Srishti whispered to herself, the words feeling strange yet necessary on her lips. "Tools for healing."

"Say it with me," Tanuja's soft encouragement echoed in her memory, guiding her from afar. Srishti's heart beat a tentative rhythm, the anticipation of change palpable in the air.

"I am capable and strong," Srishti declared, the simple phrase cutting through years of self-criticism. The sound of her own voice startled her, as if these words belonged to someone else—someone confident, someone whole.

Again, she said it, this time with more conviction, "I am capable and strong." The words felt like a lifeline, pulling her from the stormy seas of doubt to the solid ground of belief. Her reflection nodded in agreement, a silent ally in this newfound pact of positivity.

Tanuja's lessons wove seamlessly into Srishti's mind, an intricately woven fabric of wisdom and self-kindness. Each syllable of affirmation stitched together the frayed edges of her self-esteem, each pause between words a moment to breathe in courage and exhale fear.

The corners of Srishti's mouth curved upwards, a tentative smile blooming like the first rays of dawn after a long night. She repeated the mantra, letting the warmth of the affirmation bask her spirit in light. "I am capable and strong."

Outside, the world continued its relentless pace, but within the confines of that small bathroom, a profound shift occurred. Srishti faced her day armed with a new weapon against the shadows of negativity: the shining shield of positive self-talk.

*****

Srishti clasped her hands together, feeling the pulse of her own heartbeat—a rhythm that spoke of life and potential. In the quietude of Tanuja's office, with sunlight filtering in through the blinds, she felt a gentle firmness take root within her.

"I believe in myself and my abilities," Srishti said, her voice a soft murmur at first, a hesitant stream trickling into existence.

"Say it again," Tanuja encouraged, her tone imbued with the warm timbre of unwavering support. "Let yourself hear the truth in your words."

This time, Srishti's declaration was stronger, the tremor of uncertainty replaced by a growing steadiness. "I believe in myself and my abilities."

"Feel the weight of those words," Tanuja guided, leaning forward slightly, her eyes reflecting the kind of belief that could ignite stars. "They are your armour, your strength."

Srishti closed her eyes, letting the affirmation envelop her. She pictured each word like a stone laid upon a foundation, building the fortress of her self-assurance. "I am worthy of success and happiness," she affirmed, her voice gaining texture and colour, painting her world with possibilities.

"Embrace that worthiness," Tanuja whispered. "It is your birthright, not a distant land to be reached but the ground on which you stand."

With her eyes still closed, Srishti nodded, a flutter of something like wings brushing against the walls of her heart. The sentence became a chant, a mantra pulsing through her veins. "I am worthy of success and happiness."

"Let that feeling spread," Tanuja said, gesturing softly as if to smooth the air around them. "Let it touch every corner of your being."

Opening her eyes, Srishti felt a warmth radiating from within, a gentle glow that seemed to push the shadows of doubt away. The room around her seemed brighter, as if her newfound belief had lit up the space.

"Remember, Srishti," Tanuja's voice was both a lighthouse and a haven, "your self-worth doesn't have to be earned; it's inherent. You don't have to chase after happiness as if it's a prize at the end of a race."

Srishti absorbed the words, feeling them settle into her bones, a sturdy framework upon which she could rebuild her self-image. She inhaled deeply, each breath like a thread weaving strength back into her spirit.

"Can you feel the difference?" Tanuja asked, her simple question a bridge to self-discovery.

"I... I can," Srishti replied, a note of wonder threading through her words. "It's like I've been carrying this heavy weight, and saying those words... it feels lighter somehow."

"Good," Tanuja smiled, her expression a reflection of the pride she saw blossoming in Srishti. "That lightness is your true essence. It's what you carry with you when the burden of negative thoughts is lifted."

Srishti nodded, a silent promise etching itself into her resolve.

She would carry this moment with her, a talisman against the darkness of her doubts.

"Keep nurturing that belief," Tanuja continued. "Water it daily with these affirmations, and watch how it grows, how it changes the landscape of your inner world."

With a newfound clarity, Srishti recognized the power she held over her thoughts, over the dialogue within. She was the author of her story, capable of rewriting the script one affirmation at a time.

"I believe in myself and my abilities," she said again, not just as an echo but as a declaration, her voice the brushstroke of an artist confident in their craft.

"And I am worthy of success and happiness," she added, the truth of it resonating deep within, a bell tolling in celebration of her awakening.

Tanuja's approving nod was the last nudge Srishti needed, a confirmation that she was on the path to healing, to owning the narrative of her life with conviction and grace.

*****

The sunlight filtered through the blinds, casting a soft glow around Tanuja's office. Srishti sat across from her, fingers fidgeting with the hem of her sleeve, a physical manifestation of her internal turmoil. She looked up, meeting Tanuja's gaze with a timid yet determined glimmer in her eyes.

"Change isn't linear, is it?" Srishti asked, her voice steadier than before. "It's more like... climbing a mountain with no clear path."

"Exactly," Tanuja affirmed, leaning forward slightly. "And every step, even the smallest, is progress."

Srishti inhaled deeply, letting the reality of her journey settle within her. "I am constantly growing and improving," she said slowly, tasting each word as if it were new to her palette. They were simple words, yet they held power—a mantra to guide her ascent.

"Those steps you're taking," Tanuja encouraged, "they're not just leading you upwards; they're also carving out a trail for you to follow back whenever you need to remember how far you've come."

"Even when I stumble?" Srishti's question was laced with the weight of past missteps.

"Especially then," Tanuja replied with a gentle firmness. "Because that's when growth happens. In the struggle, in the recovery. Each time you rise again, you're stronger, wiser."

"Stronger," Srishti echoed. She considered her previous challenges, the ones that had once seemed insurmountable. Now, they were markers of her resilience, reminders of her capacity to overcome.

"Decisions feel like these... forked paths," Srishti continued, gesturing with her hands as if unveiling a map only she could see. "And I'm scared of choosing wrong, of falling."

Tanuja nodded, her expression a blend of empathy and assurance. "Trust isn't built overnight. It grows, like a seed into a tree, with each choice you make. Tell yourself, 'I trust myself to make good decisions.'"

"I trust myself to make good decisions," Srishti repeated. The affirmation felt like a key unlocking a door she had long been afraid to open. With each repetition, her self-doubt shrank, overshadowed by the burgeoning confidence within.

"Good," Tanuja smiled warmly. "Remember, making a decision is also a decision to trust in your ability to navigate the outcome, whatever it may be."

"Even if I'm not sure?" Srishti's voice was a whisper, a thread of uncertainty still lingering.

"Certainty isn't a prerequisite for trust," Tanuja countered gently. "Sometimes, the best choices are made with hope rather than certainty."

"Hope," Srishti mused. A soft laugh escaped her, the sound mingling with the light in the room. She felt it then, the shift from fear to faith, from doubt to determination.

"Then, I choose to hope," she declared, the words anchoring her resolve. "To believe in the growth I can't see yet."

"Beautiful choice," Tanuja said, her pride evident.

The session drew to a close, but the impact of their conversation lingered. Srishti stood, feeling the solidity of the ground beneath her feet. She carried with her the knowledge that each step was a testament to her growth, each decision a reflection of her newfound trust.

"See you next week, Srishti," Tanuja called out as Srishti opened the door.

"See you," Srishti replied, stepping into the light of the hallway, the words 'constantly growing' and 'good decisions' her silent companions, echoing with every beat of her heart.

*****

Srishti paused by the mirror in the quiet hallway, her reflection catching her off-guard. For a moment, she simply looked at herself, really looked—past the practiced smile and the carefully chosen attire to the woman beneath.

"Look at you," Srishti whispered to her reflection, her voice tinged with a revelation that felt both foreign and deeply familiar. "You've come so far."

Her eyes traced the lines of determination etched softly around her mouth—the same mouth that had spoken words of comfort to a friend in distress just yesterday. It had been a small act, yet it rippled through her memory, reminding her of the strength she often failed to acknowledge.

"Remember the presentation last month?" she continued, her gaze unwavering. "Everyone said it was impossible, but you did it. You made it happen."

A sense of warmth spread through her as she recounted the accomplishments, each one a stepping stone that had brought her here. She hadn't merely survived the challenges; she'd thrived, turning every setback into a lesson, every doubt into determination.

Tanuja's words echoed in her mind, a soothing balm to the chaos of self-critique that used to dominate her thoughts. "Pride is not about grandiosity; it's recognizing the value of your journey and honouring your efforts."

"I am proud," Srishti affirmed, her voice steadier now, a soft but unyielding force. "I am proud of what I have accomplished."

She turned from the mirror, the ghost of uncertainty still lurking at the edges of her consciousness. But today, it was met with a newfound ally—a gentle yet insistent whisper that spoke of worthiness and sufficiency.

"Enough," she murmured as she walked down the corridor, her steps echoing lightly on the tile floor. "I am enough just as I am."

*****

"Good afternoon, Tanuja," Srishti greeted as she entered the therapist's office, the natural light spilling across the room like a welcoming embrace.

"Good afternoon, Srishti," Tanuja replied, her eyes reflecting the depth of her understanding. "How are we feeling today?"

"Hopeful," Srishti said, settling into the familiar chair, its cushions now holding the imprint of her growth. "And... content."

"Contentment is a beautiful space to inhabit," Tanuja noted, her pen poised above her notebook. "Would you like to share what brings about this feeling?"

"It's strange," Srishti began, her hands folded in her lap. "I looked at myself in the mirror earlier, and instead of nitpicking every flaw, I found myself... appreciating my journey. The struggles, the wins—I'm learning to see them all as valuable."

"Valuable indeed," Tanuja smiled, her voice warm as sunlight. "It sounds like your inner dialogue is becoming kinder, more affirming."

"Yes, it's like I can finally hear my own voice over the noise of expectation and doubt." Srishti's lips curved upward, a testament to her resilience. "And it tells me I'm enough."

"Beautiful," Tanuja said, nodding in agreement. "That voice is your truth, Srishti. Hold onto it."

They delved deeper into conversation, exploring the intricate layers of Srishti's progress. Each word exchanged built upon the foundation of acceptance and self-compassion that they had been constructing together, brick by brick.

Srishti's fingers tapped a steady rhythm on the ceramic mug, the warmth seeping into her palms. Tanuja watched from across the room, her expression serene like the surface of a still lake.

"Tell me, Srishti," Tanuja began, her voice soft yet clear, "what does deserving mean to you?"

Srishti paused, considering the question. She lifted her gaze, meeting Tanuja's steady eyes. "Deserving... it's like saying 'yes' to the good without feeling guilty."

"Exactly," Tanuja affirmed. "And how does that 'yes' feel?"

"Scary," admitted Srishti, "but right. Like I'm opening doors for myself instead of waiting for someone else to do it." She took a deep breath, and as she exhaled, her shoulders relaxed.

"Good," Tanuja encouraged. "Now, think about those doors opening. What is on the other side?"

" Opportunities," Srishti replied. " Happiness, love, success—things I've worked hard for."

"And are you ready to walk through those doors?"

Srishti nodded, her heart rate picking up with the thrill of affirmation. "I am deserving of all the good things in life," she said, the words more than just sounds—they were an invocation, a claim she laid upon the world.

Tanuja's smile widened, mirroring the breakthrough in Srishti's heart. "Remember, challenges will arise. How will you meet them?"

"Challenges..." Srishti mulled over past obstacles, the times she stumbled, but now viewed them through a lens of strength. "I handle challenges with grace and strength," she declared, the conviction in her voice resonating in the quiet room.

"Say it again," Tanuja urged, leaning forward slightly, as if to catch every syllable.

"Grace and strength," Srishti repeated, her voice firmer this time. "I handle challenges with grace and strength."

"Beautiful," whispered Tanuja. "You're redefining your experiences, reshaping your narrative."

They sat in silence for a moment, allowing the power of the spoken truths to settle between them. The sunlight filtering through the blinds cast a warm glow on the scene, a physical embodiment of the internal shift taking place within Srishti.

"Today, you've embraced two powerful beliefs," Tanuja noted, standing to signal the end of the session. "Carry them with you, and let them guide your steps."

Srishti rose, her back straighter, a lightness in her step. As she reached the door, she glanced back at Tanuja, gratitude shining in her eyes.

"Thank you," she said, her voice steady and full of newfound confidence. "For helping me see what I deserve and how to face what comes my way."

With a final nod, Srishti stepped out, each stride carrying her further into a life where she was not just enough, but deserving—a world where she faced each challenge not just with resilience, but with grace and strength.

*****

Srishti paused at the edge of the park, her breath misting in the cool morning air. She watched as joggers passed by, their steady rhythm a reminder of life's continuous flow. Her hand closed around the small notebook in her pocket, its pages filled with affirmations and reflections—a testament to her journey with Tanuja.

"Every mistake is a step forward," she whispered to herself, the words a gentle incantation against the hum of self-doubt that had once filled her thoughts.

With each step on the gravel path, Srishti felt the weight of past failures grow lighter. The echo of harsh judgments, once loud within her mind, now seemed distant. She had come to understand that stumbling was not a sign of weakness but an opportunity to rise stronger.

"Control," she murmured, her pace slowing as she approached a bench overlooking the tranquil pond. "It begins here, with my thoughts... with my emotions."

Seated, she gazed out at the water, its surface rippling with the traces of a passing breeze. A family of ducks glided by, unfazed by the ripples, navigating with ease—a visual cue for Srishti's own journey through the turbulence of her inner world.

"Tanuja says, 'Our emotions need acknowledgment, not judgment,'" Srishti recalled, drawing out her notebook. She penned down the scene before her, ducks and ripples alike, anchoring the metaphor to the page.

"Good morning," a familiar voice called out, pulling Srishti from her reverie. It was Tanuja, her presence a comforting reminder of the support that surrounded Srishti's path to healing.

"Morning," Srishti replied, closing her notebook with a soft smile. "I was just... practicing."

"Practicing?" Tanuja prompted, taking a seat beside her.

"Learning. From everything around me, from everything inside me," Srishti said, gesturing to the pond. "Like them," she nodded toward the ducks, "moving forward, regardless of the ripples."

"Beautifully put," Tanuja replied with an approving nod. "And how does it feel, this learning?"

"Empowering," Srishti answered, the word tasting like freedom on her tongue. "It's like I'm finally steering my own ship, even when the waters get rough."

"Remember, Srishti, you are the captain of your soul," Tanuja said, her eyes reflecting pride. "Your thoughts, your emotions—they're the winds and tides. You've learned to navigate them with skill."

Srishti soaked in Tanuja's words, letting them reinforce the foundations of her newfound confidence. She had battled the stormy seas of her mind, and now, she sensed calm waters ahead.

"Thank you, Tanuja," Srishti said, standing up and feeling the strength in her legs, the steadiness of her heartbeat. "For guiding me towards this... control."

"Always remember, Srishti," Tanuja stood as well, her gaze holding Srishti's, "you have the power to learn and to move forward. Every single day."

As they parted ways, Srishti clutched her notebook a little tighter, her steps more assured than ever. With each affirmation, with each breath, she was rewriting her story—one where mistakes were merely signposts and control was a truth she held within.

*****

As Srishti sat across from Tanuja in the soft light of the therapist's office, a hint of sunlight found its way through the blinds, casting gentle lines across the room. She watched the dust dance in the beams, particles swirling in silent chaos before settling down again—a delicate reminder that even in disturbance, there's a return to order.

"Tanuja," Srishti began, her voice steadier than it had been in weeks, "I'm trying something new."

"Oh?" Tanuja prompted, her hands folded in her lap, her presence an anchor in the quiet space.

"I choose to focus on the positive," Srishti declared, her own words surprising her with their firmness. It was as if saying them out loud gave the thoughts solidity, power.

"Those are strong words," Tanuja acknowledged with a slight tilt of her head. "Tell me, what brought you to this choice?"

"Every morning, when I wake up," Srishti explained, "the first thing I do is think of one good thing—no matter how small." She paused, searching for the right words. "Today, it was the warmth of my coffee mug. It felt like... holding a tiny sun."

"Beautiful," Tanuja smiled encouragingly. "And in focusing on that warmth, what happens to the shadows?"

"They're still there," Srishti admitted, "but less intimidating. They don't consume me anymore. Instead, they're just... part of the landscape."

"Part of a landscape filled with many different elements, including warmth and light," Tanuja added gently, guiding Srishti's realization.

"Exactly." Nodding, Srishti felt an internal shift, a lightness she hadn't known in a long time.

"And in those moments," Tanuja continued, "do you feel alone?"

Srishti reflected, allowing herself to sink deeper into the question. "No," she said at last. "I am surrounded by love and support. It's like the people who care about me—they're the rays of that same sun, reaching out to touch me, even when they aren't physically close."

"Love and support can be powerful allies in our journey," Tanuja affirmed. "How does acknowledging this change the way you see your challenges?"

"It..." Srishti paused, feeling a swell of emotion. "It makes them seem more manageable. Like I have an army behind me, even if all they're armed with are kind words and shared cups of coffee."

"Sometimes, those are the most powerful weapons we have against doubt and fear," Tanuja noted, her voice a soothing melody.

"Speaking of armies," Tanuja added with a glimmer in her eyes, "how do you marshal your thoughts throughout the day?"

Srishti chuckled softly. "Well, I've started to greet each negative thought with a positive one. For every 'can't,' I offer a 'can.' For every fear, a hope."

"An excellent strategy," Tanuja commended. "It's not about denying the negative, but about balancing the scales, giving equal weight to the positive forces in your life."

"Balance," Srishti repeated, rolling the word around her tongue. "I like that. It feels... attainable."

"Indeed, it is," Tanuja said with a nod. "Balance isn't static. It's dynamic, ever-shifting, and that's what makes life rich and full."

"Rich and full," Srishti echoed, a smile playing on her lips. She could almost taste the words, sweet and ripe with promise.

"Remember, Srishti," Tanuja concluded, her voice wrapping around the young woman like a comforting shawl, "positivity, like sunlight, is always there. Sometimes hidden behind clouds, but never gone. And love—it has a way of finding us, especially when we're open to receiving it."

"Open," Srishti whispered, the idea taking root. Open to the light, to love, to the myriad possibilities that each day held. In that moment, with the dust motes dancing and the world outside continuing its relentless spin, Srishti felt a profound sense of peace settle over her. She was ready to face the days ahead, not just with endurance, but with anticipation—for she was no longer merely surviving; she was thriving.

*****

Srishti's fingers hovered over the keyboard, her gaze flitting between the screen and the small sticky note affixed to its corner. On it, in her neat cursive, read the words: "Celebrate every victory." She inhaled deeply, taking a moment to absorb the enormity of what she was about to do.

"Submit," she whispered, clicking the button before her. The dissertation she'd toiled over for months was now on its journey to the review committee. A surge of accomplishment washed over her like a gentle wave, leaving behind a froth of pride that tingled through her body.

"Did you do it?" Tanuja's voice emerged from the laptop's speakers, warm and expectant.

"I did," Srishti replied, her smile audible.

"Then let's celebrate this success, no matter how small you may think it is," Tanuja encouraged. "This moment—it's yours. Embrace it."

"Small?" Srishti chuckled softly, feeling the shift within herself. "No, this is monumental for me." Her heart swelled with an unfamiliar sense of gratification. She allowed herself to bask in it, the warmth of self-recognition kindling something bright inside her.

"Rightly so," Tanuja agreed. "Each step you take is a testament to your growth, Srishti. Your journey isn't just about reaching destinations; it's about acknowledging the strides you've made along the way."

The therapist's words resonated within Srishti, echoing through the chambers of her once-doubtful heart. She glanced around her room, at the walls adorned with charts and diagrams, the bookshelf brimming with well-thumbed volumes, each a milestone on her academic path, each a silent witness to her resilience.

"Today," Srishti declared, her voice gaining strength, "I'm proud of myself."

"Beautiful," Tanuja said, her tone imbued with genuine delight. "And while we're on the subject of love and acceptance—what are your thoughts?"

"Love and acceptance..." Srishti pondered the concept, turning it over in her mind like a precious gem catching light from different angles. "It means embracing who I am, the flaws and all. It's giving myself permission to be human, to falter, to learn."

"Exactly." There was a smile in Tanuja's voice. "Self-love isn't conditional. It doesn't demand perfection. It's an unconditional embrace."

"Unconditional embrace," Srishti repeated, savouring the phrase. She pictured wrapping her arms around herself, the version of her that struggled, that doubted, that fought bravely against the whisperings of inadequacy. In that internal hug, she found a compassion she'd often reserved only for others.

"Every scar, every tear, every laughter line—they're part of my story," Srishti continued, a newfound tenderness threading through her words. "I love and accept myself unconditionally."

"Your story," Tanuja echoed, "is one of triumph, Srishti. Remember that when the inner critic speaks. Drown out those harsh words with love, with acceptance, with the truth of your own worth."

"Triumph," Srishti breathed out, letting the notion seep into her bones. The idea of it fortified her, a solid foundation upon which she could build her tomorrows.

"Shall we end today's session with a reminder of your progress?" Tanuja suggested, her voice a beacon guiding Srishti back to the present.

"Let's," Srishti agreed, straightening her posture. "I celebrate my successes, no matter how small. I love and accept myself unconditionally."

"Perfect," Tanuja affirmed. "Carry these affirmations with you, Srishti. Let them guard your heart and guide your steps."

"I will," Srishti promised, her spirit lighter than it had been in years. As the call ended, she sat there with the silence, feeling it envelop her—not as an adversary, but as a companion, a quiet witness to the new chapter unfolding within her.

*****

Srishti stood before the mirror, now a place where her inner self found its loudest voice. The morning light spilled across the contours of her face, illuminating the resolve in her eyes.

"Repeat them daily," Tanuja's words echoed in her mind, a gentle nudge towards a new ritual.

With a deep inhale, Srishti began, her voice a soft but unwavering murmur. "I celebrate my successes, no matter how small." She watched her lips move, forming each word with care as if stitching a tapestry of self-love.

"I love and accept myself unconditionally." The phrase wrapped around her like a warm blanket, soothing old wounds.

She reached for the elegant journal that lay open on her vanity—a book once blank, now brimming with the chronicles of her healing. With each affirmation she penned, the ink seemed to dance, weaving strength into the fibres of the paper. Her hand moved rhythmically, affirming her commitment to this act of recovery.

"Every day," she whispered to herself, closing the journal with a sense of completion. This simple, yet profound act was a promise to her heart, a daily tending to the garden of her soul.

"See you tomorrow," she said to her reflection, a smile gracing her features. It was a vow to return, to continue nurturing the voice within that championed her worth.

The clock ticked softly in the background, a metronome to her newfound cadence of self-compassion. As she turned from the mirror, the lightness carried through her steps, a symphony of hope playing to the rhythm of positive change.

*****

Tanuja leaned forward, her gaze locked on Srishti's, who sat across from her in the cozy therapy room. The walls, adorned with serene paintings, seemed to embrace the quiet moment between them.

"Believe in what you affirm," Tanuja encouraged, her voice a steady beacon amidst Srishti's sea of doubts. "Visualize yourself as the person who embodies these statements. They are your truth."

Srishti nodded, her eyes closing softly as she inhaled a deep, purposeful breath. A gentle exhale carried her words into the space around them. "I am capable and strong," she murmured, her voice gaining conviction with each repetition.

"Good," Tanuja smiled gently. "Now, make it personal. Reflect on those moments when you've shown strength. Recall them with each affirmation."

Srishti's brows knitted together in concentration as memories flickered behind her closed lids. "I handled the Jenkins project confidently," she began, a personal triumph colouring her tone. "I believe in myself and my abilities." The memory of her successful presentation at work infused the words with genuine pride.

"See? You're not just saying the words; you're living them," Tanuja affirmed, acknowledging Srishti's progress.

"Each step I take is towards success and happiness, unique to my journey," Srishti continued, embracing the tailoring of affirmations to her narrative.

"Exactly," Tanuja said, her nod encouraging Srishti to delve deeper. "Your path, your milestones."

"Despite the challenges, I grow," Srishti spoke, her voice steadier now, "and I trust myself to make good decisions, like seeking guidance here."

"Your growth is evident, Srishti," Tanuja responded warmly, her heart buoyant with hope for the young woman's journey.

"Every day, I am more me than ever before," Srishti declared, a newfound sense of identity emerging through personalized affirmations.

"Remember this feeling," Tanuja advised. "Carry it with you, beyond these walls."

Srishti opened her eyes, their clarity reflecting the internal shift. "I will," she promised, the simplicity of the phrase holding the weight of her commitment.

"Your story, your affirmations, your power," Tanuja said, her parting words an echo of the empowerment that filled the room.

*****

Srishti's fingers trembled above the keyboard, the cursor blinking like a relentless metronome. The email from her supervisor, terse and demanding, highlighted an error in her latest report—a minor oversight now magnified into a mountain of self-reproach. Old voices whispered accusations, their volume rising to a familiar crescendo.

"Stop," she whispered, shutting her eyes against the tide of negativity. "I am capable and strong." The words felt like a shield, deflecting the barbs of criticism.

Tanuja had taught her this; to catch the critical whispers before they became shouts. Srishti breathed deeply, each affirmation a step away from the precipice of doubt. "I believe in myself and my abilities," she affirmed, her voice steadier.

Opening her eyes, she read the email again. The error was there, certainly, but it did not define her. With a quiet determination, Srishti began crafting her response, addressing the mistake with professionalism and poise.

"I am growing from this," she typed, the affirmation imbued in her action. "I learn from my mistakes and keep moving forward."

"Remember, challenges are opportunities for growth," Tanuja's voice echoed in her memory, a comforting presence.

"Exactly," Srishti murmured to herself. She was no longer the child fearful of imperfection, but a woman embracing her journey—one paved with resilience and self-compassion.

"Every challenge I overcome strengthens my confidence," she said, feeling the truth of the words fill her with warmth.

"Very good, Srishti," Tanuja would have said, her encouraging tone a balm to frayed nerves.

With the email sent, Srishti leaned back in her chair, allowing herself a moment of pride. The mistake had been acknowledged, corrected, and now it was time to move on. She had not let the negative self-talk spiral out of control, instead halting it with the practiced ease of positive affirmations.

"Consistency," she reminded herself, the word a commitment to maintain this new habit. "This is how change happens."

"Indeed," Tanuja's voice resonated within her, testament to the many sessions spent internalizing this wisdom. "You're rewriting your narrative, one affirmation at a time."

Srishti stood up, stretched, and smiled. The office around her buzzed with the hum of productivity, but inside, she harboured a quiet triumph. Today's challenge was met with strength, not fear

.

"Each day, I build more self-confidence, more self-worth," she declared softly, her once faltering belief now a burgeoning certainty.

"Bravo," Tanuja's imagined applause filled the corners of Srishti's mind, as tangible as if she were right there beside her.

"Thank you," Srishti said, though the room held only her own reflection. But it was enough, for the gratitude was also for herself—for being open, for being brave, for beginning to truly heal.

13

BARRIERS TO EMOTIONS

Tanuja leaned forward, her hands clasped together on the polished surface of her desk. The afternoon sun filtered through the blinds, casting a warm glow that danced across the room's tranquil space. "We've covered a lot," she began, her voice a soft timbre that carried the weight of reflection. "From understanding our emotional responses to recognizing the significance of self-care." Her eyes, always so expressive, met those of her client with an unwavering gaze that seemed to say, 'I'm here with you.'

"Emotions," she continued, "are like threads in an intricately woven fabric. They add colour and depth to our lives." She paused, allowing the metaphor to settle in the air between them. "But as we've discussed, mastering these threads can be quite the challenge." The rhythmic cadence of her words was soothing, each sentence flowing seamlessly into the next.

"Imagine a garden," Tanuja suggested, her hands unfolding as if to reveal an unseen landscape. "A place of potential growth and beauty. Yet sometimes, there are barriers—thorny bushes, weeds—that prevent us from tending to the flowers." She gestured gently, her movements painting the picture clearer, "These obstacles in our garden are like the barriers to mastering our emotions."

She leaned back slightly, her presence still commanding attention despite the shift. "Deep-rooted beliefs, societal pressures, personal trials—they can all hinder our progress." Her fingers tapped lightly against the desk, a subtle reminder of the persistence required to face such hurdles.

"However," she said, the hopeful lilt in her voice unmistakable, "by acknowledging these barriers, we empower ourselves to begin the work of overcoming them." She offered a warm, encouraging smile. "And that is where true mastery begins."

"Each barrier," Tanuja explained, "is a lesson waiting to be learned." She folded her hands once more, her demeanour embodying both empathy and authority. "Together, we can develop strategies to dismantle them, one by one, until the path to your emotional garden is clear." Her words were not just instructions; they were an invitation to a journey of transformation.

"Remember," Tanuja concluded, her tone imbued with conviction, "this journey towards emotional mastery is uniquely yours. It may take time, patience, and a generous dose of self-compassion." She stood up, her figure a silhouette of empowerment against the descending light. "But the benefits—oh, the benefits—are boundless. And I believe, with all my heart, that you have what it takes to reach them."

As the session drew to a close, the room seemed to echo with a newfound sense of possibility—an echo that spoke of barriers ready to be crossed and emotions waiting to be mastered.

*****

Tanuja shifted slightly in her chair, bridging the space between her and Srishti. The room was quiet, save for the gentle hum of the air conditioner—a soothing background to their conversation.

"Let's talk about emotional unawareness," she started, her voice even and steady, "It's like walking through a dense fog, unable to see the path ahead." She watched Srishti's face, the flicker of recognition in the younger woman's eyes. "Not recognizing your own emotions, or understanding what triggers them, can leave you feeling lost, can't it?"

Srishti nodded, her almond-shaped eyes reflecting a mixture of curiosity and apprehension. "I often don't realize I'm upset until it's too late," she admitted, the words tumbling out. "Then, I'm just reacting without thinking."

"Exactly," Tanuja affirmed, her nod encouraging. "And that's where mindfulness comes into play. It helps clear the fog. When you reflect, when you're willing to explore your inner experiences, you start to recognize patterns."

"Patterns?" Srishti echoed, tilting her head, a strand of hair falling across her forehead.

"Emotional patterns," Tanuja clarified, her hands gesturing as if drawing a map in the air. "Identifying them is the first step to managing your reactions more effectively."

Srishti's posture relaxed, her shoulders dropping away from her ears. "So, it's about becoming more aware?"

"Exactly," Tanuja smiled. "Awareness brings control—control over impulsive actions, control over misunderstandings in your relationships."

The room felt warmer, the atmosphere charged with the promise of progress. Tanuja's expressive eyes held Srishti's gaze, imparting strength.

"Then there are the wounds of the past," Tanuja continued, her voice dipping into a softer register. "They're like shadows that follow us, aren't they? Traumatic events that leave emotional scars."

"Shadows," Srishti whispered, looking away. Her hands fidgeted in her lap, betraying the turmoil beneath her composed exterior.

"Those shadows can trigger intense reactions when we least expect it," Tanuja acknowledged, her tone compassionate. "But remember, healing is possible. Through therapy, through effort, you can develop healthier ways to cope."

"Is it... is it really possible to heal completely?" Srishti's voice was tentative, seeking assurance.

"Complete healing takes time," Tanuja replied, her honesty gentle but unwavering. "But each small step makes the shadows less intimidating, less defining."

Srishti met her therapist's gaze again, hope glimmering in the depths of her eyes. "Small steps," she repeated, a mantra of possibility.

"Every day, every moment you choose to be mindful, to reflect, you're taking a step forward," Tanuja said, rising to signify the end of their session. "Your journey is yours alone, Srishti, but you are not walking it alone."

As Srishti stood, there was a new steadiness to her posture, a readiness to face the fog and the shadows alike. Tanuja's belief in her was a beacon, guiding her towards a future where emotional mastery was not just a distant dream, but an achievable reality.

*****

Tanuja settled back into her chair, a serene presence in the sunlit room. Srishti sat across from her, feet planted firmly on the floor, hands clasped tightly as if holding back the tide of her own emotions.

"Let's talk about vulnerability," Tanuja began, her voice a soft invitation to open up. "It's tough, isn't it? To peel away the layers and show your true self."

Srishti nodded, her eyes reflecting a familiar wariness. "It feels like every time I've let my guard down, I've been hurt. It's easier to just... keep everything inside."

"Safer, perhaps, in the moment," Tanuja agreed, "but not without its cost. When we lock our emotions away, we deny ourselves the chance to truly connect. To heal."

"Connect," Srishti echoed, the word resonating with a longing she'd long buried. "That's what I want, but fear always gets in the way."

"Creating a safe space is key," Tanuja explained, leaning forward slightly. "A space where you're heard, understood, not judged. Can you think of a time when you felt that safety?"

"Once or twice," Srishti admitted, "with friends who cared. But even then, I was scared they'd see me differently if they knew... everything."

"Trust takes time to build," Tanuja encouraged gently, "and being vulnerable is part of that process. With each small act of courage, confidence grows. You're not your fears, Srishti."

"Small acts of courage," Srishti repeated softly, a mantra blooming in her chest.

"Exactly." Tanuja's smile was warm, reassuring. "It's not about grand gestures. It's about those moments when you choose to share a little more, to be true to yourself."

The room seemed to hold its breath as Srishti pondered, her internal walls quivering at the prospect of allowing someone in.

"And what about when those walls are so thick, so high, that even I can't see over them?" Her voice trembled, betraying years of practiced suppression.

"Those walls were built for a reason, weren't they?" Tanuja asked, acknowledging the depth of Srishti's inner fortress. "To protect, to survive. But now, they also isolate. It's time to create windows in those walls, to let light in."

"Windows," Srishti mused, considering the metaphor. "I guess I never thought about it that way."

"Emotional suppression is like living in a house with boarded-up windows," Tanuja continued. "It might feel secure, but it's dark, and the air is stale. To live fully, we need fresh air, light. We need to experience all emotions, not just the easy ones."

"Even the painful ones?" Srishti's question hung between them, laden with memories of past hurts.

"Especially those," Tanuja affirmed. "Acknowledging them, feeling them, that's where healing begins. It's a slow process, but it brings us back to life."

Srishti absorbed the words, a seed of understanding taking root. The idea of dismantling her defenses was daunting, yet the image of a house bathed in sunlight was undeniably appealing.

"Will you help me?" Srishti asked, vulnerability creeping into her voice for the first time.

"Every step of the way," Tanuja promised, her commitment steady as the earth itself. "Together, we'll find the tools you need to gently pry off those boards, one by one."

"Okay," Srishti breathed out, a single word heavy with the weight of decision. "I'm ready to try."

"Then let's begin," Tanuja said, her eyes shining with pride for the bravery unfolding before her. "Let's start by letting in just a sliver of light."

"Let's," Srishti agreed, a tentative smile curving her lips, the first rays of hope piercing through the cracks in her carefully constructed walls.

Srishti perched on the edge of the cushioned chair, her hands knotted together like a bundle of live wires. Tanuja sat across from her, the light from the window haloing her as if she were part guardian angel, part therapist.

"Sometimes," Srishti began, voice tremulous, "I feel... stuck. I don't have the words."

"Words give shape to our emotions," Tanuja said gently. "Without them, feelings can become a tangled mess."

Srishti nodded, her eyes reflecting a familiar frustration.

"Think of it like learning a new language," Tanuja suggested. "We start with basics, building up, word by word."

"Where do I even begin?" Srishti's voice was a whisper of vulnerability.

"Let's explore together," Tanuja encouraged, reaching for a book on the shelf behind her. "This is a start."

She handed Srishti a thin volume, the cover adorned with a tranquil sea. 'The Language of Emotions,' it read. Srishti traced the title, the coolness of the letters grounding her.

"Every day," Tanuja instructed, "find a word that resonates with you. Write it down, say it out loud, embrace its meaning."

"Sounds simple enough," Srishti admitted, flipping through the pages.

"Simple steps lead to profound journeys," Tanuja affirmed.

They delved into a passage, dissecting the nuances between 'joy' and 'contentment,' 'anxiety' and 'apprehension.' Each term, a tool; every definition, a stepping stone.

As the session waned, Srishti's posture loosened, an ease seeping into her bones. She found solace in clarity, power in articulation.

"Negative self-talk," Tanuja shifted gears, "it's a barrier many face."

Srishti's eyes darkened momentarily. "It's like I'm my own worst enemy."

"Those harsh words," Tanuja said, leaning forward, "would you offer them to a friend?"

"Never," Srishti replied, aghast at the thought.

"Then why accept them from yourself?" Tanuja posed the question softly, letting it hang like a delicate chime in the air.

Srishti pondered, struck by the simplicity yet profundity of the idea.

"Try this," Tanuja continued, handing Srishti a small mirror.

"Look at yourself and offer kindness, as you would to a dear friend."

Hesitant, Srishti lifted the mirror, her reflection gazing back, expectant. The words stumbled at first, awkward and foreign.

"I am capable. I am learning. I am enough."

With each affirmation, the weight of years of self-doubt seemed to lift, making room for something lighter, something akin to hope.

"Affirmations are powerful," Tanuja reassured. "They remind us of our worth, especially when we forget."

"Thank you," Srishti said, her gratitude as palpable as the warmth of the sun streaming through the window. "For helping me see that."

"Self-compassion is a practice," Tanuja concluded, her voice imbued with an unwavering belief in Srishti's potential. "And you're already on your way."

As Srishti clutched the book to her chest, she felt armed with more than just words—she carried a newfound resolve to redefine the language of her inner world.

*****

Tanuja watched as Srishti's chest rose and fell, the rhythm slower now, more deliberate. The room was silent except for the soft whisper of their synchronized breathing. Inhale. Hold. Exhale.

"Notice the space between," Tanuja said, her voice a gentle nudge in the quiet. "The moment of stillness before the next breath."

Srishti's eyes fluttered open, a flicker of clarity within them. "It's like...a pause," she murmured, the realization dawning on her.

"Exactly," Tanuja affirmed with a nod. "Emotions can surge like waves. Learning to ride them, to find that pause, is a skill—one that you can master."

"Even when it feels overwhelming?" Srishti asked, skepticism lining her words.

"Especially then," Tanuja replied. "Mindfulness isn't about avoiding the wave. It's about learning to surf it."

Srishti mulled over the metaphor, envisioning herself atop the tumultuous sea of her emotions, steady and balanced.

"Can we try something?" Tanuja proposed, sensing Srishti's readiness.

"Okay," came the cautious response.

"Think of a recent time when your emotions felt out of control," Tanuja instructed.

Srishti closed her eyes once more, her forehead creasing as she delved into the memory. "I was so angry," she confessed, "it was blinding."

"Where do you feel that anger in your body?"

"Here," Srishti placed a hand over her heart, "and here," moving it to her clenched jaw.

"Let's welcome that anger," Tanuja suggested softly. "Breathe into those spaces."

With each breath, Srishti's features softened, the tightness in her jaw easing, the armour around her heart melting.

"Anger is energy," Tanuja continued. "You've held it gracefully. Now let's transform it."

"Transform?" Srishti echoed, seeking.

"Into assertiveness, perhaps. Or passion. Choose its new shape."

"Passion," Srishti decided, the word resonating with her. She imagined the fiery anger reshaping into a vibrant, driving force.

"Beautiful," Tanuja commended. "Now, take that passion and tell me—what will you do with it?"

"Use it to fuel my goals," Srishti declared, her voice stronger, surer than before. "To speak up for myself."

"Resistance often masks fear," Tanuja gently steered the conversation toward the remaining barrier. "Change is unsettling, but it's also where growth happens."

"I know I hold onto old patterns," Srishti admitted, "even when they hurt."

"Because they're familiar," Tanuja acknowledged. "But you've shown courage today, stepping into the unknown of your emotions."

"Courage," Srishti repeated, tasting the word, letting it settle into her being.

"Remember, change doesn't happen all at once," Tanuja reminded her. "It's a series of steps, and you're taking them."

"Steps," Srishti mused, picturing a path unfolding before her, each one laid with intention and self-care.

"Each day, a choice," Tanuja concluded, her belief in Srishti unwavering. "And I believe in your choices."

"Thank you," Srishti said, her gratitude lacing the air with its sincerity. "For believing, even when I falter."

"Always," Tanuja affirmed, her smile an echo of hope in the room. "Shall we continue this journey together?"

"Let's," Srishti agreed, rising from her seat with newfound resolve, ready to embrace whatever lay ahead.

14

SRISHTI'S TRANSFORMATION

Srishti's eyes fluttered open to the soft whisper of rain against her bedroom window. A peacefulness, unfamiliar yet deeply welcomed, nestled within her chest as she lay there for a moment, watching the rhythmic dance of droplets tracing paths down the glass pane. It was a stark contrast to the mornings past when anxiety would greet her before the sunlight ever could.

Over countless hours in Tanuja's nurturing presence, Srishti had learned to recognize the ebb and flow of her emotions, like the tide responding to the moon's distant pull. She had cultivated an awareness that now allowed her to observe her feelings without being capsized by them.

"Emotions are messengers," Tanuja's voice echoed in her memory—a mantra that had slowly seeped into her very pores.

Rising from bed, Srishti embraced the day with a gentle stretch, feeling the tension release from her shoulders. The demands of her job no longer loomed over her as insurmountable peaks but rather as challenges she was equipped to navigate.

In the office, the hum of productivity buzzed around her, a symphony of keystrokes and murmured conversations. When a surge of overwhelm threatened at the sight of her overflowing inbox, Srishti paused, closed her eyes, and took a deep breath—inhaling possibility, exhaling doubt.

"Identify, don't amplify," she whispered to herself, recalling Tanuja's guidance on regulating turbulent emotions.

With each breath, clarity blossomed, and she meticulously organized her tasks, prioritizing with precision. As the day unfolded, Srishti found herself in the heart of a project meeting, ideas ricocheting across the room like a spirited tennis match. She felt the familiar flutter of excitement, tempered by the weight of responsibility.

A suggestion sparked disagreement, igniting a flare of frustration in her chest. But this time, Srishti recognized the emotion, inviting it to sit beside her rather than take the lead. She listened, observed, and when she spoke, her words were measured and thoughtful, a bridge rather than a barrier.

"Perhaps we can find a middle ground," she proposed, her tone even, embodying the balance she had laboured to achieve.

Her colleagues paused, considered, and slowly, nods circled the table. In that moment, Srishti realized the profound shift within her—the metamorphosis from reactive to responsive.

Later, as she walked through the quiet park on her way home, Srishti reflected on the day's triumphs. She acknowledged the growth that had sprouted from seeds of self-awareness, watered diligently by sessions with Tanuja. With every step, her heart swelled with gratitude for the emotional tools she now wielded with confidence.

"Every challenge is an opportunity to practice," she reminded herself, the words forming a smile on her lips.

And with the city lights beginning to twinkle like stars fallen to earth, Srishti continued her journey home, not as the woman she once was, but as the one she was becoming—resilient, mindful, and whole.

*****

The morning sun spilled golden light across Srishti's workspace, casting long shadows over the stack of project files that awaited her attention. She was the nucleus of a hive of activity, her team buzzing with questions and deadlines looming. A promotion was on the horizon, a testament to her dedication and talent, but it was tethered to the success of their current endeavour—a demanding initiative that demanded precision and leadership.

"Let's review our progress," Srishti announced, her voice steady despite the flutter of nerves in her stomach. She scanned the room, making eye contact with each member of her team, seeking engagement, encouraging ownership. They had hit a snag—a critical piece of data was elusive, hiding like a shy creature amongst the thicket of numbers and reports.

"Rohan, can you walk us through the latest analysis?" she asked, directing her attention toward a colleague known for his meticulous work yet equally for his prickly demeanour when under pressure.

"Again?" Rohan's response held an edge of irritation, his brow creasing into a familiar frown. "I've already explained this twice."

Srishti felt a familiar heat rise within her, a remnant of her old self who would have bristled at the tone, ready to snap back with equal force. But now, she breathed in deeply, embracing the pause, allowing space between stimulus and response.

"Rohan, your expertise is invaluable to us," she said calmly, affirming his role. "A fresh perspective might uncover what we're missing. Let's approach it together, as a team."

Rohan hesitated, then nodded, perhaps recognizing the olive branch extended in Srishti's words. The tension dissolved, replaced by a renewed focus that pulsed through the room.

As the meeting progressed, Srishti led with a quiet confidence, her words infused with the emotional intelligence that had become her compass. When opinions clashed, she listened intently, her empathy bridging gaps between differing viewpoints.

"Thank you all for your hard work," Srishti concluded, her gaze sweeping the room. "Every challenge is a stepping stone towards our goal."

Afterward, her manager pulled her aside, his expression serious yet soft around the edges. "You handled that well, Srishti. Your ability to keep the team aligned is impressive."

"Thank you," she replied, feeling the weight of his words settle into a sense of pride. "I've been working on my communication skills—trying to create an environment where everyone feels heard."

"Keep it up. It's making a difference," he said, offering a nod that seemed to carry the promise of the recognition she sought.

As the day drew to a close, Srishti sat alone, reflecting on the interactions, the delicate dance of dialogue and decision. She thought about the promotion, not just as a personal achievement but as a milestone on her journey of growth.

"Every step forward," she murmured to herself, a mantra of perseverance, "is a testament to change."

In the silence of her office, with shadows lengthening and the hum of computers winding down, Srishti allowed herself a moment to savour the quiet triumphs of the day—the way she navigated the choppy waters of professional dynamics with grace, the way she articulated her needs without diminishing others.

"Tomorrow," she whispered, a smile playing at the corners of her mouth, "is another opportunity to be better." And with that, she gathered her things and stepped out into the fading light, ready to meet whatever challenges awaited with resilience and hope.

*****

Srishti's hands trembled slightly as she traced the rim of her coffee mug, the ceramic cool against her fingertips. Amith sat opposite her, his brow furrowed in frustration. The sun had dipped below the horizon, casting a soft glow that wrapped the small balcony in a blanket of serenity—a stark contrast to the tension between them.

"Another late night at work?" Amith asked, his voice tinged with disappointment.

She inhaled deeply, grounding herself in the therapy techniques that had become her lifeline. "I know it's been hard on us," Srishti began, her voice steady and sincere. "I'm trying to balance everything, but I see how it affects you, and I'm sorry."

Amith's expression softened as he reached across the table, his fingers brushing against hers. "I just miss spending time with you, Srishti. It feels like we're losing 'us' in the hustle of your job."

Her heart ached at his words, but instead of the familiar surge of defensiveness, there was clarity. She recognized his need for connection, for reassurance. "Let's plan a weekend getaway, just the two of us. No emails, no calls," she proposed, a gentle smile curving her lips.

"Really? You'd do that?" Hope flickered in Amith's eyes.

"Absolutely," she affirmed. The promise of dedicated time together seemed to bridge the gap that crept into their lives, linking them back to each other.

The conversation shifted then, Srishti actively listening as Amith shared stories from his day, speaking animatedly about a new project. She nodded, engaging with thoughtful questions, her empathy shining through as she celebrated his excitement.

It wasn't long before a delicate issue surfaced—their differing views on finances causing a rift that was all too familiar. Amith wanted to invest in a property, while Srishti urged caution, wanting to save for potential emergencies.

"I hear your concerns," Srishti acknowledged, her tone even, respectful. "And I understand the importance of investing in our future. Could we meet with a financial advisor? Find a plan that accommodates both our needs?"

Amith considered this, the edge of conflict blunting into contemplation. "That sounds fair," he conceded. "We'll make an informed decision together."

The air between them cleared, charged now with collaborative energy. They discussed potential advisors, their dialogue flowing smoothly—a dance of compromise and mutual support.

As they stood to clear the table, Srishti caught Amith's eye, a silent communication passing between them. There was gratitude there, and love—emotions once buried beneath misunderstandings, now brought to light by her willingness to be vulnerable, to listen, to speak with intention.

"Thank you for being open to finding a middle ground," Amith said, his voice warm.

"Thank you for helping me see beyond my own perspective," she replied, her growth evident in her response.

Their bond reaffirmed, they leaned into each other, a shared laugh escaping as they reminisced over past adventures. In that moment, their connection felt unshakeable, fortified by Srishti's emotional transformation and the strength it inspired in them both.

*****

Srishti's laughter mingled with the scent of freshly cut grass as she and Amith challenged each other to a game of badminton in the park. The shuttlecock flew back and forth, a symbol of the playful give-and-take that now characterized their relationship. She lunged for a particularly ambitious shot, racket slicing through the air, and missed by inches. Falling onto the soft earth, she looked up to see Amith extending a hand, his eyes crinkling with amusement.

"Nice try," he teased, pulling her up. "You've definitely improved."

"Thanks to you," Srishti replied, brushing the dirt from her knees, her tone light and appreciative. They resumed their game, the rhythm of their banter matching the steady thwap of the shuttlecock. Here, amid friendly competition and shared smiles, they found common ground, an easy camaraderie born of countless similar moments.

As the sun dipped lower, painting the sky with strokes of orange and pink, they paused, breathless from exertion and joy. Amith reached for the water bottle and handed it to Srishti first, a small gesture that spoke volumes. She took a grateful sip, feeling the cool liquid quench more than just physical thirst.

"Beautiful sunset," Amith remarked, and they stood side by side, watching the day wane, revelling in the silent language of companionship.

Later, sitting alone on her balcony, wrapped in the comfort of a plush throw blanket, Srishti reflected on the transformation she had experienced. The city lights below twinkled like stars grounded to earth, mirroring the sparks of realization that flickered within her. She thought of the therapy sessions with Tanuja, the challenging emotional work, the revelations that sometimes came in whispers and other times in roars.

"Look how far you've come," she murmured to herself, acknowledging the journey with gentle pride. Her internal dialogue, once a critic's harsh voice, now spoke with kindness and encouragement. She had learned to embrace her emotions as guides rather than enemies, to listen to the whispers of her heart with respect and curiosity.

"Emotional intelligence," she whispered, a smile touching her lips. It was not just a concept but a lifeline, one that had anchored her in stormy seas and now propelled her forward with confidence. The gratitude she felt for this growth enveloped her, a warm embrace from within.

"Thank you," she said aloud, though there was no one else present. It was an offering to the universe, to Tanuja, to her own resilient spirit. With each sunrise, she greeted a world rich with possibilities, her heart open, her mind clear, and her soul ready for whatever lay ahead.

*****

The fluorescent lights of the office hummed a monotonous tune, a stark contrast to the cacophony brewing in the conference room. Srishti sat at the head of the table, her fingers rhythmically tapping against the polished wood surface, a silent symphony to accompany the tension in the air.

"Unfortunately, the client isn't happy with our proposal," her colleague, Rajan, said with an edge of frustration in his voice. "They're considering other agencies."

A knot tightened in Srishti's stomach—a familiar sensation, a visitor from her past that would have once unravelled her composure. But this time, she breathed deeply, feeling the cool air fill her lungs, grounding her to the present moment. She drew upon the lessons etched into her mind like sacred mantras: acknowledge, assess, act.

"Thank you for bringing this to my attention, Rajan," Srishti replied, her voice steady. "Let's view this as an opportunity to refine our approach." Her eyes scanned the room, meeting those of her team members, each one a reflection of shared concern and resolve.

"Any ideas on how we can turn this around?" she encouraged, inviting collaboration. The room began to buzz with suggestions, the setback morphing into a brainstorming session. Srishti facilitated the conversation with grace, her newfound confidence an invisible but palpable presence among them.

Days later, the fruits of their labour blossomed. Srishti stood by the window, gazing out at the cityscape as her phone chimed with an email notification. It was from the client, a beacon amidst the sea of mundane correspondence. They were impressed with the revisions, praising the team's responsiveness and creativity. And at the heart of their commendation was Srishti—the architect of recovery.

"Exceptional leadership, Srishti," her boss said, entering her office with a smile that reached his eyes. "Your ability to rally the team and pivot strategy under pressure did not go unnoticed."

A wave of warmth rushed over her, a pleasant tingling that danced along her spine. She allowed herself a moment to bask in the glow of recognition, her hard work reflected in the words of gratitude and respect.

"Thank you, sir," she responded, her heart swelling with pride. "I couldn't have done it without the team's support and your guidance."

"Keep this up, and there's a bright future ahead for you here," he affirmed before exiting, leaving a trail of potential in his wake.

Alone once more, Srishti turned back to the window, her reflection superimposed on the glass—a mirror of progress. She whispered a silent thank you to the woman staring back at her, the one who had braved the depths of her own mind to emerge enlightened and empowered.

"Every challenge is a step forward," she recited softly, a testament to her emotional resilience. The journey wasn't without its thorns, but each one had taught her to heal, to grow. And as she stood there, the city below her witness, Srishti knew that the greatest recognition came from within—the acknowledgment of her evolution, a triumph of spirit and self.

*****

Srishti cupped the steaming mug of tea between her palms, relishing its warmth as she sat across from her Cousin, Anusha. The monsoon rain tapped a gentle rhythm against the windowpane, a soothing backdrop to their heartfelt conversation.

"Remember how I'd spiral at the smallest setback?" Srishti began, her voice steady and imbued with a quiet strength. "Tanuja helped me see those moments differently—as opportunities to grow, not just obstacles."

Anusha leaned in, her curiosity piqued by the evident change in her cousin's demeanor. "But how did you actually do it?" she asked, mirroring Srishti's posture, elbows resting on the kitchen table.

"It's about understanding your emotions, not letting them control you," Srishti explained, her almond eyes reflecting the flicker of candlelight. "I learned to pause, to breathe, to ask myself why I felt a certain way."

"And that made a difference?"

"More than I thought possible," Srishti affirmed, a smile tugging at the corners of her lips. "The clarity that comes from self-awareness—it's liberating."

Anusha sipped her tea contemplatively, the steam fogging her glasses momentarily. "Maybe I should try talking to someone like Tanuja," she mused, the seed of inspiration taking root.

Srishti reached out, placing a reassuring hand atop Anusha's. "I believe it could help you, just like it did for me," she said, her tone as comforting as the warm beverage they shared.

As the evening deepened, the cousins talked, laughter and earnest words twining together. Srishti shared tales of triumphs and trials, each anecdote sprinkled with newfound wisdom. And within those shared confidences, the ripple effect of her journey became tangible, touching Anusha's heart and kindling a hope for transformation.

Later, alone in her room, Srishti stood before her window, the city lights a constellation of life below. She drew in a deep breath, her chest expanding with a sense of anticipation for the future. Embracing the silence, she allowed herself to feel the full weight of her experiences—the tears, the laughter, the lessons learned.

"Life will always have its ups and downs," she whispered to her reflection, a gentle reminder of the truth Tanuja had instilled in her. Each word was a stepping stone, a promise of resilience. "But I am equipped now, stronger and wiser."

With a nod to her past self, Srishti turned from the window, her heart buoyant with hope. The journey ahead would no doubt bring its share of challenges, but she faced them armed with an arsenal of emotional intelligence, an unwavering support system, and the enduring guidance of her cherished therapist.

"Here's to growth," she said softly, her voice a blend of gratitude and determination. "Here's to becoming who I'm meant to be."

She closed her eyes, envisioning the path ahead not as a series of hurdles, but as a landscape ripe with possibility—a horizon wide and welcoming, ready to be met with grace and courage. And in that moment of stillness, Srishti felt the full magnitude of her evolution, a testament to the power of healing and the human capacity for change.

*****

As the soft morning light filtered through the sheer curtains, Srishti sat cross-legged on her living room floor, a gentle hum of serenity in her space. Weeks, months had passed, each therapy session with Tanuja weaving a stronger fabric of resilience within her. Where once confusion reigned, clarity now blossomed, each petal a lesson learned, a tool grasped. Her emotions, once wild horses without reins, now galloped at her command, powerful and directed.

"Today," she whispered to herself, "I navigate my journey with grace." The affirmation was a silken thread spun during her sessions, one that connected her present resolve to a future bright with promise.

At work, the challenge arrived as an unexpected email, its subject line like a storm cloud on the horizon: "Project Revision Needed – Urgent." Srishti's pulse quickened, but she inhaled deeply, recalling Tanuja's analogy of emotional waves—observe them, ride them, do not let them sweep you away.

"Alright," she murmured, clicking open the message. As she read through the feedback, her mind's eye pictured Tanuja's nurturing gaze, her voice steady and calm, "What is this situation asking of you?"

"Perspective," Srishti answered aloud, as if in dialogue with her therapist. She acknowledged the frustration nipping at her heels, gave it a nod, and then turned her focus to solution-finding. The task was daunting, but she broke it down, piece by piece, employing strategies from her mental toolkit with meticulous care.

"Let's look at this as an opportunity," she said in the meeting that followed, surprising even herself with the confidence in her tone. They leaned in, listening as she outlined a plan, her words painting a path through the thicket of complications.

"Thank you for stepping up, Srishti," her boss said afterwards, a note of respect threading his words. "You've really turned this around."

She smiled, feeling the weight of her progress, as tangible as the congratulatory pats on her back.

"Every setback is a setup for a comeback," she thought, remembering Tanuja's encouraging mantra. And in that bustling office, amidst the clatter of keyboards and the whirl of minds at work, Srishti found a quiet corner of victory—a triumph not just of circumstance, but of her own emotional mastery.

*****

The following week, amidst the hum of fluorescent lights and the shuffle of papers, Srishti found herself at another crossroads. A key client project was teetering on the brink of disaster, deadlines looming like dark clouds. Her team looked to her, eyes wide with panic.

"Okay, let's take a moment," she said, her voice cutting through the chaos. She stood at the head of the conference table, drawing from the well of confidence she had been nurturing. "We can handle this. Let's prioritize our tasks and tackle them one by one. Who can take on the financial report?"

As hands raised and assignments were delegated, Srishti charted their course with a clear mind and a proactive stance. When the meeting adjourned, there was a collective breath of relief, a shared sense of direction replacing the earlier frenzy.

"Great job handling that, Srishti," her colleague Ravi murmured as they left the room, his admiration genuine. "You kept us focused and moving forward."

"Thanks, Ravi," Srishti replied, allowing herself a moment of pride. She recognized these milestones now, the fruits of her labor in therapy with Tanuja, the emotional intelligence she wielded like armor against life's slings and arrows.

Later, alone in the quiet of her office, Srishti allowed herself a smile. The growth within her resonated in harmony with each challenge faced, each conflict resolved. She had learned to navigate the waters of life with grace, her sails catching the winds of change, steering her ever onward.

*****

The sun was setting, splashing amber hues across the sky, when Srishti felt the first ripple of unease. She had just hung up from a call with her mother, the kind that usually left her drowning in self-doubt. But this time, she caught the wave before it could crash over her. She took a deep breath, recognizing the familiar trigger in her mother's subtle tone of disappointment.

"Is everything alright?" she murmured to herself, mimicking the gentleness Tanuja would often use. Srishti stepped away from the phone, her heart rate slowing as she acknowledged the emotion without letting it define her response. "It's just a feeling," she reasoned. "And feelings are not facts."

With a newfound clarity, Srishti decided to engage in one of the self-care practices Tanuja had championed. She chose her balcony garden, where tendrils of jasmine scented the air, and sank into a comfortable chair. Her fingers found the soft, leather-bound journal gifted by Tanuja on her birthday—a token and a tool for reflection.

Pen in hand, Srishti began to write, her thoughts flowing freely onto the page. Each word was a step back from the emotional precipice, a reaffirmation of her journey towards well-being. As the sky darkened, the flicker of candlelight danced across the pages, a visual reminder of the peace she had cultivated within.

"Emotions are like passing clouds," she wrote, recalling Tanuja's analogy. "Observe them, let them be, but do not cling to them."

Finishing her entry, Srishti closed the journal with a soft thud, a sense of accomplishment enveloping her. She then reached for the small terracotta pot housing a delicate bonsai, her hands working the soil, pruning and shaping with care. It was a hobby that brought her joy, a silent conversation with life itself.

"Grow at your own pace," she whispered to the plant, smiling at the echo of self-advice. It was a mantra she had adopted, a promise to honour her own rhythm.

As night settled in, Srishti leaned back, her gaze lost in the stars above. The practice of mindfulness, once foreign and elusive, now wove seamlessly into the fabric of her days. And in these quiet moments of solitude, she found strength and serenity.

"Thank you, Tanuja," she said softly, her voice carrying gratitude into the calm of the evening.

"Thank you, me," she added, giving credit where it was due—to the woman she was becoming, resilient and whole.

*****

Srishti stood before the mirror, her reflection an echo of recent trials. Stray wisps of hair framed her face, and there were shadows beneath her almond-shaped eyes—silent witnesses to sleepless nights spent wrestling with doubt. Yet, as she traced the contours of her own gaze, a gentle acceptance settled upon her features.

"Perfect in your imperfection," she murmured, a smile playing at the corners of her lips. The mantra was a gift from Tanuja, a seed planted that had taken root in fertile soil. She watched as her reflection mimicked the rise of her chest—a deep, grounding breath—and felt the weight of self-criticism lift.

"Progress, not perfection," Srishti affirmed, turning away from the mirror with a renewed sense of self-compassion.

Later that day, a challenge arose. The Peterson project, her brainchild at work, faltered under unexpected technical difficulties. In the crowded meeting room, tension hung thick in the air, and accusatory glances sliced through the space like arrows seeking a target.

Srishti's pulse quickened, a familiar anxiety gnawing at her edges. But then she remembered Tanuja's words: "Obstacles are opportunities for growth." She closed her eyes for a brief moment, summoning the tools she had honed—mindful breathing, clear-headed analysis, openness to solutions.

"Let's view this as a chance to innovate," Srishti suggested, her voice steady despite the storm of stress surrounding her. "We've hit a snag, but together we can turn this around."

Her colleagues exchanged looks of scepticism and curiosity, but Srishti's confidence was contagious. Ideas began to flow, and the setback became a detour leading to creative problem-solving.

As the meeting dispersed, Srishti's boss lingered, his expression one of impressed regard. "Good recovery, Srishti. Your resilience is what this team needs."

"Thank you," she replied, acknowledging not just the praise but her own ability to navigate the choppy waters of failure and emerge unscathed.

That evening, as she reflected on the day's events, Srishti allowed herself a small, private celebration. There was no grand victory, no triumphant fanfare—just the quiet recognition of her own emotional fortitude.

"Every stumble," she wrote in her journal, "is a step forward if you choose to keep walking."

She set the pen down, her heart full of hope and possibility. The journey wasn't easy, the road often winding and obscured, but Srishti walked it with grace—a traveller transformed by the power of emotional mastery and self-discovery.

*****

Srishti stood before the bathroom mirror, the fluorescent lights casting a sterile glow on her features. Her eyes locked with her reflection as a familiar wave of self-doubt threatened to engulf her. The project she had poured her heart into was facing criticism, and the voices of disapproval echoed in her mind.

"Maybe I'm not good enough," she whispered, the words leaving a bitter taste.

But then she paused, taking a deep breath that filled her lungs with resolve. She recalled Tanuja's words, the gentle prompts that nudged her towards kindness for herself.

"Stop," Srishti commanded softly to her reflection. "I am capable. I am resilient. Growth is carved from challenges."

With each affirmation, the crease between her brows softened, and the shadows beneath her eyes seemed less pronounced. A small smile played on her lips — not one of mirth, but of determination. She had planted seeds of positivity in the fertile soil of her mind, and she felt them rooting deeply, sprouting confidence.

Later that day, at a quaint café awash with the aroma of roasted coffee beans, Srishti noticed her friend Ananya's shoulders drooping under an invisible weight. Over steaming cups of cappuccino, Ananya's words tumbled out like dominos, each one knocking down her spirit further. Work pressures were mounting, personal life teetering, and the balance she strove for seemed an illusion.

"I just can't catch a break," Ananya sighed, stirring her coffee listlessly.

Srishti reached across the table, her fingers briefly squeezing Ananya's hand. "You're navigating through a storm right now," she said empathetically, her voice a lighthouse amidst the fog of Ananya's worries. "Remember how you've sailed through rough seas before? You have that same strength now."

Ananya looked up, her eyes searching Srishti's for certainty. "How do you do it, Srishti? After everything?"

"By believing I can," Srishti replied, her tone imbued with warmth. "And so can you. Let's break it down together—where can we find small victories in your day?"

As they spoke, Srishti listened intently, offering insights that were both practical and tender. She shared her own journey without overshadowing Ananya's plight. Ananya's posture gradually shifted, her back straightening as if each word of encouragement fortified her spine.

"Thank you, Srishti," she said finally, a glimmer of hope flickering in her gaze. "You always know how to shine light on the path ahead."

"Sometimes all we need is a reminder that the sun still rises," Srishti offered with a soft chuckle, feeling the truth of her words resonate within her own heart.

Together, they crafted a plan, small steps that would lead Ananya back to steadier ground. And as they parted ways, Srishti felt a renewed sense of purpose. Her own trials were not just solitary battles; they were lessons she could share, echoes of resilience that could uplift others.

Walking home, Srishti looked up at the sky, its expanse a canvas painted with hues of twilight. She let out a contented sigh, knowing that every challenge surmounted didn't just fortify her own walls, but also built bridges to those who might need her light to find their way.

*****

Srishti perched on the edge of her bed, fingers tracing the delicate embroidery of her comforter. The soft fabric was a familiar tactile reminder of how far she had come. In the stillness of her bedroom, with the muted city sounds filtering through her window, she allowed herself a moment to reflect—a mental inventory of the emotional milestones she had triumphed over.

"Look at you, Srishti," she murmured, a smile tugging at the corners of her mouth. "Bruised, yes, but oh so much stronger."

She closed her eyes, taking in a deep breath that filled her lungs with the scent of jasmine from her nightstand. Gratitude swelled within her chest, not just for the tangible achievements but for the intangible shifts in her heart. She had learned to navigate the stormy seas of her emotions with a newfound grace, no longer capsizing under their weight but riding them like waves.

"Thank you," she whispered to the universe, or perhaps to Tanuja, her therapist, whose wisdom had become a beacon in her darkest times. "Thank you for the tools, for the courage, for the understanding."

The gratitude was not just for the support she had received, but for her own spirit that had refused to falter. Her resilience had been tested, yet here she stood, more centred and self-aware than ever before.

"Life's challenges," she recalled Tanuja saying, "are not stop signs, but guidelines." With this mantra etched into her mind, Srishti felt a surge of empowerment. Every setback had transformed into a stepping stone, leading her to this very moment of quiet triumph.

"Emotional mastery," she contemplated aloud, the words feeling like a sacred vow, "is not about conquering feelings, but about harmonizing with them." This harmony had brought her peace, had taught her to dance with her shadows instead of fearing them.

The therapeutic journey had unlocked doors within her, each key a lesson of self-discovery that she now carried in an invisible keyring around her heart. And it wasn't just her own locks that these keys could open; they were universal, able to guide others out of their emotional labyrinths as well.

"Readers," Srishti thought, imagining those who would one day walk paths parallel to hers, "embrace the lessons life offers. Embrace your feelings, both the light and the dark. They are part of the beautiful mosaic that is you."

"Allow yourself to feel," she would tell them if she could, "and allow yourself to heal. Your emotions are not your enemies; they are your guides, whispering secrets of who you are and who you can become."

"Resilience," she concluded, standing up now, stretching her arms towards the ceiling as if reaching for the stars that had watched over her journey, "is our shared inheritance. May we all learn to wield it with grace."

With a gentle exhale, Srishti embraced the night that lay ahead, her heart full, her mind clear, and her soul ready for whatever tomorrow might bring.

*****

Srishti stood by the window, the first light of dawn casting a soft glow on her face. She watched as the sky turned from a dusky purple to shades of pink and orange, a daily rebirth that mirrored the awakening she felt within herself. The world outside was waking up, and so was she—more alive and attuned than ever before.

"Today is unwritten," she whispered to her reflection, a mantra that filled her with a sense of hope and possibility. She had learned to greet each day like a blank page, ready to be filled with new stories, lessons, and growth.

The aroma of freshly brewed coffee beckoned her to the kitchen, where she wrapped her hands around the warm mug and breathed in deeply. Gone were the mornings overshadowed by dread, replaced now by quiet anticipation for what lay ahead.

"Every challenge," Srishti mused aloud, "is an invitation to become more of who I am meant to be." Her voice resonated with newfound conviction, a testament to the emotional resilience she had cultivated through her therapy sessions with Tanuja.

She visualized the readers who might one day find solace in her journey, those navigating their own tumultuous seas of emotion. "You're not alone," she'd say if they were sitting across from her at the kitchen table. "The waves may be high, but you have the strength to ride them."

Srishti's story, like the breaking dawn, was a beacon of light. It promised that even the longest night would eventually give way to morning. Her experiences were echoes, emotional reverberations that would resonate far beyond the confines of her own life. They would inspire, empower, and offer companionship to others on the winding road of self-discovery.

Moving to her small desk, she flipped open a journal, its pages witness to her transformation. With every entry, she had charted her course, navigated through storms, and now, she was sailing into calmer waters. Her pen danced across the paper, a celebration of all she had overcome and all that was yet to come.

"Let your heart be your compass," she wrote, her words a guiding star for anyone lost in the dark. "It knows the way, even when your mind is clouded with doubt."

A smile curled at the corners of her mouth as she closed the journal, her story etched within it, but also stretching outwards, infinite in its potential to touch lives. She knew that every person's path was unique, but the journey toward emotional well-being was a shared human experience, universal and timeless.

"Keep walking," she thought, her gaze returning to the horizon where the sun now climbed higher, bathing the world in golden light. "With every step, you are rewriting your destiny."

And with that, Srishti stepped away from the window, ready to meet the day, her spirit a symphony of hope, her steps echoing the rhythm of possibility. She left the chapter of her past behind, stepping into a future where every emotion, every struggle, and every triumph was a part of her unfolding masterpiece of self.

*****

SRISHTI'S TRANSFORMATION

Srishti flipped through the pages of her journal, each word a testament to her growth. The ink bore witness to her tears, her laughter, and the silent transformations between therapy sessions. She paused, her finger tracing the arc of a sentence that shimmered with newfound wisdom: "Emotions are the language of the soul—listen."

"Indeed," Tanuja's voice resonated across the room, both a balm and beacon. "Understanding that language is key to unlocking the richness of life."

"Richness," Srishti repeated softly, as if tasting the word for the first time. Her gaze lifted from the journal to meet Tanuja's steady eyes. "I used to think it meant success, accolades... but it's so much more, isn't it?"

"Absolutely," Tanuja affirmed, her nod slow and deliberate. "It's the full spectrum of experience, the depth of connection with yourself and others. Your emotional intelligence has become your most precious asset."

Srishti closed her eyes briefly, letting the truth sink in. When she reopened them, a clear light shone within—the reflection of an inner fire that had been stoked by challenge and nurtured by self- discovery.

"Emotional intelligence," she mused aloud, "it's what allows us to navigate life not just with our minds, but with our hearts. To live fully, deeply, meaningfully."

"Exactly." Tanuja's smile was warm as sunlight. "And remember, Srishti, this journey doesn't end here. Self-discovery is a continuous path, rich with lessons and opportunities for growth."

"Opportunities," Srishti echoed, and in that one word lay acceptance, readiness, the promise of horizons yet to be explored. Her heart felt expansive, ready to embrace whatever came next.

"Life will always have its ups and downs," she said, her tone threaded with resilience. "But now I feel equipped to face them. To learn from them."

"And that," Tanuja spoke gently, "is the essence of living a fulfilling life. Embracing each moment, each emotion, as a gift that shapes who you are."

"Who I am," Srishti whispered, and there was reverence in her voice—a profound recognition of her own being. She stood up, placing the journal on the desk, a symbol of chapters completed and those yet to be written.

"Thank you, Tanuja," she said sincerely, "for teaching me the importance of emotional intelligence and self-discovery."

"It has been my honour to witness your transformation," Tanuja replied, her voice tinged with pride.

As Srishti walked towards the door, she turned back once more, her words floating in the air like a gentle benediction for all who would walk this path after her.

"May we all find the courage to listen to our emotions, to understand their wisdom, and to let them guide us toward a life of true fulfilment and meaning."

With her hand on the doorknob, Srishti smiled, her heart full. The chapter may close, but the story—her story—was infinite in its potential, a narrative of hope and effort transforming the quality of life.

15

EPILOGUE

Tanuja paused, her expressive eyes reflecting the soft glow of her office lamp. She leaned forward slightly, a gesture that bridged the distance and invited confidence. "As we draw this chapter to a close," she began, her voice wrapping around each word like a warm embrace, "I want to underscore the importance of emotional intelligence in our lives."

"Emotional Echoes" was more than just a section title; it encapsulated the reverberations of our innermost feelings through the caverns of our existence. Tanuja's gaze softened as she thought of Srishti, who had navigated those very echoes with such bravery. "Self-discovery is a journey," she continued, "one that requires patience, introspection, and an unwavering commitment to oneself."

She rose from her chair, the movement fluid and purposeful, and walked toward the window. Outside, the city thrummed with life, each light a story, each story a lesson in living. "You've seen how Srishti's understanding of herself brought clarity and direction to her life. Now, it's your turn." Tanuja's reflection in the glass nodded affirmatively.

"Take these lessons," she urged, turning back to face the room, her sanctuary of healing. "Apply them. Grow from them. Emotional mastery isn't about controlling your feelings but rather letting them inform your actions with wisdom."

"Remember," Tanuja concluded, her tone imbued with hope, "within you lies the power to change, to heal, to flourish. Your emotions are your compass; learn their language, and they will guide you to a life rich with purpose and joy."

Her words hung in the air, simple yet profound—a call to action for anyone seeking to reclaim their narrative, just as Srishti had. With a final, encouraging smile, Tanuja closed the book on "Emotional Echoes" but opened the door to countless journeys of transformation.

Printed in the USA
CPSIA information can be obtained
at www.ICGtesting.com
CBHW031337260924
14965CB00037B/237